Lecture Notes in Computer Science 5830

Commenced Publication in 1973
Founding and Former Series Editors:
Gerhard Goos, Juris Hartmanis, and Jan van Leeuwen

Tsvi Kuflik   Shlomo Berkovsky
Francesca Carmagnola   Dominikus Heckmann
Antonio Krüger (Eds.)

Advances in Ubiquitous User Modelling

Revised Selected Papers

 Springer

Volume Editors

Tsvi Kuflik
The University of Haifa
Management Information Systems Department
Mount Carmel, 31905 Haifa, Israel
E-mail: tsvikak@is.haifa.ac.il

Shlomo Berkovsky
Tasmanian ICT Centre, CSIRO
Castray Esplanade, Hobart 7001, Australia
E-mail: shlomo.berkovsky@csiro.au

Francesca Carmagnola
University of Turin, Department of Computer Science
Corso Svizzera 185, 10149 Turin, Italy
E-mail: carmagnola@di.unito.it

Dominikus Heckmann
German Research Center for Artificial Intelligence
Intelligent User Interfaces
Stuhlsatzenhausweg 3, 66123 Saarbrücken, Germany
E-mail: dominikus.heckmann@dfki.de

Antonio Krüger
German Research Center for Artificial Intelligence
Innovative Retail Laboratory (IRL)
Stuhlsatzenhausweg 3, 66123 Saarbrücken, Germany
E-mail: antonio.krueger@dfki.de

Library of Congress Control Number: 2009936326

CR Subject Classification (1998): H.5.2, I.2, H.5, H.4, I.6, J.4, J.5, K.4, K.6

LNCS Sublibrary: SL 3 – Information Systems and Application, incl. Internet/Web and HCI

ISSN   0302-9743
ISBN-10   3-642-05038-7 Springer Berlin Heidelberg New York
ISBN-13   978-3-642-05038-1 Springer Berlin Heidelberg New York

springer.com

© Springer-Verlag Berlin Heidelberg 2009
Printed in Germany

Typesetting: Camera-ready by author, data conversion by Scientific Publishing Services, Chennai, India
Printed on acid-free paper   SPIN: 12777464   06/3180   5 4 3 2 1 0

Preface

In today's information world, small personal computerized devices, such as PDAs, smart phones and other smart appliances, have become widely available and essential tools in many situations. The ongoing penetration of computers into everyday life leads to so-called ubiquitous computing environments, where computational power and networking capabilities are available (and used) everywhere to support the environment's "inhabitants." The strive to provide personal services to users made user modelling capability an essential part of any ubiquitous application. Ubiquitous user modelling describes ongoing modelling and exploitation of user behavior with a variety of systems that share their user models. These shared user models can either be used for mutual or for individual adaptation goals. Ubiquitous user modelling differs from generic user modelling by three additional concepts: ongoing modelling, ongoing sharing and ongoing exploitation. Systems that share their user models will improve the coverage, the level of detail, and the reliability of the integrated user models and thus allow better functions of adaptation. Ubiquitous user modelling implies new challenges of interchangeability, scalability, scrutability and privacy.

During the past few years ubiquitous user modelling is an ongoing series of workshops focusing on the above challenges. It serves as a meeting place for ubiquitous user modelling researchers, for discussing new challenges and research directions and setting up the UbiqUM research agenda. This book presents a selection of papers representing the Ubiquitous User Modelling Workshop series.

We would like to thank the authors that contributed to the workshops and to this book, and to the reviewers that helped improve the extended original workshop papers.

September 2009

Tsvi Kuflik
Shlomo Berkovsky
Francesca Carmagnola
Dominik Heckmann
Antonio Krüger

Organization

Reviewers

Federica Cena
Amruth Kumar
Melanie Hartmann
Geert-Jan Houben
Bhaskar Mehta
Sergey Sosnovsky
Vassileios Tsetsos
Kees van der Sluijs
Julita Vassileva
Michael Yudelson

Table of Contents

Addressing Challenges of Ubiquitous User Modeling: Between Mediation and Semantic Integration

Shlomo Berkovsky[1], Dominikus Heckmann[2], and Tsvi Kuflik[3]

[1] CSIRO – Tasmanian ICT Centre, Hobart, Australia
shlomo.berkovsky@csiro.au
[2] DFKI GmbH, Saarbruecken, Germany
heckmann@dfki.de
[3] The University of Haifa, Mount Carmel, Haifa, Israel
tsvikak@is.haifa.ac.il

Abstract. Ubiquitous User Modeling aims at providing personalized services to inhabitants of smart environments. Current research in ubiquitous user modeling focuses on two directions. The first is a practical approach that tries to resolve current problems of sparseness of data and heterogeneity of user modeling techniques and representations by mediation of user models or building hybrid systems. The second approach is based on semantic standardization of user modeling enabling user modeling data exchange and sharing by using a common user modeling ontology and language. Although both approaches have their limitations, their integration has the potential to leverage their advantages and overcome the limitations. This paper discusses initial work done in this direction, suggests a path for such integration, and points out research directions aimed at bridging the gap between these approaches.

1 Introduction

Ubiquitous user modeling aims at providing personalized services to inhabitants of smart environments. Interest in ubiquitous user modeling is growing rapidly, mainly due to the fact that mobile and pervasive computers are widely spread and their users may benefit from personalized "information-on-the-go" services. To provide personalized services, there is a need for knowledge about the specific user, the application domain of the service, and the specific context in which the service will be provided to the user. For example, consider a user visiting an ethnographical museum exhibition with his/her family. For the provision of personalized information services, gastronomical preferences of the visitor seem irrelevant, whereas his/her historical knowledge is relevant. The artistic properties of the presented cave paintings may not be relevant to the average visitor, whereas they may be very relevant if art is the main interest of the visitor. Turning to context, although the visitor may be a knowledgeable art expert, the context of a family visit may affect the provided service, such that the delivered information will use lay terms rather than more appropriate for the visitor artistic knowledge.

In general, some user characteristics, (such as preferences for instance), represented by a user model may be valid only within specific contextual conditions, such as spatial, temporal, emotional, and other conditions. That is, a user's preferences stored in

T. Kuflik et al. (Eds.): Advances in Ubiquitous User Modelling, LNCS 5830, pp. 1–19, 2009.

the user model may change as a function of various contextual conditions. The challenges of such user modeling data representation were discussed and exemplified by the multi-dimensional *experience* model suggested by Berkovsky et al. [2006; 2008], which extended traditional two-dimensional recommender systems approach addressing users and items only [Adomavicius et al., 2005]. When attempting to personalize a service provided to a user, there are several aspects that should be taken into account: 1) personal characteristics of the user requesting the service, 2) characteristics of the service itself, and 3) contextual aspects. In the context of recommender systems, [Berkovsky et al., 2008] defined experience as a function that maps the tuple {*user* that had the experience, *item* experienced, *context* of the experience}, to the *evaluation* of the experience. Formally, the experience was represented by:

$$Exp: User_{feat} \times Item_{feat} \times Context_{feat} \rightarrow evaluation.$$

$User_{feat}$, $Item_{feat}$ and $Context_{feat}$ refer to the representations of, respectively, the user features, item features and context features, while *evaluation* represents the feedback provided. Figure 1 schematically illustrates the above three-dimensional representation of experiences.

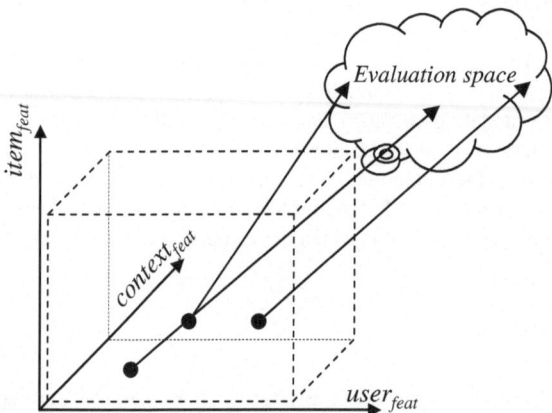

Fig. 1. Representation of Context-Aware Experiences in Three-Dimensional Space

The specific dimentions, $User_{feat}$, $Item_{feat}$ and $Context_{feat}$, in turn, may be described using a multidimensional representation by sets of features. Hence, a user model, a domain description, and contextual conditions of the experiences are referred to as subspaces of this three-dimensional space. For instance, in the above mentioned family museum visit example, only one contextual feature of *companion* out of a large $Context_{feat}$ set of contextual features is used. When the *companion* feature is assigned the value of *colleagues*, the evaluation of the delivered information using the artistic terminology may be positive, while when the *companion* features has the value *family*, the evaluation may be negative.

One of the most challenging questions in this setting is the initialization of the user models. In other words, how can the system provide an accurate personalized service to a user on his/her first interaction with the system, when none or little information about him/her is available to the system? In order to do that, the system needs to acquire some contextualized information about the user (while application domain characteristics may be available). Traditionally, personalization services were initialized by explicitly providing personal information or rating sample items. However, this is impractical or time- and effort-consuming in a ubiquitous computing environment. Hence, there is a need for a fundamentally different approach, where the user model initialization task is rather based on interoperability of personalization systems, i.e., deriving the missing information from information previously acquired by other systems, or possibly the user's personal devices. This implies bridging between the differences and discrepancies in terminologies, concepts, and user modeling approaches used by various systems, since nowadays personalization systems are typically designed to deliver their own personalized service, making user modeling information sharing practically impossible.

Recent research outlines two major approaches for such interoperability. The first calls for using a generally agreed, standard user modeling ontology, as suggested by Heckmann [2005], while the second addresses the practical limitations of personalization services by suggesting the idea of mediation [Berkovsky et al., 2008]. Heckmann [2005] suggested a rich and standardized ontology for user modeling, augmented by XML-based a user modeling language for information sharing [Heckmann and Krueger, 2003]. The benefits of this approach are clear: the agreed upon ontology and standardized XML-based representation pave the way for user modeling information sharing. An obvious limitation of this approach is that it requires all systems to adhere to the standard user model ontology, which brings up the question whether service providers will accept this requirement. Berkovsky et al. [2008] idea of mediation addresses the challenges of user modeling information sharing across applications in a practical way. Mediation deals with transferring user modeling data from one representation (for example, collaborative filtering) to another (for example, content based filtering) in the same domain, or across domains. Although the mediation does not imply standardized ontology, practical mediation scenarios require a large number of transfer mechanisms to be developed.

Both approaches have various variants implemented, demonstrated, and evaluated. However, both approaches could benefit from bridging the gaps between them and integrating components of one into another. Such an integrated user modeling data interoperability framework will enable developers of personalized services to use the level of abstraction and generality that best suits their case. This paper suggests integrating both approaches, and points out a research agenda for bridging that gap between them, while demonstrating initial steps already taken in this direction. The rest of the paper is organized as follows: Section 2 provides background and related work; Section 3 provides a description of initial step towards bridging the gap by smart situation retrieval with semantic conflict resolution; Section 4 concludes with suggestions for future work required to further bridge the gap between the two extremes.

2 Background and Related Work

Integration and reuse of user modeling mechanisms and data are drawing research interest for more than a decade. Various approaches were explored over time and it seems that two orthogonal approaches have evolved: (1) a comprehensive user modeling ontology that strives to provide rich semantics for standardization of user modeling, and (2) user modeling mediation, aimed to resolve the practical problems of heterogeneity in both user modeling representation and user modeling techniques. Both approaches are overviewed below, as well as additional related work.

2.1 Generic User Models and User Modeling Servers

User model initialization is a well known problem in personalization. Over the years, various approaches have been suggested to address it and shorten the process. As surveyed by Kobsa [2001], pioneering work of generic user models started as early as the mid-1980s, with the intention to allow re-use of already developed user modeling components and systems, thus focusing on technology re-use, rather than on the re-use of precious user modeling data collected in practice. It could be understood at that time, when in general, applications were stand alone and specific and user modeling capabilities were integrated into the application. The first step into ubiquitous user modeling was made by decoupling the linkage between the application and the user modeling component and introducing the general user modeling shell systems [Kobsa 2001]. Such shells, servers and toolkits were developed starting at the early 1990s. Kobsa [1995] performed a brief domain analysis of generic user modeling shells and listed the common core of services. This was later on extended by Kobsa [2001] that defined more abstract requirements. However, until this point the focus was the system – generic mechanisms for user modeling that could potentially be applied in different domain applications "as is", as needed, provided that the relevant domain knowledge and users' personal data are available. During the late 1990s, commercial user modeling shell systems started to appear, applying client-server architecture. This architecture provided the initial step towards sharing and re-using user modeling data for personalization by different applications [Pazani 2000, Kobsa 2001].

Kobsa [2001] also brought up the need to import and export existing user data as a requirement from user modeling server, but without suggesting any mechanism or framework for that process. He states correctly that processing done by current servers cannot be used outside the context of the specific domain and application due to the lack of abstract representation of learned users' characteristics. [Kobsa 2001] also details the requirements that will facilitate wide dissemination of generic user models. Originally, the requirements were split between academic and commercial applications, but since both groups of requirements were complimentary, they are integrated below into one list (omitting the technical performance requirements):

- Generality – domain independence, compatibility with as many as possible applications and domains, and for as many as possible user modeling tasks.
- Expressiveness – ability to express as many as possible types of facts and rules about the user.
- Inferential capabilities – capability of performing various types of reasoning and resolving the conflicts when contradictory facts or rules are detected.
- Import of external data – ability to integrate the user modeling data collected by the system with the data collected by other systems.
- Privacy – support of privacy policies and conventions, national and international privacy legislations, and privacy-supporting tools and service providers.

- Quick adaptation – ability to quickly adapt services to new users, personalization functionalities, applications, and domains.
- Extensibility – provide application programmer interfaces (APIs) and interfaces that allow (possibly bi-directional) exchange of user information between user-modeling tools, thus allowing the integration of variety of user modeling techniques.

Kobsa [2001] concludes his survey of generic user modeling systems with fairly accurate predictions of the evolvement of networked computers and especially mobile computing. He suggests two options for ubiquitous user modeling with a user model residing on the server side or on the client side, e.g., on the mobile device carried by the user. Furthermore, he presents the issue of personalization of smart appliances and the potential of multiple-purpose usage of users characteristics and discusses in light of this the pros and cons of client side versus server side user models [Yimam and Kobsa, 2003]. The survey is summarized with "...*one can expect to find a wide variety of generic user modeling systems, each of which is going to support only a few of the very different future manifestations of personalization and other applications of information about the user*". The conclusion from the above, (on the one hand, the expected variety of limited user modeling servers, and, on the other hand, the usefulness of re-using already available precious user modeling data), brings forward the need for some kind of generic mechanism for user modeling data sharing, conversion and exchange.

Recently, Van der Sluijs and Houben [2005] introduced Web 2.0 technology into user modeling servers when they introduced GUC – a Generic User Modeling Component. They suggest a user modeling server using OWL for user models representations stored in user models repository and applying schema matching techniques for finding appropriate user models in the repository as a response to a service request. This is in fact a suggestion how to apply novel web 2.0 technology for the above described user modeling servers' idea.

2.2 Semantically Enhanced User Modeling

Standardization and "common language" is one of the key issues in integrating information sources in every domain, including user modeling. The state-of-the-art approach for the problem of standardization of domain-specific knowledge representation is the use of ontologies. According to Gruber [1993], ontology is a formal representation of a set of concepts within a domain and the relationships between those concepts. These concepts constitute the domain vocabulary, whereas the relationships link them into a meaningful domain structure. Ontologies and common language communication protocols are among the commonly expected approaches, while the advent of the semantic web provided a common platform that encourages and supports this approach.

Ontology-based representation of user modeling was discussed by Kay [1999], which motivated ontology-based reusable and scrutable, i.e., understandable, modeling of students. Reusability allowed separating the representation of the user model from the personalization task in a particular application or domain. The structure of the user models was based on a set of predefined and agreed upon ontologies facilitated access to a customized explanation of the meaning of the user modeling components in each domain. However, despite the great potential in the use of on-tologies, they did not become widely used in user modeling tasks, possibly due to the considerable initial effort required in the construction of any ontology.

The notion of generic ontology-based user models was first developed by Razmerita et al. [2003] that presented a generic ontology-based user modeling architecture called OntobUM. OntobUM integrated three ontologies: user ontology characterizing the users, domain ontology defining the relationships between the per-sonalization applications, and log ontology defining the semantics of user-application interaction. Mehta et al. [2005] and Mehta and Nejdl [2007] also suggested the use of ontology for standardization of user models and to ease information exchange be-tween applications. A similar, but way more extensive approach for ontology-based representation of the user models was presented by Heckmann et al. [2006]. Heck-mann [2006] suggests GUMO[1] that seems to be the most comprehensive publicly avail-able user modeling ontology to date. Vassileva et al. [2003] also noted the need for a standard catalogue for user modeling, which defines relevant parameter values, and mechanisms for different user modeling purposes, as a necessary tool for integrating user models fragments.

The above works are natural extensions of earlier works on general user modeling systems of [Kay, 1995], [Kobsa, 2001], [Jameson, 2001], and others. Such ontology may be represented in a modern semantic web language like OWL, and thus be avail-able for all user-adaptive systems at the same time. The major advantage of such approach would be the simplification of exchanging user model data between different user-adaptive systems. Even though this is a desired situation and GUMO seems to be a major step in enabling the achievement of such a goal, the current state of the art is different. So far, there is a great deal of syntactical and structural differences between existing user modeling systems that cannot be overcome simply be introducing a com-monly accepted taxonomy, adapted to user modeling tasks as suggested by Heckmann, [2006]. In addition to GUMO, the UbisWorld[2] knowledge-base has been designed to complement GUMO and model contextual characteristics of a user, including their activity, as well as the environmental context. It also provides a symbolic spatial model to express location. Heckmann [2006] acknowledges the need for a relevant domain-specific ontology, as part of the overall framework, but rightfully recognizes the problem of including such ontologies in a user model. Heckman's compromise is to include a general interest model in the user model, a solution that needs to be extended for specific applications (by adding domain-specific ontology) in order to allow the application of GUMO in every specific domain.

2.3 User Models Integration and Mediation

Vassileva et al. [1999; 2001; 2003] pointed out the future situation of fragmented and inconsistent user models in ubiquitous computing. They suggested a distributed Multi-Agent approach for addressing the challenges of ubiquitous computing where large number of inconsistent user model fragments may be available and there will be a need to integrate them for an ad-hoc personalized service delivery. They presented

---

[1] GUMO homepage: http://www.gumo.org
[2] UbisWorld homepage: http://www.ubisworld.org

I-Help [Vassileva et al., 2003], a system providing access to help resources for students. The user modeling information included preferences, rankings, ratings and numeric overlays on course topics. The system is based on matchmaking – a variety of broker agents that keep track of user models and are able to map help requests to possible service providers. This matchmaking is based on domain taxonomy (provided by an instructor/teacher in I-Help). In their view, user modeling is a process that involves computation over subjects, objects, purposes and resources, where the I-Help is a specific demonstration. In order to generalize the approach, they noted the need for a "catalogue of purposes for user modeling" that needs to be manually constructed and be a standard reference to user modeling.

While Vassileva et al. [1999; 2001; 2003] and McCalla et al. [2000] focused the discussion on an abstract user modeling process, Berkovsky et al. [2008], suggested a practical approach aimed at overcoming the sparseness problem in recommender systems, by using *mediation* of the user models and other user modeling data. The exact definition of mediation is formulated as follows: "*mediation of user models is a process of importing the user modeling data collected by other (remote) recommender systems, integrating them and generating an integrated user model for a specific goal within a specific context.*" In this definition, the term integration refers to a set of techniques aimed at resolving the heterogeneities and inconsistencies in the obtained data. The mediation process facilitates the instantiation of user models by inferring the required user modeling data from past experiences and their evaluations in a three-dimensional context-aware representation space. Hence, the mediation enriches the existing (or bootstraps empty) user models in a target recommender system using the data collected by remote systems. This, in turn, facilitates provision of better context-aware recommendations.

The main obstacle for materializing the mediation ideas is overcoming the heterogeneity of the user modeling data. For example, recommender systems from different application domains imply different user modeling data stored in the models. Within the same domain, different systems may store different information in their user models, according to the specific recommendation technique being exploited (e.g., collaborative filtering ratings [Herlocker et al. 1999] versus domain/item features in content-based systems [Morita and Shinoda 1994]). Moreover, even the models of two recommender systems from the same application domain exploiting the same recommendation technique may use different terms to describe equivalent underlying objects, i.e., users, items, or domain features. Hence, successful completion of the user model mediation task requires (1) developing and applying reasoning and inference mechanisms for converting user modeling data between various representations, applications and domains, and (2) exploiting semantically-enhanced knowledge bases, actually facilitating the above reasoning and inference.

In the domain of recommender systems, prior research tried to integrate multiple recommendation techniques in the recommendation generation process. These systems are referred to in the literature as hybrid recommender systems [Burke 2002]. Although hybrid recommenders typically combine several recommendation techniques into a single recommender system for the sake of improving the accuracy of the generated recommendations, they are not concerned with the conversion of user modeling data between independently operating recommender systems. Hence, it should be noted that the mediation of user modeling data is more generic, dynamic and flexible approach than the data hybridization methods presented in [Burke 2002]. In a mediation scenario, the user model data a system received may be originated by various systems using different recommendation techniques and the mediation implies an ad-hoc application of dynamically selected mediation modules converting the user modeling data from a source to the target system, whereas classical hybridizations integrate specific techniques and approaches.

3 Smart Situation Retrieval with Semantic Conflict Resolution

The above two approaches refer to the issue of interoperability of personalization and user modeling systems in two orthogonal ways. Every approach has its own inherent limitations. Ontology-based standardization depends on a voluntary adoption of some kind of user modeling data representation standard by personalized service providers. Although GUMO currently represents a major step towards such standardization, at the current state of affairs this is a wishful thinking, since served eproviders need to adopt the standards and agree to share information. Mediation, on the other hand focuses on transforming specific models (or parts of such models) between applications, hence a mediator is needed between every two methods and user modeling data representation and terminology pose another challenge on practical mediation. The possible benefits of combining domain specific knowledge and more abstract user model knowledge were noted already both by Heckmann [2006] and by [Berkovsky et al., 2007]. The natural question we are facing is how to enhance the mediation mechanisms with semantic knowledge, in a way that will allow gradual adoption of standard tools like GUMO and UserML, while allowing the continuous use of the specific user modeling techniques applied in specific applications. In other words, how can an application be enhanced without the need to completely replace personalization mechanisms?

The *SmartSituationRetrieval* [Heckmann and Blass, 2008], is an example of a step towards this direction of semantic abstraction of user modeling for personalization. In this specific case, semantic abstraction is used for contextual conflicts resolution process. One class of problems that may occur in the challenge of context integration is the problem of *semantic conflicts* that occur in a case where several context statements use different words, concepts, ranges or values to describe the same situation. For example if one system claims that "Peter is happy," and the other system says "Peter is not happy," it is a classical conflict that has to be detected and resolved (which is reasonably easy in this case). On the contrary, if the other system says "Peter is sad," the system has to understand the semantic relation between happiness and sadness to detect these two statements as being conflicting. Consider another example, where one system talks about blood pressure while the other talks about pulse and both mean the same context dimension. Finally, consider a third example, where one system says "Peter is in the grocery store, " while the other system only reports "Peter is in a shop ." The crucial point is that these contextual dimensions are semantically related. In order to handle these relations there is a need for an ontology that will cover this semantic information.

UbisWorld's user model exchange and context management system UbisMEMORY is based on the semantic web ontology GUMO that describes the user model and context dimensions, but not the semantic relations between the different dimensions. However, these relations are defined and collected in the WordNet ontology, which will be presented in the following sub-section.

3.1 WordNet

The basic concept of WordNet is a collection of *SynSets*. A SynSet groups words with synonymous meaning. For example, "heartbeat, pulse, pulsation, beat" would be one SynSet of the word heartbeat. However, heartbeat is also a part of another SynSet "heartbeat, flash, blink of an eye, split second," in the meaning of *"Everything went so fast, in a heartbeat it was over."* To distinguish between the different meanings of the same word in different SynSets, one talks about *WordSenses*. Hence, SynSet contains one or more WordSenses and each WordSense belongs to exactly one SynSet. In turn, each WordSense has exactly one *Word* that represents it lexically, and one Word can be related to one or more Word-Senses [Van Assen, 2002]. Figure 2 schematically presents a graphical representation of Words, WordSenses and SynSets as part of the above example. Since both RDF/OWL extension of WordNet and the general user model and context ontology GUMO are represented in RDF/OWL, the representation used for both ontologies hereafter will be in RDF/OWL.

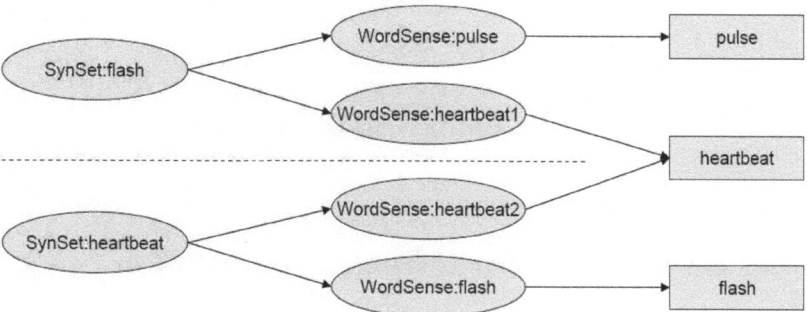

Fig. 2. Example of WordNet: The three words pulse, heartbeat and flash and their corresponding WordSenses and SynSets. The WordSense pulse is synonym to one of the WordSenses of heartbeat, so is flash with another WordSense of heartbeat. [Blass 2007]

As indicated by the symbols used in figure 2, there exists a model of WordNet using RDF and OWL. Every *SynSet*, every *WordSense* and every *Word* have unique identifiers and become RDF resources. Every *SynSet* holds the information which *WordSenses* are contained in it with the help of an RDF relation *containsWordSense*. The *WordSenses* point to the *Words* via *word* relation, which is related to the string literal it represents by *lexicalForm* relation. In addition to the relations *containsWordSense*, *word*, and *lexicalForm* there exist a number of additional relations. Some of the most widely used relations are briefly exemplified below. *Hyponym* describes a word or phrase whose semantic range is included within that of another word. For example: 'banana', 'apple', and 'grape' are all hyponyms of 'fruit'. In this example 'fruit' would be the *hypernym* of the other words. *Antonyms* are word pairs that are opposite in meaning, such as 'hot' and 'cold' or 'happy' and 'sad'. The *antonymOf* relation models this. *Meronym* denotes a constituent part or a member of something. That is, *{A}meronymOf{B}* if A is either a part or a member of B. For example, 'finger' is a meronym of 'hand' because a finger is part of a hand. Similarly 'wheel' is a meronym of 'automobile'. A further discussion on WordNet relations can be found in [Van Assen, 2002].

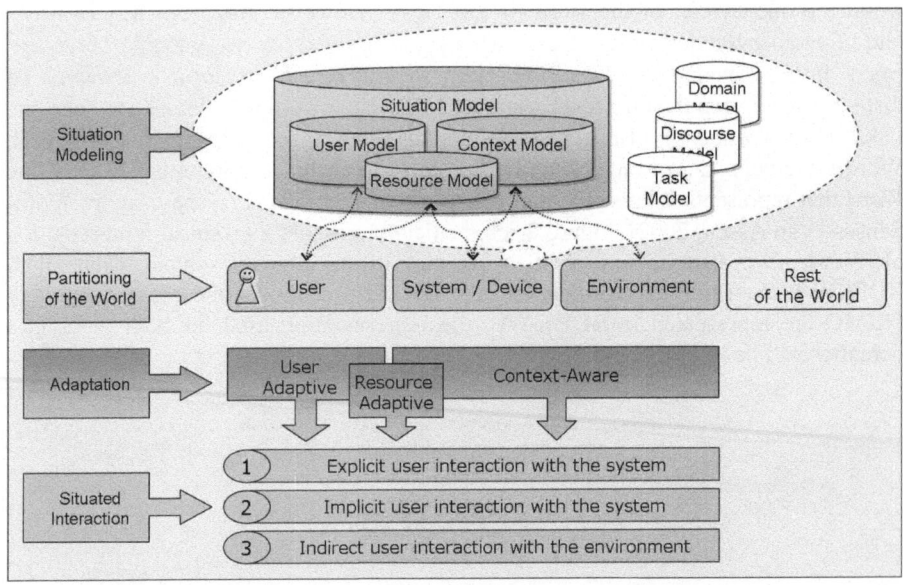

Fig. 3. Situated interaction and the system's situation model for mobile computing

3.2 Integrated Model for Context-Awareness and User-Adaptivity

The research areas of *user-adaptivity*, *context-awareness* and *ubiquitous computing* find their intersection in the concept of context, while *semantic web* technology could serve as a mediator between them. In [Kray, 2003] it is pointed out that throughout the different research communities and disciplines, there are various definitions of what exactly is contained in the *context model* [McCarthy and Buvac, 1998], the *user model* [Day, 1999], and the *situation model* [Jameson, 2001]. Therefore, it is necessary to clarify how those terms will be used in our approach. A *situation model* is defined as the combination of a *user model* and a *context model*. Figure 3 presents a diagrammatic answer to the question *"What is situated interaction and how can we conceptualize it?"* Resource-adaptivity overlaps with *user-adaptivity* and *context-awareness* because the human's cognitive resources fall into the user model, while the system's technical resources can be seen as part of the context model. The fundamental data structure is the SITUATIONALSTATEMENT (see [Heckmann, 2003]) that collects apart from the main contextual information also meta-data like temporal and spatial constraints, explanation components, and privacy preferences. Distributed sets of SITUATIONREPORTS form a coherent, integrated, but still hybrid accretion concept of ubiquitous situation (user and context) models.

3.3   User Modeling and Context Modeling with GUMO and UserML

GUMO, the general user modeling ontology allows user modeling applications to collect the user's dimensions modeled by user-adaptive systems like the *heartbeat rate, age, current position, birthplace, ability to swim,* and many others. The contextual dimensions like *noise level* in the environment, *battery status* of the mobile device, or the *weather* conditions are modeled as well. The main conceptual idea in SITUATION-ALSTATEMENTS is the division of user model and contextual dimensions into three parts: `auxiliary`, `predicate` and `range`. Apart from these `main` attributes, there are predefined attributes about the `situation`, the `explanation`, the `privacy` and the `administration`. Thus, our basic context modeling is more flexible than simple attribute-value pairs or RDF triples. If one wants to say *something about the user's interest in football,* one could divide this into the `auxiliary`=*hasInterest*, the `predicate`=*football* and the `range`=*low-medium-high*.

GUMO is designed according to USERML approach, as an XML application (see [Heckmann and Krueger, 2003]), to facilitate easy exchange of user modeling data. Approximately one thousand groups of `auxiliaries`, `predicates` and `ranges` have so far been identified and inserted into the ontology. However, it turned out that actually everything can be a `predicate` for the `auxiliary` *hasInterest* or *hasKnowledge,* what leads to a problem if work is not modularized. The suggested solution is to identify basic user model dimensions on the one hand, while leaving the more general world knowledge open for already existing other ontologies on the other hand. Candidates are the general suggested upper merged ontology SUMO [Pease et al., 2002] and the UBISONTOLOGY[3] [Stahl and Heckmann, 2004] used to model intelligent environments. Identified user model and context `auxiliaries` are, for example, *hasKnowledge, hasInterest, hasBelief, hasPlan, hasProperty, hasPlan,* and *hasLocation.* A class defines a group of individuals that belong together because they share some properties. Classes can be organized in a specialization hierarchy using the `subClassOf` `relation`.

3.4   Smart Situation Retrieval Process

In an "open world assumption" together with an "open to everyone assumption", every user and every system is allowed to enter statements into repositories (that contain partial user models), where some of this information might be contradictory. Conflicts among the statements like, for example, a contradiction caused by different opinions of different creators or changed values over time, are loosely categorized in the following listing.

1. On the semantic level: the systems do not use the same ontology to represent the meaning of the concepts, which leads to the user model integration problem.

---

[3] UbisWorld homepage: `http://www.ubisworld.org`

2. On the observation and inference level: several sensors interpret the same observations differently, measurement errors occur, or systems have preferred information sources
3. On the temporal and spatial level: information is out of date or out of spatial range.
4. On the privacy and trust level: information is hidden, incomplete, secret or falsified on purpose.

The architectural diagram in Figure 4 shows the SMARTSITUATIONRETRIEVAL or in other words: how the conflict-free partial user models are generated. Not all of these modules are explained here in detail. See [Heckmann 2006] for a detailed description. The focus in our discussion is set on the semantic conflict resolution part. *Note that the oval numbers indicate the reading order.*

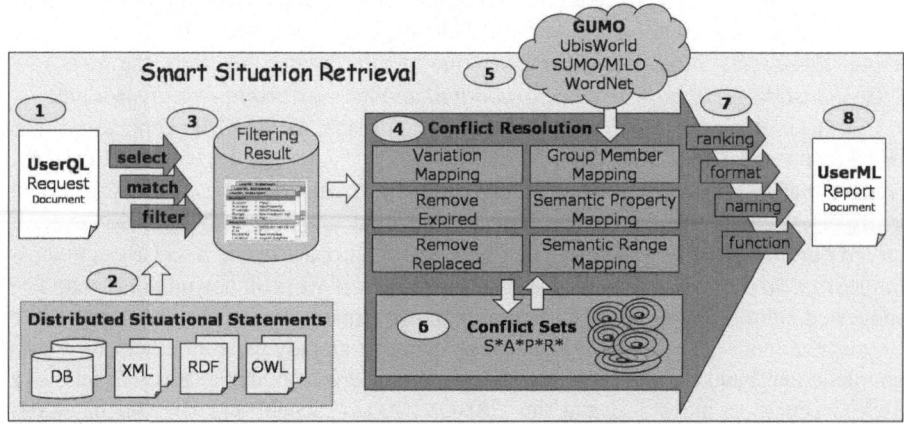

Fig. 4. Smart Situation Retrieval with Focus on Semantic Conflict Resolution

Item (1) shows a request that has to be parsed. It is given in UserQL, the query language that has been defined in analogy to UserML. Item (2) refers to the distributed retrieval of SITUATIONALSTATEMENTS (accumulated over time, entered by different sources) . In the retrieval case, that we are discussing here, we can see (1), (2) and (5) as given and the others as being calculated. Item (3) summarizes the three macro-steps, i.e., `select`, `match`, and `filter`, and presents the FILTERINGRE-SULT as input to the follow up conflict resolution process. The filtering result contains all statements that fit to the UserQL query, however with possible conflicts and contradictions.

Now, the conflict resolution phase starts. Item (4) stands for three syntactical procedures VARIATIONMAPPING, REMOVEEXPIRED and REMOVEREPLACED. These three procedures align the statements syntactically, and remove outdated and replaced statements. Item (5) represents three semantic procedures GROUPMEMBERMAPPING, SEMANTICPROPERTYMAPPING and SEMANTICRANGEMAPPING that base on the data represented by the knowledge base of WorldNet and GUMO, UbisWorldOntology, and SUMO/MILO ontologies. Item (6) shows the detection of syntactic and semantic conflicts and the construction of the conflict sets. Item (7) refers to the post-processing of `ranking, format, naming` and `function` that control the output format. Item (8) forms the resulting `UserML` report, that is send back to the requestor.

A simplified example will demonstrate the process. Assume there are two statements: "Peter is 30% happy" and "Pedro is almost sad" that are stored as distributed statements in the repository (facts that were inserted sometime before) (2). Now, our system receives a UserQL request (1) like "Is Peter happy?". The select and *matching procedure (3)* compares all given match attributes with the corresponding statement attributes – in our example, the following attributes may be compared: happy and sad, Peter and Pedro (which are the only informative attributes in these statements). The *filtering procedure* operates on the matching results. Each statement is individually checked if it passes the *privacy filter*, the *confidence filter,* and the *temporal filter (in our case the temporal characteristics of the statements, whether any of them is outdated)*. Now we look closer to the conflict resolution step (4), the "variation mapping" can map "Peter" in system A to "Pedro" in system B, if both denote the same person (should be reasoned about). Now, the semantic property mapping has to map "happy" and "sad" to each other, which makes sense only if there is a strong semantic relation between the two properties. The last step would be the semantic range mapping that maps "almost" onto the scale of percentage, such that it can be directly compared with "30%".

The question that arises: how do we resolve conflicts that we have found in (6) together with the defined semantics in (5). In our example, we can conclude that Peter is not happy. Independently of who has claimed which statement, like a novice versus an expert. If we also take such meta-information into account we can resolve further conflicts. *Conflict resolvers* were developed to control the *conflict resolution process* such that an ordered list of resolvers defines the *conflict resolution strategy*. These resolvers are needed if the *match process* and *filter process* leave several conflicting statements as possible answers. The *most(n)*-resolvers use meta data for their decision. Several most(n)-resolvers are presented in the following listing.

- **mostRecent(n).** If sensors send new statements on a frequent basis, values tend to change more quickly as they expire. This leads to conflicting non-expired statements. The *mostRecent(n)* resolver returns the n newest non-expired statements, where n is a natural number between 1 and the number of remaining statements.
- **mostNamed(n).** If there are many statements that claim A and only a few claim B or something else, than n of the most named statements are returned. Of course, it is not sure that the majority necessarily tells the truth but it could be a reasonable rule of thumb for some cases.
- **mostConfident(n).** If the confidence values of several conflicting statements can be compared with each other, it seems to be an obvious decision to return the n statements with the highest confidence value.
- **mostPersonal(n).** If the `creator` of the statement is the statement's `subject` (a self-reflecting statement), this statement is preferred by the *mostPersonal(n)* resolver. Furthermore, if an *is-friend-of relation* is defined, statements by friends could be preferred to statements by others.

Although these conflict resolver rules are based on common sense heuristics, they do not necessarily need to be true for specific sets of statements. An important issue to keep in mind is that the resolvers and their strategies imply uncertainty. To reflect this, the `confidence` value of the resulting statement is changed appropriately and the conflict situation is added to the `evidence` attribute.

To come back to the discussion about WordNet: the semantic conflicts are resolved using WordNet query expansion algorithm. The query expansion algorithm posts four queries to the WordNet repository: one query for synonyms, one for hyponyms, and the other two for antonyms. The two queries are shown in Figure 5. *Predicate* denotes the input of the function. It is assumed to be a string representing the full identified of the resources annotating the WordSense. All results, that is, the identifiers of related WordSenses, are added to the output.

```
SYNONYMS:
SELECT DISTINCT WS2
FROM {SynSet} wn20schema:containsWordSense
{<predicate>},
{SynSet} wn20schema:containsWordSense {WS2}
USING NAMESPACE
wn20schema =
<http://www.w3.org/2006/03/wn/wn20/schema/>

HYPONYMS:
SELECT DISTINCT WS2
FROM {SynSet} wn20schema:containsWordSense
{<predicate>},
{SynSet2} wn20schema:hyponymOf {SynSet},
{SynSet2}wn20schema:containsWordSense {WS2}
USING NAMESPACE
wn20schema =
<http://www.w3.org/2006/03/wn/wn20/schema/>";
```

Fig. 5. Queries for synonyms and hyponyms of a given *predicate[Blass2008]*

Statements that have predicates synonym, hyponym and antonym to the given one are found by posting queries with replaced predicates to our basic matching query engine. It could be hypothesized that synonyms, hyponyms and antonyms would improve the performance of our search, since statements with predicated synonym are semantically equivalent to the ones with the base predicate. Antonyms correspond to negation and hence if used as predicates, only the object needs to be inverted in order to gain a semantic equivalence. The hyponym of a predicate is more specific than the predicate itself and can be also useful. However, hypernyms are not so helpful, as one's interest in a certain concept does not necessarily imply his/her interest in a more general concept.

4   Future Research Directions

The above example introduced an initial work geared towards introducing an integrated architecture for *Situation Modeling* and *Smart Context Retrieval*, taking advantage of GUMO and UserML. A model for situated interaction and context-awareness was suggested, using WordNet and GUMO for supporting semantic conflict resolution of ubiquitous user and context models.

There are several kinds of conflicts that arise in a standard retrieval approach. Semantic conflicts are statements that are difficult to detect. If a system querying a ubiquitous user model is unaware of these problems it is hard to give correct recommendations based on the results of retrieval. The approach suggested above is based on semantic web technology and a complex conflict resolution and query concept, in order to be flexible enough to support adaptation in human-computer interaction in ubiquitous computing.

It is reasonable to presume that user modeling mediation may be enhanced by additional knowledge. The simplest example is the use of linguistic knowledge for identification of synonyms, antonyms etc. A step further may be the use of domain taxonomy for the mediation of user models. Furthermore, similarity of domains and mediation of domain-related user models from one domain in another domain requires additional knowledge about how to translate and interpret the information from the source domain in the target domain. This brings up the issue of what a domain is, how domains can be characterized and modeled, and how these definitions can be used for user modeling. The issue of context is another issue of great importance, since the same user may have different preferences for the same item in a different context [Berkovsky et al., 2006]. Figure 6 illustrates a semantically enhanced user modeling mediation, where, in addition to the specific mechanism used to transform the user modeling data from remote systems to the target system (may be regarded as a part of the catalogue suggested by Vassileva et al. [2003]), all various types of knowledge are used to select the right user attributes that are relevant to a given situation.

In the following list we sample and briefly discuss future research directions for ubiquitous user modeling that may help, in turn, to bridge the knowledge gap and allow building true ubiquitous user models, which may be stored on a user device or distributed in the environments:

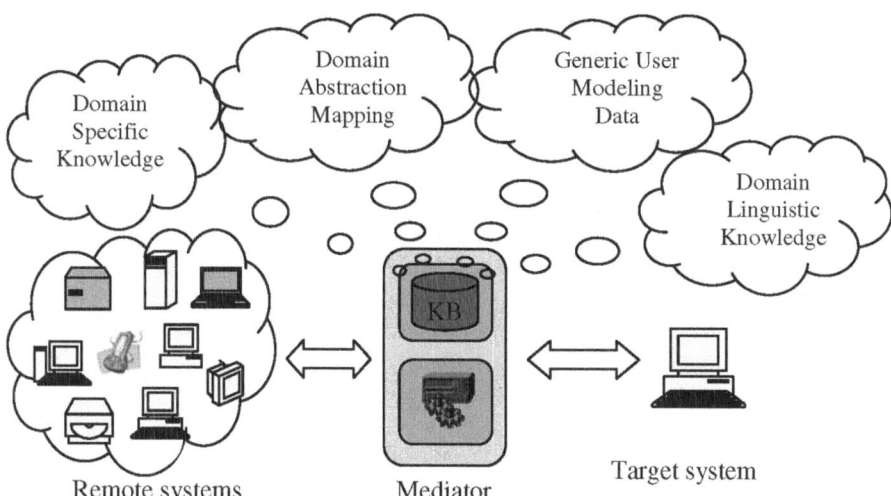

Fig. 6. Semantically enhanced user models mediation

- **Use of Domain Thesauri and Ontologies.** Different domains may have their own thesauri and ontologies. These are needed not only for user modeling purposes, but in general for standardization and common understanding of the domain. A good example is the medicine, where there is a systematic development of vocabularies. Although thesauri provide only linguistic information, they can standardize the domain terminology. Even WordNet can be used for identifying synonyms and enhance reasoning and mediation of content-based user modeling data. In particular, these ontologies can be used for a two-stage mediation: (1) bottom-up inference from the available user modeling data to the values of the ontology slots, and (2) inverse top-down inference from the inferred values of the ontology slots to the user modeling data required by the target personalization system.

- **Mapping GUMO Attributes to Specific Domains.** While GUMO provides a comprehensive user modeling ontology, different domains, situations, and even constraints of a certain situation may require to use different components of GUMO. Moreover, they may lead to different interpretations of the same slots of GUMO and their values. Hence there is a need to develop flexible mechanisms that will allow applying GUMO in different domains, situations, and constrains. This can be done, for instance, by a rule-based inference mechanism using GUMO attributes in specific conditions. These rules will lead to dynamically created localized views of GUMO, which can be applied for specific domains, situations, and constraints.

- **Contextual Aspects.** As already mentioned, different context may lead to different uses and interpretations of user modeling data. This is especially important for ubiquitous computing where the users' context changes frequently and dynamically. GUMO is naturally extensible for modeling various dimensions of contexts. This modeling, in turn, facilitates cross-context mediation of user modeling data, as suggested by Berkovsky et al [2006]. There, two complementary mediation types are presented: rule-based inference according to the rules crafted by domain experts or similarity-based reasoning applying statistical learning methods using previously collected user experiences.

- **Applying Machine Learning Approaches for Mediation Techniques.** Taking a closer look at content-based user modeling, a variety of machine learning techniques may be applied for user modeling purposes. Learning techniques used in the implemented mediation scenarios were quite simplistic and used intuitive reasoning mechanisms and shallow knowledge bases. However, this may hamper the accuracy of the derived user modeling data and, in turn, of the personalized services provided to the user. A natural question may be how to apply more accurate approaches and elicit the information using, for instance, Artificial Neural Network or the Support Vector Machine. While initial ideas were suggested by [Berkovsky et al., 2007], there are still a number of practical issues, machine learning approaches, and mediation scenarios to deal with.

- **Privacy Aspects.** With the evolvement of ubiquitous computing and user modeling, comes the issue of privacy. Personalized service requires the service provider to have a decent amount of personal information about the user, which can be provided by the user or by other systems, if the user is identified and allows such information transfer. Hence, mechanisms for preserving the privacy of the user and his/her personal information should be developed in parallel. However, the goals of the privacy-preserving mechanisms contradict the goals of the personalization systems, leading to privacy versus accuracy trade-off. One possible compromise may be that the user will have a comprehensive representation of his/her model and allow parts of it to be provided anonymously to the service provider, if requested.

General user modeling ontology and user modeling mediation seem to be two orthogonal approaches to materialize the user modeling data interoperability in personalization systems. Each approach bears its own inherent advantages and limitations. This work presented a list of research issues that may help bridging the gap between the two approaches. We believe that incremental research efforts in these areas may gradually bridge the gap and allow applying both the semantics provided by GUMO and the user modeling mediation ideas in practice.

Acknowledgements

This work has partly been supported by the EU-funded FP7 Project "GRAPPLE" which stands for "Generic Responsive Adaptive Personalized Learning Environment" and by the Australian Government through the Intelligent Island Program (administered by the Tasmanian Department of Economic Development and Tourism) and CSIRO. A special gratitude goes to Christian Blass and his work on semantic conflict resolution with WordNet in his Bachelor thesis [Blass, 2007].

References

Adomavicius, G., Sankaranarayanan, R., Sen, S., Tuzhilin, A.: Incorporating Contextual Information in Recommender Systems using a Multidimensional Approach. ACM Transactions on Information Systems 23(1), 103–145 (2005)

Berkovsky, S., Aroyo, L., Heckmann, D., Houben, G.J., Kröner, A., Kuflik, T., Ricci, F.: Predicting User Experiences through Cross-Context Reasoning. In: Proceedings of ABIS 2006 - 14th Workshop on Adaptivity and User Modeling in Interactive Systems, Hildesheim, Germany, October 9-11 (2006)

Berkovsky, S., Kuflik, T., Ricci, F.: Mediation of user models for enhanced personalization in recommender systems. User Modeling and User-Adapted Interaction 18(3), 245–286 (2008)

Blass, C.: Ubiquitous User Modeling: Semantic Conflict Resolution with WordNet, Bachelor Thesis, Saarland University (2007)

Burke, R.: Hybrid Recommender Systems: Survey and Experiments. User Modeling and User-Adapted Interaction 12(4), 331–370 (2002)

Dey, A.K., Abowd, G.D.: Towards a better understanding of context and context-awareness. Technical Report GIT-GVU-99-22, College of Computing, Georgia Institute of Technology, Atlanta, Georgia, U.S.A (1999)

Fellbaum, C. (ed.): WordNet – An Electronic Lexical Database. The MIT Press, Cambridge (1998)

Gruber, T.R.: A translation approach to portable ontologies. Knowledge Acquisition 5(2), 199–220 (1993)

Heckmann, D.: Ubiqutous User Modeling. Akademische Verlagsgesellschaft Aka GmbH, Berlin (2006) ISBN 3-89838-297-4 and ISBN 1-58603-608-4

Heckmann, D., Blass, C.: Context Integration for Ubiquitous User Modeling: Solving Semantic Conflicts with WordNet and GUMO. In: 5th International Workshop on Ubiquitous User Modeling, UbiqUM 2008, Gran Canaria, Spain (2008)

Heckmann, D., Krueger, A.: A User Modeling Markup Language (UserML) for Ubiquitous Computing. In: Brusilovsky, P., Corbett, A.T., de Rosis, F. (eds.) UM 2003. LNCS (LNAI), vol. 2702, pp. 393–397. Springer, Heidelberg (2003)

Heckmann, D.: Introducing situational statements as an integrating data structure for user modeling, context-awareness and resource-adaptive computing. In: Hoto, A., Stumme, G. (eds.) LLWA Lehren - Lernen - Wissen - Adaptivität (ABIS 2003), Karlsruhe, Germany, pp. 283–286 (2003)

Herlocker, J.L., Konstan, J.A., Borchers, A., Riedl, J.: An Algorithmic Framework for Performing Collaborative Filtering. In: Proceedings of the Annual International ACM SIGIR Conference on Research and Development in Information Retrieval, Berkeley, CA (1999)

Jameson, A.: Modeling both the context and the user. Personal Technologies 5(1), 29–33 (2001)

Kay, J.: The UM toolkit for reusable, long term user models. User Modeling and User-Adapted Interaction 4(3), 149–196 (1995)

Kobsa, A.: Generic user modeling systems. User Modelling and User-Adapted Interaction Journal 11(1-2), 49–63 (2001)

Kray, C.: Situated Interaction on Spatial Topics. DISKI, vol. 274. Aka Verlag, Berlin (2003)

McCarthy, J., Buvac, S.: Formalizing context (expanded notes). In: Aliseda, A., van Glabbek, R.J., Westerstahl, D. (eds.) Computing Natural Language. CSLI Lecture Notes. Center for the Study of Language and Information, vol. 81, Standford University, CA, pp. 13–50 (1998)

McCalla, G., Vassileva, G., Greer, J., Bull, S.: Active Learner Modelling. In: Gauthier, G., VanLehn, K., Frasson, C. (eds.) ITS 2000. LNCS, vol. 1839, pp. 53–62. Springer, Heidelberg (2000)

Mehta, B., Niederee, C., Stewart, A., Degemmis, M., Lops, P., Semeraro, G.: Ontologically-Enriched Unified User Modeling for Cross-System Personalization. In: Ardissono, L., Brna, P., Mitrović, A. (eds.) UM 2005. LNCS (LNAI), vol. 3538, pp. 119–123. Springer, Heidelberg (2005)

Mehta, B., Nejdl, W.: Intelligent Distributed User Modelling: from Semantics to Learning. In: UbiDeUM, Corfu, Greece (2007)

Morita, M., Shinoda, Y.: Information Filtering Based on User Behavior Analysis and Best Match Retrieval. In: Proceedings of the Annual International Conference on Research and De-velopment in Information Retrieval, Dublin, Ireland (1994)

Muhammad, T., Vassileva, J.: Policies for Distributed User Modeling in Online Communities. In: Proc. Workshop UbiDeUM 2007, at the 11th International Conference UM 2007, Corfu (2007)

Pease, A., Niles, I., Li, J.: The suggested upper merged ontology: A large ontology for the semanticweb and its applications. In: AAAI 2002 Workshop on Ontologies and the Semantic Web. Working Notes (2002),
http://projects.teknowledge.com/AAAI-2002/Pease.ps

Stahl, C., Heckmann, D.: Using semantic web technology for ubiquitous location and situation modeling. The Journal of Geographic Information Sciences CPGIS: Berkeley 10, 157–165 (2004)

van Assem, M., Gangemi, A., Schreiber, G.: Rdf/owl representation of wordnet. Technical report, Vrije Universiteit Amsterdam (2002)

van der Sluijs, K., Houben, G.J.: Towards a Generic User Model Component. In: Workshop on Personalization on the Semantic Web (PerSWeb 2005), at the 10th International Conference on User Modeling (UM 2005), Edinburgh, Scotland, July 25-26, pp. 43–52 (2005)

Vassileva, J., Greer, J.E., McCalla, G.I.: Openness and Disclosure in Multi-agent Learner Models. In: Proceedings of the Workshop on Open, Interactive, and Other Overt Approaches to Learner Modeling, International Conference on AI in Education, Lemans, France (1999)

Vassileva, J.: Distributed User Modeling for Universal Information Access. In: Stephanidis, C. (ed.) Universal Access in Human - Computer Interaction (UAHCI), Proceedings of the 9th International Conference on Human-Computer Interaction, New Orleans, USA, vol. 3, pp. 122–126. Lawrence Erlbaum, Mahwah (2001)

Vassileva, J., McCalla, G., Greer, J.: Multi-Agent Multi-User Modeling. User Modelling and User Adapted Interaction 13(1), 1–31 (2003)

Yimam-Seid, D., Kobsa, A.: Expert Finding Systems for Organizations: Problem and Domain Analysis and the DEMOIR Approach. Journal of Organizational Computing and Electronic Commerce 13(1), 1–24 (2003)

Handling Semantic Heterogeneity in Interoperable Distributed User Models

Francesca Carmagnola

Department of Computer Science, University of Turin, Italy
carmagnola@di.unito.it

Abstract. Due to the overspread of user adaptive systems user data are collected and processed in diverse settings and from different platforms. The computational effort to extract user models is commonly repeated across applications and domains, mainly due to lack of interoperability and synchronization among user-adaptive systems. One way of achieving a complete picture of a user's experience is to allow systems to share user data to obtain maximum leverage and reuse of information. We address this process as user model interoperability. One of the major challenge to user models interoperability is handling semantic heterogeneity. The paper proposes a new approach for user model interoperability which deals with the semantic heterogeneity of user models and automates the user model exchange across applications.

1 Introduction

Nowadays user-adaptive systems have been deployed in several areas. This enables information about the user to be collected and processed in diverse settings (home, work, travel, leisure) and from different platforms (web, mobile devices, sensors). The computational efforts to extract user models is commonly repeated across applications and domains, mainly due to lack of interoperability and synchronization among user-adaptive systems. There is no common "memory" of all the user activities, preferences and characteristics, which would allow effective and adequate adaptation to the users current state [1]. One way of achieving a rather complete picture of a users experience is to allow systems to share user data to obtain maximum leverage and reuse of information. [2], [3], [4], [5], [6]. In this way users can be offered with better adaptation results without being annoyed by directly asking data (such as interests and preferences) or waiting a lot of time before obtaining personalized information and services.

Gathering and making sense of this distributed user information entails the capability of interpreting the information from heterogeneous sources and integrating them into a user model of a proper granularity. We denote this process as *user models interoperability*, and the systems exchanging knowledge about a user as *interoperable user-adaptive systems*.

Interoperability is, in general, a challenging task which turns out to be even more complex when dealing with knowledge-based systems that collect data about users.

One of the major challenge to user model interoperability is handling the semantic heterogeneity of the user models. Systems may represent user data in different ways by using various syntactic and conceptual structures, rarely share vocabularies (even when

T. Kuflik et al. (Eds.): Advances in Ubiquitous User Modelling, LNCS 5830, pp. 20–36, 2009.

dealing with the same domains), and often make different interpretations of the same terminology. This may hinder the exchange and reuse of user models, and can have a negative impact on the practical applications of interoperable distributed user models.

The paper proposes a new approach for user model interoperability which deals with semantic heterogeneity of user models and automates the user model exchange across applications.

The paper is structured as follows. In Section 2 we present an application scenario of user model interoperability. In Section 3 we position our work in the relevant literature. The framework and the architecture we propose are described in Section 4. Section 5 presents the algorithm for handling semantic heterogeneity in user model interoperability. Finally, Section 6 concludes the paper providing some future directions and open issues of the current research.

2   Application Scenario

As an example of user models interoperability among user-adaptive systems, let us consider the following scenario. We consider iCITY, an adaptive social mobile guide that provides personalized information and suggestions about cultural events of the city of Torino (Turin) [7].

Suppose a scenario showing iCITY wishes to decide whether to show an advertisement for an incoming Rock concert to a novice user called Carlo. In a typical recommender system, a correct assumption about user's interests can be estimated only after a reasonably high number of user's interactions within the system. In this example use case, no information about Carlo's interest for Rock music is available in Carlo's user model since Carlo is a novice user. This situation addresses the well known "cold start problem" which occurs when, at the beginning of the users interactions, the user model stores little data about the user [8].

Thus, the possibility of gathering knowledge about Carlo from the other adaptive systems he interacts with may be extremely helpful.

Assuming Carlo is used to interact with another user-adaptive system, named UbiquiTO [9]. UbiquiTO is a mobile tourist guide which supports users in visiting the city of Torino, according with her interests, preferences, needs. In a interoperability scenario, iCITY will query UbiquiTO to retrieve Carlo's interest for Rock music. Thanks to the derived information, iCITY becomes aware of Carlo's great likelihood for Rock music and it is finally able to inform him of the presence of a rock band concert in Torino.

3   Related Work

To benefit from distributed user information, a system must be able to access and interpret information derived from multiple heterogeneous sources and to integrate this information into a model of proper granularity [10]. This is the so-called interoperability. Interoperability has been variously addressed in the literature. Greaves relates the concept of interoperability with three main issues [11].

Syntactic interoperability, which refers to the capability of different information systems to interpret the syntax of the delivered data in the same way. Syntactic interoperability can be achieved, for instance, through the definition of a common interchange formalism, or through APIs [12].

Semantic interoperability, which regards the possibility for systems to bridge differences between information systems on the meaning level. It refers to the "capability for different systems to entail a co-ordination of meaning on the basis of shared, pre-established and negotiated meaning of terms and expressions"[13]. It is often achieved through multiple controlled vocabularies.

Logical interoperability regards the possibility for systems to share a common content model. Thus, it regards the possibility to bridge differences between information systems on the meaning level.

In the user modeling community, researchers have mainly focused on proposing solutions to achieve syntactic and semantic interoperability. To this purpose, we can distinguish among two approaches: a *shared format approach* vs. a *conversion* approach [14]. While the former imposes the use of a shared syntax and semantics to represent user model and user profile data; in the latter there is not a shared representation for the user model and suitable algorithms and techniques are employed to convert the syntax and semantics of the user model data used in one system into those of another system.

3.1 Shared Format Approach

Suppliers and consumers of user profiles have recently shown an increased awareness of the need for standards for representing and exchanging user model data with the aim of achieving a unified user profile which is easily exchangeable and interpretable [15].

Many efforts have been devoted in standardizing user model related aspects, mostly in application-specific areas [16,17,18,19,20]. Some examples of standards used especially in e-learning domain are vCard [16], IMS LIP [17], IEEE PAPI [18] and FOAF [21].

Although these standards are universally acknowledged, they have some limitations. vCard is best suited for light weight user profiles like contact information or directories, while IMS and PAPI are more generic but they are not conceptually extensible. Moreover, all these standards are not conformed to represent dynamic user data, like preferences and interests which are required in present-day user-adaptive systems.

More recent works, exploit the standard languages of Semantic Web, such as, RDF [22], RDF [23], DAML [24], OWL [25] to provide an extended representation of the user which includes several relevant user aspects, together with a wide representation of the domain knowledge. In this direction we can cite GUMO [20], the General User Model Ontology. GUMO represents the user model in a standard and commonly accepted way, in several semantic web languages, and it is available via Internet for several user-adaptive systems at the same time [20]. The classes and properties of GUMO are employed into the user model exchange language called UserML [26] which supports the user model data exchange across systems.

A further example of the exploitation of the lingua franca approach was proposed by Metha et al. ([27]). As a basis for the exchange of user profile information between multiple systems, the authors define an ontology-based user context model, the unified user context model (UUCM). UUCM is published as a shared ontology all participating systems should rely on to represent and exchange user model data.

3.2 Conversion Approach

The major advantage of the shared format approach is that no syntactic and semantic heterogeneity issues need to be solved since there is a unified user profile that is easily exchangeable and interpretable [28]. Indeed, user model interoperability is strongly streamlined. However, in open and dynamic environments, such as the Web or decentralized ubiquitous settings, it is impractical, and in many cases impossible, to create a unified user profile infrastructure and to enforce applications to adhere to a shared vocabulary [29].

The opposite approach excludes the use of any semantic representation or of a shared representation for the user model. On the contrary, it defines proper algorithms and techniques to convert the syntax and semantics of the user model data used in one system into those used in another system. Along this line, we can mention the work of Berkovsky et al. [30] which defines hybrid recommendation algorithms to bootstrap user models in one system by using information from other systems. This approach however does not take into account the richness of semantics and domain specific knowledge the systems have accumulated about the user [29]. Another example of conversion approach is given in Stewart et al. [15], where the interoperability of user models between different Adaptive Educational Hypermedia systems is done via a one-to-one conversion. The conversion is performed identifying a core set of common variables among the user models of the two systems and then through a simple peer-to-peer interaction.

An intermediate solution would be to combine the benefits of both approaches to allow flexibility in representing user models and to provide *semantic mapping* of the user data from one system to another [29]. Recent proposals along this line of research exploit Semantic Web techniques.

For example, [5] suggests that the exchange of user model data is facilitated by an additional phase where the user model schemata of different systems are mapped. More specifically, the author develop the Generic User Model Component (GUC), a generic component which provides the user model with storage facilities for applications. Each application can use its own vocabulary, e.g. a proprietary format for its user models. The user-adaptive systems that aim at exchanging user data can "subscribe" to GUC. The mapping of the user data are performed translating the instance data of one application to the instance data of another application through a procedure which builds a graph view over the application schemes, then it creates a common graph by using graph-matching techniques, and finally it semi-automatically creates the mappings among the schemes. Even if this is a promising solution to handle data heterogeneity issue, the mapping requires additional human effort and may not always be feasible. Instead, [31] proposes the use of a semantics-based dialog for exchanging and clarifying user model data between applications. The authors introduce a specific dialogue game, called "concepts-explorative game" to solve semantic interoperability issue. When a semantic conflict among user model data is detected, the requestor systems starts such a game in order to find out any related concepts in providers' user model ontology. Once the closest concepts have been identified, it starts the exchange of the values of the related concepts. However, the dialog planning mechanism assumes that the applications share a common domain ontology, which may not always be the case.

The approach proposed in this paper is inspired by advances in the Semantic Web and contributes to research along the agenda of finding an intermediate solution combining both a flexibility in representing user models and providing a *semantic mapping* of the user data from one system to another.

4   A Framework for User Model Interoperability

The work presented in this paper is part of a larger research [32] which developed a framework for user model interoperability, including a mechanism to identify the user whose data and information are shared across systems in absence of a unique user identifier [33], a mechanism for the exchange of user data, conflict detection and resolution for data integration and a real evaluation of the user model interoperability process.

This paper focuses on the core phase of the user model interoperability process, that is the exchange of user data. We will present in this section its main principles and architecture.

In the scenario we envision, data about a user can be stored in more than one application and can be used in different ways and for different purposes. According to the user model interoperability process, an application which we will call *receiver* R, may request data about a user U from other systems, called *providers* P.

4.1   Data Representation

According to our approach, systems are not required to share a common user model representation. Indeed, every systems can represent the user model according to the proprietary format they wish. However, to ensure syntactic interoperability systems need to adhere to a standard for the exchange of semantic-enriched user data. To this purpose, we exploit RDF[1], which is one of the most widely used Semantic Web languages which ensures interoperability of semantic data.

We consider that to take part in the interoperability process every provider system maintains a *shareable user model* which includes those fragments of the user model that can be shared[2] with other systems as RDF statements. We will denote the collection of shared statements of provider P as

$$S_P = \left\{ s_P^1, s_P^2, s_P^3, \ldots s_P^n \right\}$$

Every statement s_P^n represents a user model data that can be shared with the other systems.

A statement may be represented using a conceptual graph approach, like in Dimitrova [34] or trough semantic relations [35]. For simplicity, we rely here on a simple linear parameters representation of a statement as a tuple

$$s = < subject, property, object, value >$$

---

[1] http://www.w3.org/RDF/

[2] Notice that systems can share only those user model data the user has explicitly given the informed consent to be shared.

like in Rich [36]. In the shareable user model, every user model data is represented as a RDF statement, where the Subject is an instance of the user model (thus a specific user); the Object represents the resource upon which the system reflects user's interests, preferences, knowledge, personal data, etc.; while the Property relates an instance of the resource User with an Object.

Each tuple can be formalized trough RDF reification.

Moreover, we assume that each shareable user model is linked to a semantic representation of the domain exported by the provider as an RDF ontology.

The following extract represents the "interest for art (value: 0.3) of a user called Carlo" into the system iCITY [3]. The statement is expressed as RDF which allows to represent it as a tuple $< subject, property, object, value >$. The class "Art" is modeled as an overlay with the domain model, i.e., Art is a class belonging to the domain ontology.

```
<rdf:Description rdf:about="http://www.di.unito.it/~carmagno/icity/carlo.rdf">
<rdf:type rdf:resource="http://www.di.unito.it/~carmagno/icity/um.rdf#User"/>
<um:has_interest rdf:resource="http://www.di.unito.it/~carmagno/icity/dm.rdf#Art"/>
</rdf:Description>

<rdf:Description rdf:about="http://www.di.unito.it/~carmagno/icity/dm.rdf#Art">
<rdf:type rdf:resource="http://www.w3.org/2000/01/rdf-schema#Class"/>
<um:has_value>0.3</um:has_value>
</rdf:Description>
```

4.2 Data Exchange

Figure 1 illustrates the mechanism for user data exchange using three providers (A, B, and C) that offer data about the same user U.

To take part in the interoperability process every provider system maintains a shareable user model including the RDF statements representing those fragments of the user model that can be shared with other systems.

We denote the collection of shared statements of a generic provider P as

$$S_P = \left\{ s_P^1, s_P^2, s_P^3, \ldots s_P^n \right\}$$

and the collection of shared statements of the receiver R as

$$S_R = \left\{ s_R^1, s_R^2, s_R^3, \ldots s_R^n \right\}$$

Every statement s^n in S_P and S_R represents a specific user model data shared with the other systems. Moreover every shareable user model is linked to a domain ontology.

When a receiver system R needs to gather a user model data from other systems, it performs the interoperability process first retrieving the shareable user model of the provider systems A, B and C the user interacts with (S_A, S_B, S_C); then searching for the specific user model data it needs into S_A, S_B, S_C.

---

[3] A complete example of the shareable user model of the user Carlo into the system iCITY can be retrieved at www.di.unito.it/~carmagno/iCITY/Carlo.rdf

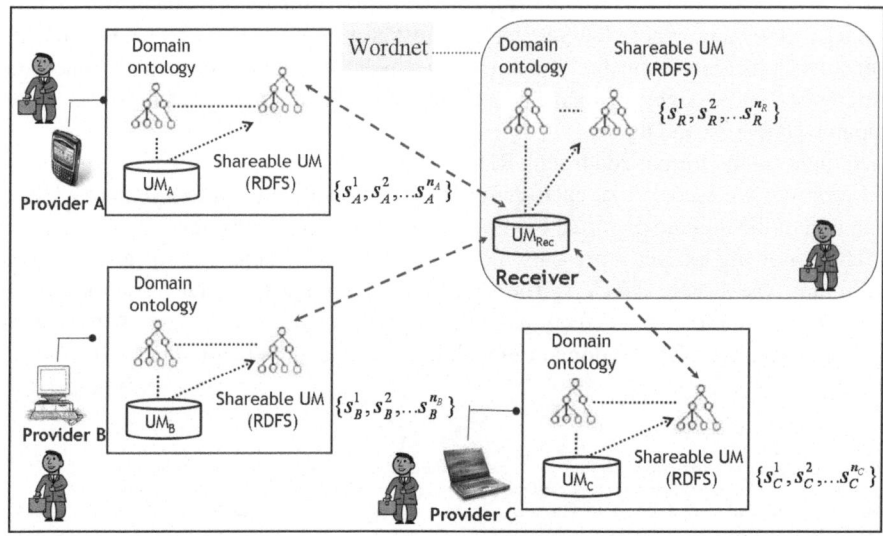

Fig. 1. Logical architecture of the framework for user model interoperability

Given the semantic representation of the shareable user models of the provider systems, the receiver need to be able to retrieve references to such semantic objects. To this purpose, we use Sesame[4], an open source Java framework that can be used as a database server which client applications can access through the HTTP protocol. Notice that the use of Sesame is suggested but not compulsory for the receivers and providers systems. Systems might use other semantic environments like Jena[5] or Mulgara[6]. We advice Sesame because it supports the storage, inferencing and querying of RDF data, which is the syntax we exploit to represent the knowledge in the framework. We hosted the Sesame Java servlet in the Apache Tomcat environment. The core module in the Sesame framework is the "repository", a Java object that stores RDF statements. The shareable user model is defined as an in-memory Sesame repository. To ensure the access to the shareable user models, they are required to be stored on remote web servers. To make systems connect to the servers, retrieve and manipulate all the data, Sesame offers APIs, which abstract from the storage format used and provide reasoning support. In particular, the APIs contain a set of available procedures that programmers can use to manage both the task of inserting RDF statements into systems repositories and the task of querying their internal repositories and those of the suppliers. We used the Sesame API to provide systems with the suitable procedures to make the shareable user models available to systems.

Access to the repositories hosted by Sesame is query driven: a SELECT-FROM clause is sent via HTTP to remote repositories and requires a short time answer.

---

[4] http://www.openrdf.org/
[5] http://jena.sourceforge.net/
[6] http://mulgara.org/

The queries are performed through SeRQL[37] (Sesame RDF Query Language), a RDF/RDFS expressive query language, with many features and useful constructs[7] [37].

The interoperability process is performed as a SeRQL query from the receiver R over the sharable user models of the provider systems.

Notice that at this stage the receiver is not aware if there is any statement s in the shareable user models of the providers dealing with the specific user data it is searching for (interest for Rock music in the scenario we depicted).

Moreover, the receiver cannot simply executes a direct query over s_P searching for that feature. Because of systems do not rely on a unique representation for the user model, they can represent different concepts and/or employ different terms to address a common concept. For such a reason, a punctual query would return misleading results. Indeed the receiver executes a generic SeRQL query in the form of:

$$select * from\{< http : //www.di.unito.it/\ carmagno/icity/carlo.rdf >\}X\{Carlo\}$$

to retrieve the complete collection of statements about the user U from each provider.

5   Handling Semantic Heterogeneity of User Models

To illustrate our proposal to perform user model interoperability despite of the semantic heterogeneity of user models, let us consider the above example where the receiver wants to know Carlo's interest in Rock music. This feature, as well as the other user model data, is represented in the shareable user model of the receiver in the form of a RDF statement. As shown, at a high level, we can represent every statement as a tuple $< subject, property, object, value >$.

The tuple s_R^1 representing this specific feature in S_R is the following:

$$s_R^1 =< Carlo, has\_interest, Rock, missingvalue >$$

As said above, R extracts from P the complete collection of the statement belonging to its shareable user model. Among them we have the following statements:

$$s_P^1 =< Carlo, interested\_in, Rock, 0.6 >$$

$$s_P^2 =< Carlo, interest, Music, 0.5 >$$

$$s_P^3 =< Carlo, knowledge, Art, 0.8 >$$

where Rock, Music, and Art are linked to P's domain ontology.

To measure the semantic similarity among s_P^1, s_P^2, s_P^3 and s_R^1, we break up every statement into Object and Property. We first calculate the similarity between the objects in S_P (Rock, Music, Art) and the object of s_R^1 (Rock); second we calculate the similarity between the properties in S_P ("interested_in", "interest", "knowledge") and the property of s_R^1 ("has_interest").

---

[7] Notice that the Java APIs that Sesame offers can be wrapped on different communication protocol, according to the implementation choices of every specific system, e.g. via peer-to-peer communication, using agent-based techniques, or using a constraint-based approach.

The first task is managed by the Object Similarity Algorithm (Osm Algorithm) (Section 5.1), while the second one is managed by the Property Similarity Algorithm (Psm Algorithm) (Section 5.2).

Finally, we combine those two similarity measures to derive an overall similarity measure expressing the measure of how much each statement in S_P is similar to s_R^1. The highest is the similarity measure of a statement s_P^i with respect to s_R^1, the highest is the relevance of this statement for the purpose of search of the receiver.

5.1   Object Similarity Algorithm

In absence of a unique user model ontology, the computation of semantic similarity among the objects of statements linked to different domain model ontologies cannot rely on direct comparison of terms. For instance, it may happen that the same term represents completely different concepts, e.g. *Rock* (music genre) and *Rock* (geological object), or different terms present similar concepts, e.g. *Rock* and *Rock and Roll*. To compare the semantics of $object(s_P)$ and $object(s_R)$ we follow the Word Sense Disambiguation Theory (WSD Theory) which postulates that two terms are semantically equivalent if their *micro-contexts* are equivalent [38].

The micro-context of a term can be defined by reliance on two major sources of information: a) the information contained within the text or discourse in which the term appears, together with extra-linguistic information about the text such as situation, etc.; b) external knowledge sources, including lexical, encyclopedic, etc. resources, as well as hand-devised knowledge sources, which provide data useful to associate words with senses.

Three main methods have been exploited by the WSD Theory: i) artificial intelligence-based methods, ii) knowledge-driven methods and iii) corpus-based o data-driven methods. We are particularly interested in knowledge-driven methods which exploit machine-readable dictionaries, thesauri, and computational lexicons to disambiguate the meaning of a word.

Knowledge-driven methods spread in the 1980's when large-scale lexical resources such as dictionaries, thesauri, and corpora became widely available, and when the automatic extraction of knowledge from these sources was made possible and supported by the technology[8].

Moving from the WSD Theory assumption that two terms are semantically equivalent if their *micro-contexts* are equivalent, the *Osm algorithm* first derives the micro-contexts for $object(s_P)$ and $object(s_R)$, and then it measures the similarity between both micro-contexts.

Step 1: Find the micro-contexts of $object(s_P)$ **and** $object(s_R^1)$**.**
We define the micro-context of a term (both $object(s_P)$ and $object(s_R^1)$ are conceived as terms) as the set of its semantically related concepts. Because of the concept representing the Object of a statement rely on the domain model, we use the domain ontologies of P and R to define the micro-contexts of $object(s_P)$ and $object(s_R^1)$.
Given an ontology Ω and a concept $C \in \Omega$, the semantically related concepts of C are

---

[8] For a detailed overview of the methods for WSD Theory, the interested reader can refer to [38].

the "neighbors" of C in Ω. In our approach, the neighbors are the Direct SuperClass, the Direct SubClasses and the Sibling of C. Thus, the micro-context of C is defined as:

$$microContext(C, \Omega) = DirectSuperClass(C, \Omega) \cup DirectSubClasses(C, \Omega) \cup Siblings(C, \Omega)$$

We find $microContext(object(s_P), \Omega_P)$ and $microContext(object(s_R^1), \Omega_R)$ by using corresponding SeRQL queries over the provider's ontology Ω_P and receiver's ontology Ω_R.

Figure 2 shows the micro-context for object Rock from s_P^1 given above.

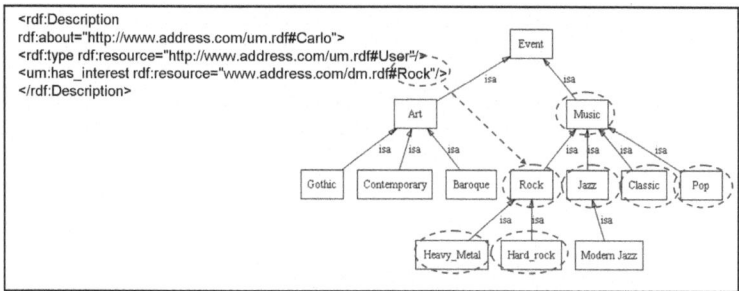

Fig. 2. Micro-context for Rock from the domain ontology of P

To widen the application of our approach, we consider that it may be possible the receiver not to have a pre-defined domain ontology. In this case, the micro-context of $object(s_R^1)$ is extracted by using `Wordnet`[9]. We consider that $object(s_R^1)$ is associated with a corresponding *word meaning* of an `Wordnet` entity[10]. To define the micro-context of $C = object(s_R^1)$ we execute a SeRQL query which extracts the neighbors [11] of $C = object(s_R^1)$.

Notice that in respect with the neighbors of C, we have the following correspondences:

$$DirectSuperClass(C, \Omega_R) \Leftrightarrow DirectHyperonim(C, Wordnet)$$
$$DirectSubClasses(C, \Omega_R) \Leftrightarrow DirectHyponyms(C, Wordnet)$$
$$Siblings(C, \Omega_R) \Leftrightarrow SisterTerms(C, Wordnet)$$

If there are any synonyms of $C = object(s_R^1)$ in Wordnet they are included as well in the micro-context.

Figure 3 shows the micro-context for object Rock in `Wordnet`.

Step 2: Calculate similarity among the micro-contexts of $object(s_P)$ **and** $object(s_R^1)$. We consider each micro-context as a vector of keywords in the form of strings. To compare the elements in the vectors, we use the *Dice coefficient* - a term based similarity measure - used in Information Retrieval [39]. It ranges from 0.0 to 1.0,

---

[9] http://wordnet.princeton.edu/

[10] Since there can be many senses for the same word, the receiver should specify which sense should be used, e.g. Rock as music genre or Rock as geological object.

[11] The neighbors of $C = object(s_R^1)$ are a sub part of the Wordnet synset of $C = object(s_R^1)$.

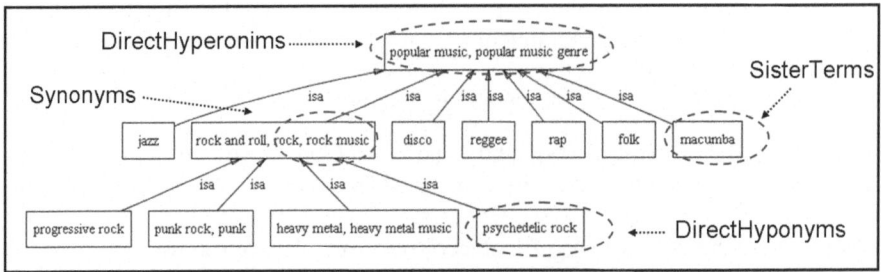

Fig. 3. Micro-context for object Rock in `Wordnet`

where a coefficient of 1.0 indicates identical vectors, whilst a coefficient of 0.0 indicates orthogonal vectors. The Dice coefficient measures the similarity of two vectors X and Y:

$$DC(X, Y) = 2 * \frac{|X \cap Y|}{|X| + |Y|}$$

The *Osm algorithm* returns the Dice coefficient of both micro-contexts:

$$Osm(object(s_P), object(s_R^1)) = DC(microContext(object(s_P), \Omega_P), microContext(object(s_R^1), \Omega_R)$$

which indicates the measure of the semantic similarity among $object(s_P)$ in S_P and $object(s_R^1)$ in s_R^1.

Notice that the Osm algorithm is performed for all the statements belonging to all the available providers systems.

The *Osm algorithm* was tested with several combinations.

An evaluation of the Osm algorithm is not simple to be carried out because it requires the user models to be represented as RDF statements. Due to the lack of availability of such representations, we searched for available ontologies over the web. We considered five huge domain ontologies mainly gathered from Swoogle[12], the semantic web search engine which makes available several RDF ontologies [40]. Three of them rely on the tourism domain, while two on the science domain. Furthermore, we considered the domain ontology of the system iCITY[13].

We carefully chose some domain ontologies which included the class *Rock* or semantically related concepts. The purpose of the test was to check if the Osm algorithm was able to overcome any syntactic and semantic heterogeneity among the concepts, as postulated. More specifically, the purpose was to verify if the Osm algorithm correctly identified as *similar* those classes representing the concept *Rock* even if with a different syntax and if it correctly identified as *not similar* those classes showing the same syntax of *Rock* but do not representing the same concept.

In the following we report the micro-context for the concept *Rock* in the receiver domain ontology (Ω_R), as well as the micro-contexts for the same concept the domain ontologies we analyzed.

---

[12] http://swoogle.umbc.edu/
[13] www.di.unito.it/~carmagno/icity/icitydm.rdfs

Table 1. Micro-context for the concept *Rock* in the analyzed domain ontologies

Ontology	Object	DirSupClass	DirSubClasses	Siblings
$\Omega_R{}^1$	Rock	Popular Music, Popular Music Genre	Heavy Metal	Disco, Disco Music, Macumba,
			Heavy Metal Music, Progressive Rock,	Pop Music, Pop, Folk Music, Ethnic Music,
			Art Rock, Psychedelic Rock,	Folk, Dance Music, Danceroom Music,
			Acid Rock, Punk Rock, Punk	Ballroom Music, Jazz, Rap Music,
				Hip-Hop, Rhythm and Blues, Rockability, Reggae
$\Omega_A{}^2$	Rock	MusicGenre		Musical, Opera,
				Popular, PunkRock,
				Rap, Reggae, Rhythm-n-Blues
$\Omega_B{}^3$	Rock	Music		Classic, Pop,
				Jazz-Blues, Reggae,
				Opera
$\Omega_C{}^4$	Rock	Contemporary	Psychedelic Rock,	Jazz, Pop, Disco
			Beat, Jazz-Rap,	
			Country, Acid-Rock,	
			Soul, Metal,	
$\Omega_D{}^5$	Rock	Thing	BedRock, PyroclasticRock,	
			SedimentaryRock, MetamorphicRock,	
$\Omega_E{}^6$	Rock	Solid	Bedrock	Ground, Litter
			Igneous, Metamorphic,	
			Sedimentary, Pyroclastics	

1 www.di.unito.it/~carmagno/icity/icitydm.rdfs
2 www.ubisworld.org/ubisworld/documents/gumo/2.0/gumo.owl
3 www.di.unito.it/~carmagno/ubiquito/ubiquitodm.rdfs
4 http://islab.dico.unimi.it/ontologies/mxonto-genre.owl
5 http://users.ecs.soton.ac.uk/ar5/aktivesa/aktivesa.owl
6 http://iri.columbia.edu/%7Ebenno/samplesweetdump.owl

The algorithm has been executed over a total amount of 120 domain model classes. Table 2 reports the result of the application of the Osm algorithm over the $microContext(object(Rock), \Omega_R)$ and the $microContext(object(Rock), \Omega_P)$ for each provider ontology presented in Table 1.

Table 2. Object similarity measures among $microContext(object(Rock), \Omega_R)$ and $microContext(object(Rock), \Omega_P)$

$microContext(object(Rock), \Omega_R)$	$microContext(object(Rock), \Omega_A)$	Osm = 0.13
$microContext(object(Rock), \Omega_R)$	$microContext(object(Rock), \Omega_B)$	Osm = 0.11
$microContext(object(Rock), \Omega_R)$	$microContext(object(Rock), \Omega_C)$	Osm = 0.21
$microContext(object(Rock), \Omega_R)$	$microContext(object(Rock), \Omega_D)$	Osm = 0.07
$microContext(object(Rock), \Omega_R)$	$microContext(object(Rock), \Omega_E)$	Osm = 0.07

As emerges from the test, the Osm algorithm correctly results a higher value in those case where $microContext(object(R), \Omega_R)$ and $microContext(object(P), \Omega_P)$ are semantically similar independently by the syntactic heterogeneity among the terms.

Moreover, since the evaluation has been performed considering a class (*Rock*) which has a different semantics according to the current domain, it has also been used to define a threshold score which warrants that the Osm algorithm lead to correct results. Indeed, the overcoming of an established threshold score is required to affirm that $object(s_P^n)$ and $object(s_R^n)$ are semantically similar. Moreover, such a threshold can be also used to represent the measure of the similarity among the compared terms. From the test we establish a threshold of 0.10[14]. Below this score the terms should not be considered as semantically related, while above this score they can be assumed as related. The highest is the Osm score, the greatest is the semantic relation among the terms.

5.2 Property Similarity Algorithm

As said in Section 4, the property of a RDF statement in the shareable user model relates an instance of the resource User with an Object.

Assuming the user be the same among two statements belonging to P and R and the Osm Algorithm results that $(object(s_P))$ and $(object(s_R^1))$ are similar. However, $property(s_P)$ and $property(s_R^1)$ may be different, as in the following example:

$$s_R^1 = < Carlo, \textbf{has\_interest}, Rock, missingvalue >$$

$$s_P^1 = < Carlo, \textbf{has\_knowledge}, Rock, 0.6 >$$

If the receiver R needs to know Carlo'interest for Rock music (expressed trough the property *has_interest*), it does not care about Carlo's knowledge in Rock (expressed trough the property *has_knowledge*) or his preferences about Rock music. Therefore, measuring the similarity among $property(s_P)$ and $property(s_R^1)$ is necessary in establishing the similarity among (s_P) and (s_R^1).

To this purpose and differently from the Osm, we cannot rely on the domain ontology of the provider, which may not include a taxonomy of the properties. There is also a high heterogeneity, both at a semantic level (different verbs may have different meanings) and at a syntactic level (a verb may assume many different forms according to the tense used). Furthermore, according to the RDF Core Working Group[15] guidelines for RDF language, properties should be represented in the form of verbs (for instance, "has_interest", "interested_in", etc.). So Wordnet similarity algorithms, which deal mostly with noun comparison, cannot be employed for understanding the semantics of the properties included in the s_P.

We assume that semantic similarity of properties dovetails to syntactic similarity, i.e. properties having a similar syntax (e.g. *has_interest* and *interested_in*) are likely to have a similar semantics.

The *Psm algorithm* measures the similarity among $property(s_P)$ and $property(s_R^1)$ using the *Levenshtein distance* [41] that assigns a unit cost to all edit operations required to convert one string $(property(s_P)$ in this case) into another $(property(s_R^1))$[16].

The Levenshtein distance is 1 when there is no similarity between the compared terms, i.e. the *Psm algorithm* returns values close to 1 when $property(s_P)$ and $property(s_R)$ are not similar at all. However, the *Osm algorithm* returns values close to 1 when $object(s_P)$ and $object(s_R^1)$ are similar. Hence, in order to combine the *Osm* and *Psm* values, the *Psm* measure is normalized, as shown below:

$$Psm = (1 - \frac{LD}{max\left\{|property(s_P)|, |property(s_R^1)|\right\}})$$

---

[14] The value has been refined in order not to be affected by the lengths of the vectors.

[15] http://www.w3.org/RDF/

[16] The Dice coefficient is not applicable in this case, as it is used to compare large vectors, while we need to compare two terms expressing a property.

The similarity of the properties in the example statements given above is:

$$Psm(property(s_P^1), property(s_R^1)) = Psm(has\_interest, interested\_in) = 0.42$$
$$Psm(property(s_P^1), property(s_R^1)) = Psm(has\_interest, interest) = 0.73$$
$$Psm(property(s_P^1), property(s_R^1)) = Psm(has\_interest, knowledge) = 0.1$$

Notice that the Psm algorithm is performed for all the statements belonging to all the available providers systems, whose Osm overcame the threshold.

Overall similarity measure among s_P and s_R^1

Finally, the similarity measure (Sm) between s_P and s_R^1 is derived as the average of *Osm* and *Psm*. The highest similarity measure between a provider's statement s_P and the receiver's statement s_R^1 gives the highest relevance of s_P for the receiver R.

The algorithms for similarity measure have been implemented in Java using Sesame and SeRQL and are described in more detail in [42].

6 Conclusion

The paper has proposed our solution to manage the semantic heterogeneity of interoperable distributed user models in order to automate the user model exchange across user-adaptive applications. With respect to the works proposed in the community, our approach is not performed through the use of a shared format approach, nor exploiting algorithms to bootstrap user models in one system by using information from other systems. On the contrary, we propose an intermediate solution inspired by evidential reasoning and recent advances in the Semantic Web to allow flexibility in representing user models and to provide semantic mapping of the user data from one system to another.

The strength of the approach is its high flexibility, which allows it to be applied to many different user-adaptive systems, and intelligent information systems in general.

Beside the great flexibility of this approach, it show some further challenges. According to the approach we propose, every system maintains its own user model. In order to take part in the interoperability process, every provider system maintains a shareable user model which includes those fragments of the user model that can be shared with other systems, represented as RDF statements. Therefore, any change over the user model data, such as values deletion or changes, need to be replicated also for the correspondent RDF data into the shareable user model. Moreover, the user models interoperability process requires many computational efforts with consequent delays in the response, even if it should be managed in a reasonable short time to make adaptation really benefit from it. A possible solution we adopted would be the execution of the whole interoperability process off line. The receiver could periodically examine the user model of each user when he/she is not interacting with the system and, if required, execute the interoperability process avoiding the slowdown of users interactions.

A final remark regards the Relevance Algorithm. The performance of the Object Similarity Algorithm is strictly related to the level of granularity used in defining the taxonomy of the classes in the ontologies. Both in the case the classes of an ontology are represented with a thick level of granularity as well as they are represented with a too low level of granularity, the comparison of vectors will be not significant and the Osm algorithm will result an *object similarity measure* that does not overcome the score of threshold. However, creating an ontology is a free cognitive process and the degree of specificity is often contingent on the purpose of usage of the ontology. In the perspective of do not enforcing user-adaptive systems to exploit a shared user model and domain model ontology, the approach we have proposed represents a possible solution for obtaining a set of comparable terms to enable user models interoperability.

In the immediate future work we are interested in considering the benefits of the user model interoperability process in improving the quality of the information provided to users for different kinds of adaptive web systems. More specifically we are currently working on investigating how to map the values of the instances of the user models if they use different scales (0.9 versus 90%, versus 5). Moroever, for the RDF query language, we are shifthig from SeRQL to SPARQL which is a W3C standard and supported by Sesame.

In the long run, we want to incorporate also the sharing of user modeling *reasoning strategies* across systems, to provide interoperability not just of user data but also of the procedures used to derive these data.

References

1. Montaner, M., López, B., de la Rosa, J.L.: A taxonomy of recommender agents on the internet. Artificial Intelligent Review 19(4), 285–330 (2003)
2. Niederee, C.J., Stewart, A., Mehta, B., Hemmje, M.: A multi-dimensional, unified user model for cross-system personalization. In: Proc. of Workshop on Environments for Personalized Information Access, in Advanced Visual Interfaces International Working Conference, Gallipoli, Italy, pp. 34–54 (2004)
3. Heckmann, D.: Ubiquitous User Modeling. PhD thesis, Department of Computer Science Saarbrucken, University of Saarlandes (2005)
4. Houben, G., Aerts, A., Aroyo, L., Sluijs, K., Rutten, B., De Bra, P.: State of the art: Semantic interoperability for distributed user profile. Technical Report 22, Telematika Institute, Netherlands (June 2005)
5. van der Sluijs, K., Houben, G.J.: Towards a generic user model component. In: Proc. of Workshop on Decentralized, Agent Based and Special Approaches to User Modelling, In International Conference on User Modelling, Edinburgh, Scotland, pp. 43–52 (2005)
6. Berkovsky, S., Kuflik, T., Ricci, F.: Mediation of user models for enhanced personalization in recommender systems. User Modeling and User-Adapted Interaction (2007)
7. Carmagnola, F., Cena, F., Console, L., Cortassa, O., Gena, C., Goy, A., Torre, I., Toso, A., Vernero, F.: Tag-based user models for social multi-device adaptive guides. User Modeling and User-Adapted Interaction (2008)
8. Salton, G., McGill, M.: Introduction to Modern Information Retrieval. McGraw-Hill Book Company, New York (1984)
9. Cena, F., Console, L., Gena, C., Goy, A., Levi, G., Modeo, S., Torre, I.: Integrating heterogeneous adaptation techniques to build a flexible and usable mobile tourist guide. AI Commun. 19(4), 369–384 (2006)
10. Vassileva, J.: Distributed user modelling for universal information access. Internation Journal of Human Compueter Interaction, 122–126 (2001)
11. Greaves, M., Holmback, H., Bradshaw, J.: What is a conversation policy? In: Dignum, F.P.M., Greaves, M. (eds.) Issues in Agent Communication. LNCS, vol. 1916, pp. 118–131. Springer, Heidelberg (2000)

12. Aroyo, L., Dolog, P., Houben, G., Kravcik, M., Ambjorn Naeve, A., Nilsson, M., Wild, F.: Interoperability in personalized adaptive learning. Educational Technology & Society 9(2), 4–18 (2006)
13. Veltman, K.H.: Syntactic and semantic interoperability: New approaches to knowledge and the semantic web. In: The New Review of Information Networking, pp. 1–32 (2001)
14. Cristea, A., Smits, D., De Bra, P.: Writing mot, reading aha! - converting between an authoring and a delivery system for adaptive educational hypermedia. In: Workshop paper at AIED (July 2005)
15. Stewart, C., Cristea, A., Celik, I., Ashman, E.: Interoperability between aeh user models. In: Proc. of International workshop on Adaptivity, personalization and the semantic Web, in Conference on Hypertext and Hypermedia, Odense, Denmark, pp. 21–30 (2006)
16. Dawson, F., Howes, T.: Vcard mime directory profile. RFC 2426, IETF (September 1998)
17. Colin Smythe, F.T., Robson, R.: I.m.s. learner information package specification (2001), http://www.imsproject.org/profiles/lipbpig01.html
18. Farance, F., Tonkel, J.: IEEE p1484.1/d9, 2001-11-30 draft standard for learning technology - learning technology systems architecture (ltsa). Technical report. IEEE Computer Society, Los Alamitos (2001)
19. Klyne, G., Reynolds, F., Woodrow, C., Ohto, H., Hjelm, J., Butler, M.H.: Composite capabilities / preferences profile working group (2003)
20. Heckmann, D., Schwartz, T., Brandherm, B., Schmitz, M., Wilamowitz-Moellendorff, M.: Gumo - the general user model ontology. In: Ardissono, L., Brna, P., Mitrović, A. (eds.) UM 2005. LNCS (LNAI), vol. 3538, pp. 428–432. Springer, Heidelberg (2005)
21. FOAF. Foaf friend of a friend vocabulary specification 0.91 (2007), http://xmlns.com/foaf/spec/
22. RDF. Resource description framework (1999), http://www.w3.org/RDF/
23. RDFS. Resource description framework (2004), http://www.w3.org/TR/rdf-schema/
24. DAML. The darpa agent markup language (2001), http://www.daml.org/2001/03/daml+oil-index.html
25. OWL. Owl web ontology language overview (2004), http://www.w3.org/TR/owl-features/
26. Heckmann, D., Krüger, A.: A user modeling markup language (userml) for ubiquitous computing. In: Brusilovsky, P., Corbett, A.T., de Rosis, F. (eds.) UM 2003. LNCS (LNAI), vol. 2702, pp. 393–397. Springer, Heidelberg (2003)
27. Mehta, B., Niederée, C., Stewart, A., Degemmis, M., Lops, P., Semeraro, G.: Ontologically-enriched unified user modeling for cross-system personalization. In: Ardissono, L., Brna, P., Mitrović, A. (eds.) UM 2005. LNCS (LNAI), vol. 3538, pp. 119–123. Springer, Heidelberg (2005)
28. Heckmann, D., Schwartz, T., Brandherm, B., Schmitz, M., von Wilamowitz-Moellendorff, M.: Gumo - the general user model ontology. In: Ardissono, L., Brna, P., Mitrović, A. (eds.) UM 2005. LNCS (LNAI), vol. 3538, pp. 428–432. Springer, Heidelberg (2005)
29. Kuflik, T.: Semantically-enhanced user models mediation: Research agenda. In: Workshop on Ubiquitous User Modeling, in International Intelligent User Interface Conference, IUI 2008 (2008)
30. Berkovsky, S., Kuflik, T., Ricci, F.: Mediation of user models for enhancing personalized services delivery. User Model. User-Adapt. Interact. (2007) (Published online)
31. Cena, F., Aroyo, L.: A semantics-based dialogue for interoperability of user-adaptive systems in a ubiquitous environment. In: Conati, C., McCoy, K., Paliouras, G. (eds.) UM 2007. LNCS (LNAI), vol. 4511, pp. 309–313. Springer, Heidelberg (2007)
32. Carmagnola, F.: From User Models to Interoperable User Models. PhD thesis, University of Turin, Italy (December 2007)

33. Carmagnola, F., Cena, F.: User identification for cross-system personalisation. Information Sciences (2008)
34. Dimitrova, V., Self, J., Brna, P.: Applying interactive open learner models to learning technical terminology. In: Bauer, M., Gmytrasiewicz, P.J., Vassileva, J. (eds.) UM 2001. LNCS (LNAI), vol. 2109, pp. 148–157. Springer, Heidelberg (2001)
35. Denaux, R., Aroyo, L., Dimitrova, V.: Owl-olm: Interactive ontology-based elicitation of user models. In: Aroyo, L., Dimitrova, V., Kay, J. (eds.) Workshop on Personalization on the Semantic Web (PerSWeb) with PROLEARN Session. UM 2005 Conference (2005)
36. Rich, E.: Users are individuals: Individualizing user models. International Journal of Man-Machine Studies 18(3), 199–214 (1983)
37. Broekstra, J., Kampman, A.: Serql: An rdf query and transformation language. In: Semantic Web and Peer-to-Peer: Decentralized Management and Exchange of Knowledge and Information, pp. 23–39. Springer, Heidelberg (2005)
38. Ide, N., Veronis, J.: Introduction to the special issue on word sense disambiguation: The state of the art. Computational Linguistics 24(1), 1–40 (1998)
39. Dice, L.: Measures of the amount of ecologic association between species. Ecology 26, 297–302 (1945)
40. Ding, L., Finin, T., Joshi, A., Pan, R., Cost, S., Peng, J., Reddivari, P., Doshi, V., Sachs, J.: Swoogle: A Search and Metadata Engine for the Semantic Web. In: Proceedings of the Thirteenth ACM Conference on Information and Knowledge Management. ACM Press, New York (2004)
41. Levenshtein, V.: Binary codes capable of correcting deletions, insertions, and reversals. Technical Report 8 (1966)
42. Carmagnola, F.: From User Models to Interoperable User Models. PhD thesis, Department of Computer Science, Torino, Italy (December 2007)

A Model for Feature-Based User Model Interoperability on the Web

Federica Cena and Roberto Furnari

Department of Computer Science,
University of Torino Corso Svizzera 185, Torino, Italy
{cena,furnari}@di.unito.it

Abstract. In this paper we present a model for User Model (UM) interoperability among feature-based adaptive applications on the Web. In order to enhance the interaction capabilities of such systems, we propose to exploit Web standards for interoperability, i.e. Web Services technologies and Semantic Web languages, together with negotiation techniques based on dialogue.

Our model is based on a Service Oriented Architecture(SOA), where a central UDDI registry, enhanced with UM specific capabilities, can be used to support the cooperation between user-adaptive applications. The proposed framework support a discovery mechanism, a simple request/response-based pattern of communication and a dialogue model.

1 Introduction

Exchanging User Models data among user-adaptive applications on the Web is very promising. The opportunities and the advantages, both for the end users and for the applications, for sharing knowledge about the users are well known: on the one hand, users do not need to waste time training each new system they deal with, and, on the other hand, the adaptive systems are able to reach a deeper understanding of users. In fact, sharing User Models enables applications to cover more aspects of the user profile, increasing, at the same time, the level of detail and the reliability of user data. All this additional information about the user leads to adaptation results that are more appropriate for her [1], [2].

However, apart from close experiments (e.g.[3]), only a very few number of adaptive applications really cooperate to share UM knowledge (see [4]). The reason is that UM interoperability in an open environment like the Web is in general extremely difficult and requires a very high degree of alignment between the applications, because of the lack of standardization [5].

The UM data exchange, in particular, could require non trivial pattern of communication between the requestor of UM data and the provider of them. For instance, they may need to clarify the requested user feature (if the systems do not share the same knowledge models), or they may need to negotiate about the response (when the exact one is not available or is not considered satisfying by the requestor). In these situations, the interacting systems could use some form of *conversation*, a complex interactions among two parties, that may evolve in different ways, depending on the state and the needs of the two participants.

T. Kuflik et al. (Eds.): Advances in Ubiquitous User Modelling, LNCS 5830, pp. 37–54, 2009.

This paper describes a model to support the User Model interoperability process on the Web, presented in a preliminary version in [6]. The core idea is to exploit Web standards for interoperability, i.e. Web Service technologies for syntactic interoperability, and Semantic Web paradigm for semantic interoperability.

In the framework we propose, we enhanced Service Oriented Architecture (SOA) to handle the peculiar needs of the UM interoperability context, giving a sound environment where it is possible to implement existing approaches for interoperability (such as the dialogue approach of [7]) and other solutions.

We propose an interoperability model that can be exploited by feature-based (or content-based) systems. In feature-based systems, the UMs are typically represented by weight assigned to item features and representing the user's level of preferences for these features ([8]).

The paper is structured as follow. We first present in Section 2 scenarios that motivate the relevance of the discussed problem. In Section 3 we provide the technological background and motivate our solution. Section 4 presents the conceptual model of the dialogue implemented in the framework. Then, Section 5 describes the model of the proposed framework, while Section 6 presents the framework in action dealing with the scenario. Section 7 presents similar existing solutions for the interoperability problem and Section 8 concludes the paper with some discussions.

2   Motivating Scenarios

In the following we describe two scenarios to clarify the problem.

Scenario 1. UbiquiTO [9], a mobile tourist recommender system for the city of Turin, is being accessed by Mary. UbiquiTO lacks some important information about her, and therefore is not able to provide an effective personalization service. The problem increases in case Mary is a new or occasional user. A possible solution (avoiding the need to bore Mary by directly asking her for the missing information) is to exchange information about her with other user-adaptive systems operating in a similar context, which know Mary because she has interacted also with them.

To do so, first of all, UbiquiTO should find out these systems. This means that UbiquiTO's developers have to explicitly encode this information in the system. For example, UbiquiTO knows about iCITY [10], a social recommender of events occurring in Turin. In order to start a collaboration, it has to contact it, and to reach an agreement on the stack of protocols to be used in the communication. Since UbiquiTO and iCITY do not share exactly the same representation of the domain, some interpretation problems may occur. For example, when the requested user feature is not represented in the same way in the two systems, some form of conversation can be useful to clarify the meaning of the used terms.

Scenario 2. A new personalization system, ArtEvent, specialized in artistic events in Turin, is under development: the designers of the new system have to decide how to represent users and domain knowledge and which technologies to implement in order to make the system able to communicate with other systems. With respect to the User

Model representation, the ArtEvent designers can decide to build some customized domain taxonomies or link to some well-known shared ontologies. Then in order to interoperate with other systems, the developers of ArtEvent have to look for the systems sharing a similar context (and probably the same potential set of users). Suppose, as example, that the systems which satisfy these requirements are UbiquiTO and iCITY, the ArtEvent developers must contact both the UbiquiTO and the iCITY developers in order to reach an agreement on the communication protocols to use. This results in extra work to provide the necessary technologies.

Note that the kind of User Model representation and domain representation used by ArtEvent will affect its future interoperability capability.

As it can be seen in the scenarios, one of the main obstacles that makes interoperability a hard issue is that an application has to discover other applications available to interoperate (i.e. the *discovery issue*) and the mechanisms and protocols to be used to interoperate (i.e. the *syntactic interoperability issue*). Theoretically, all the agreements have to be taken in a peer-to-peer way, which is time consuming and requires a big overwork when dealing with a large number of services. This becomes impossible in a dynamic environment as the Web.

Another problem is related to the content of communication (*semantic interoperability issue*). There are no problems when the knowledge model is shared, and thus the involved services agree on the meaning of terms. In this case, it is possible to exploit simple *atomic communication* (where a system merely asks for the value of a property and the other system provides it) by means of standard *request/response* invocation.

Instead, when the knowledge models are note shared, atomic communication is not sufficient since systems have to agree on the meaning of each single property. *Conversation* can be used in order to negotiate the meaning (i.e. finding similar concepts, reasoning on concepts in order to find an agreement [11]) and also to approximate the response when an exact one is not available.

The requirements for atomic communication and conversation are different: for the former, systems must only know how to ask for the desired property; for the latter, in addition to the previous information, systems must also know how to structure the conversation, how to express a message, and the allowed order of messages.

3   Key Elements for a UM Interoperability Solution

In recent years two main technologies and tools have changed the way the applications can interact in distributed (and open) environment as the Web: Web Service technologies and Semantic Web languages. In a typical Service Oriented Architecture [12], an application that aims at offering its functionalities to other applications is defined as a Service.

Each service provides a WSDL[1] (Web Service Description Language) description that defines the service interface, i.e. the offered operations and the input and output parameters for each operation. Every application, which wants to exploit the operations offered by the service, looking at its WSDL definition is able to pack the required

---

[1] http://www.w3.org/TR/wsdl

SOAP[2] (Simple Object Access Protocol) messages. In the SOA environment, UDDI[3] (Universal Description Discovery and Integration) registries are defined to play the role of discovery agencies and they are used to store the information about the available services. Each service may publish its description and its WSDL interface in such registries. The other applications can find a particular service via such registries, and use its WSDL description to known how interact with it.

It is important to note that Web Service interface and the service publication standards support only the specification of static interfaces of elementary services. They allow only simple *one- shot* interactions, structured as *request/response* pairs, but they are not expressive enough to define conversations including more than two turns [13]. In fact such standards cannot support rich interactions requiring a more proactive, dynamic modality of communication with complex patterns of interaction [14].

Thus, Web services technologies can be used successfully to solve the problem of a common syntax to describe the interfaces and the format of the exchanged messages, providing a set of common standards that are nowadays widely accepted.

At the same time, the Semantic Web initiative [15] deals with the meaning of the exchanged concepts, in order to have a common understanding among different applications. Resources from the Semantic Web, such as ontologies[4], metadata and specification languages (like RDF[5], RDFS[6], OWL[7]), are based on open standards and have been developed to allow common understanding among distributed systems in open environments.

On account on these considerations we think that Semantic Web and Web Service tools should be the basis of a solution for interoperability. The loosely coupled structure and the well accepted stack of standards (SOAP, WSDL and UDDI) underlying Web Services represent a solution to the *syntactic interoperability issue* with respect to the exchange of UM knowledge among various personalization systems. The usage of Web Service techniques for reaching UM interoperability means that user adaptive systems must make their UMs available as services. Thus, each user-adaptive system has to provide to other user-adaptive systems a set of WSDL operations to access the data stored on its User Model.

In order to deal with the *semantic interoperability issue* we propose to use Semantic Web tools. This implies that the user-adaptive systems must represent the knowledge in the User Model (and in the Domain Model related to the User Model) with standard xml-based formal languages, and to organize this knowledge in structures such ontologies.

Such a solution seems to be sufficient to address interoperability when systems share the same knowledge representation and atomic communication can be exploited: the *requestor* asks for a specified concept related to the user feature (by means of the

---

[2] http://www.w3.org/TR/soap/

[3] http://uddi.org/pubs/uddi-v3.0.2-20041019.htm

[4] An ontology represents a knowledge schema, expressed with standard formal languages, that represents relations among concepts and a set of constraints over the domain.

[5] Resource Description Framework, http://www.w3.org/RDF/

[6] RDF-Schema - http://www.w3.org/TR/rdf-schema/

[7] Web Ontology Language - http://www.w3.org/2004/OWL/

opportune SOAP message, formatted according to the WSDL interface description), and the *responder* answers with the requested value.

Unfortunately, this is not always sufficient. In fact, even if suppliers and consumers of user profiles have shown an increasing awareness of the need for standards for representing and exchanging UM data, the heterogeneity of user-adaptive applications on the Web makes the use of such standards very difficult [16]. Currently in such an environment there is not a single universally shared ontology that is agreed upon by all the involved parties. Every system typically uses its own private ontology, which may not be understandable by other applications. Thus, some kind of alignment among ontologies becomes necessary.

As mentioned in the introduction, other forms of interaction are needed. We propose to use a *conversation* in the following situations:

– to negotiate the meaning of an exchanged concept (when the knowledge representation is not shared between systems);
– to approximate the response when the exact one is not available or to find better results when the available one is not reliable enough (in case of a shared knowledge representation).

In the framework we propose, some predefined conversation schemes to address these problems are shared among the systems.

Finally, another problem it is necessary to solve to enable interoperability is the discovery of systems. In order to solve such *discovery issue* we propose to use a centralized registry where all the user-adaptive systems publish their description. We propose to enrich the traditional functionalities offered by a standard UDDI registry with a set of novel functionalities useful in the User Model interoperability scenario. The idea is to publish on such a registry the description of the conversation schemes (Section 4), and for each service, the references to the Domain Model and to the supported conversation schemes. Thus, in order to improve the discovery capability of the registry, we propose to extend the registry by means of a shared network space, based on the tuple space model [17], that the user-adaptive applications can exploit in order to discover which systems can maintain the desired user features. In such a way we offer to user-adaptive systems a central shared place used to discover other systems available to interoperate, and we provide the systems with all the information needed to contact them.

4   The Conversation Model

One of the main novelties of our solution for interoperability is the capability to support complex interactions as conversation. In particular, in our framework we instantiated the dialogue model presented in [7]. Such a model adapts to UM interoperability context the diagnostic learning dialog model of [18], based on Dialogue Games [19] and Speech Acts theory [20]. In the following we present such conversation model, providing the definition of its main components: *Speech Acts*, *Dialogue Rules* and *Dialogue Games*.

4.1   Speech Acts

The basic dialogue primitive in the model is the Speech Act [20]. A Speech Act consists of a proposition representing the intention of a system. Each participant in a dialogue produces Speech Acts at her turn. In this model, a Speech Act is represented as a quadruple

$$<requestor,\ responder,\ move,\ statement>.$$

where

- *requestor/responder* identify the dialogue participants. In the context of UM inter-operability, the requestor is the user-adaptive system asking for information about a user, while the responder is the provider of UM data.
- *move* is a verb expressing the intention of the Speech Act. Starting from the defi-nition of moves by [18], [7] identifies a set of moves appropriate for the UM inter-operability context. By means of moves, a system may express its intentions (for instance to *inquire*, to *deny*, to *accept*, to *inform*, to *explain*, to *challenge*).
- *statement* is a claim over concepts of the knowledge models (User Model and cor-respondent domain models) the requestor and the responder use to communicate. Statements are dependent on the specific application domain, but independent of the representational language used for the knowledge representation. In the model, statements are represented by means of linear parameters [21] as:

$$<property(topic),\ value,\ belief>$$

where *property* is a feature of the User Model, *topic* is a concept of the domain model the property refers to, *value* indicates the value assumed by the property, *be-lief* measures how much the system believes that its assumption about the specific value is correct.

A sample *statement* about the User Model could be $<interest(art),0.8,0.2>$, which means that the value of the property *interest in art* is high with low certainty.

An example of Speech Act could be the following:

$$system1,\ system2,\ inquiry,\ (interest(art),\ value=?,\ belief=?)$$

which means that *system1* asks *system2* the value and belief of the UM property *interest* in the domain concept *art*.

4.2 Dialogue Rules

The Dialogue Rules define the communication protocol of the dialogue. They express the allowed moves in Speech Act and how to sequence them. A dialogue rule is defined as *if(m1,s1) then (m2, s2)* and postulates that a Speech Act with move *m2* and statement *s2* is permitted if the previous turn has included the move *m1* and the statement *s1*.

Dialogue Rules are public and all the systems involved in the dialogue have to follow them in order to be able to communicate correctly.

Possible Dialogue Rules in the UM interoperability context are for instance:

- *if (inquiry, s) then (inform, s);*
- *if (inquiry, s) then (deny);*

stating that when a participant receives the request to provide information about a statement *s* (*inquiry, s*), it is allowed to provide the required information (*inform, s*) or to refuse the request (*deny*) (for instance, it could not have the requested value).
Other possible rules can be for instance:

- *if (inform, s) then (challenge, s)*;
- *if (inform, s) then (accept, s)*;

stating that when a participant receives a statement *s* (*inform, s*), it can accept the statement (*accept, s*) or it can challenge it (*challenge, s*) (since, for instance, the received value is different from the one already present in the system).

Note that the rules just prescribe the allowed sequences of moves in a dialogue and do not state which rule to select in case of multiple applicable rules or how to evaluate its parameters; this task is delegated to the internal business logic of each system.

4.3 Dialogue Games

The building blocks of the model are the *Dialogue Games*: templates defining the sequence of Speech Acts to be exchanged for reaching a particular goal. A Dialogue Game, from a conceptual point of view, is characterized by three parts: *specifications*, *parameters*, and *components*.

- *Specifications* are the elements that remain constant during the game and are represented as predicates on the game parameters. They represent the *pre-conditions* of the game, i.e. the specific situation triggering a Dialogue Game.
- *Parameters* are the elements of a dialogue which can vary during the same game. They express i) the goal the requestor wants to achieve by means of the Dialogue Game; ii) a list of concepts that can be discussed during the game (*focus space*).
- *Components* are the elements changing in a systematic way during a game. They are a set of sub-goals that determine the sequence of Speech Acts to be generated during the game. They are defined by three typologies of strategies:

  • strategies to retrieve the necessary pieces of information for the construction of each Dialogue Game: strategies for retrieving all the concepts that will compose the *focus space* of the game (*focus strategies*), and strategies for extracting from the set of concepts in the focus the specific concept to use as statement of each Speech Act (*scope strategies*).
  • strategies to determine the Speech Acts to produce. For example, a system may apply the following rule: if the belief in the statement is under a particular threshold, the next Speech Act must be a challenge of the statement. That is:
  if (belief < 0.7) then
  (SpeechActsList = add <requestor, responder, challenge, s>, SpeechActsList)
  • strategies to determine how the dialogue participants' knowledge base changes at the end of the dialogue (*post-conditions*).

In particular, in the UM interoperability context, three main goals systems may desire to achieve have been identified [22]: i) to clarify the request; ii) to approximate the response; iii) to explain the response. Three different Dialogue Games were then defined to reach such goals:

– *Clarification Game.* It supports the goal of refinement of the request[8]. The rationale of the game is the use of concept properties to disambiguate the meaning of the requested topic, since two concepts sharing the same properties have a high probability of being the same concept. The responder can use this game to disambiguate the exchanged concept, when systems do not share the same knowledge model.

The strategies that determine the content of the clarification dialogue consists in disambiguating the concept starting from identifying its features. Thus, the focus will be constituted by the properties of the concept. For example, if we want to identify the concept of *painting*, a possible focus could be composed by all the properties of the concept: *style*, *author*, *date of creation*, *title*, *techniques*. See Section 6 for an example of this game.

– *Explorative Game.* It supports the goal of approximation of concepts by collecting information about the concepts and relations in the knowledge base to find an approximate answer. The rationale of the game is that if there is not the value of the requested concept, the values of related concepts can be used instead. We can consider that if the user expresses an interest in a subclass, this interest can be extended with high degree of certainty to the upper class, since children concepts are subclasses of a class and the subclasses inherit attributes of the upper classes. Thus, the interest of a user in *ancient art* can be assumed to be similar to the interest in its parent concept *art*.

The strategies that determine the content of the explorative dialogue consists in retrieving information related to the context of the concept. Thus, the focus space will be composed by all the concepts related to the topic. For example, if a starting topic is the concept of *cubism* (an artistic movement) a possible focus could be composed by other artistic movements with similar principles (e.g., *elementarism*); sharing the same historical period (e.g., *futurism*) , or all the concepts that are more generic than the starting one (for example, *contemporary art*).

– *Explicative Game.* It clarifies why a particular user features value or belief is present. This Dialogue Game can start when there is a discrepancy in the participants' beliefs that need justification. This game is out of scope of the paper.

5   A Framework for UM Interoperability

Taking into account the considerations made in Section 3, we can say that a framework which supports UM interoperability on the Web should i) support the discovery of systems with the needed User Model features; ii) provide shared way to describe the interoperability capabilities of applications; iii) support *atomic communication* and *conversation*. Moreover, it is important to respect the privacy policies of the involved services, protecting the UM features and the sensitive data.

The model of the framework we propose has the following features:

– it is based on Web Services and Semantic Web standards;

---

[8] A query refinement task is the process of searching for queries that are more relevant for an entity's needs than the initial query, by specialization of the query's scope [23].

- it uses a UDDI registry which stores information about all the available services; in this central registry each service declares, beside its WSDL interface, the ontologies it uses and its communication ability (the supported Dialogue Game);
- it enhances the central registry with discovery functionalities, that can be exploited to help systems in finding available services to interoperate with;
- it provides a clear, centralized and shared definition of the tools supporting complex form of communication. In particular the framework is designed to support the implementation of complex interactions using the conversation model described in Section 4. To this purpose, we made some simplification to the original conceptual model (see Section 5.1).

Each user-adaptive application running in our framework should be a *Web Service* (see figure 1) and has to support the web service strandards (WSDL, SOAP) and provide the basic operation to support atomic communication to share UM knowledge (e.g. *getValueOf(property,...)*. Furthermore the applications aiming at collaborating in the interoperability framework model must:

- refer at least conceptually to an ontology regardless of the inner knowledge representation;
- use a mechanism to provide a common user identification;
- refer to the Public General User Model Ontology GUMO[9] for the definition of the UM features.

As illustrated in Figure 1 each application has to correctly interact with a central registry, the *Enhanced User Model UDDI Registry* (*EUMUR*). This is a UDDI registry (used as a standard discovery tool) enhanced according to the peculiarity of the UM context. Beside the declaration of all the services cooperating in the framework, here we can find the definition of all the tools that can be used as model for the communication between services. EUMUR has three main components: the *Dialogue Game*, the *Services Declaration*, and the *Search Network Buffer*.

5.1 Dialogue Game

This component contains the definition of the elements needed to implement the Dialogue Game model presented in Section 4. The main parts of the Dialogue Game are:

- *Conversation Rules*, the definition of the conversation expressed in terms of messages exchanged, i.e. the allowed moves in Speech Act and how to order them, from the different point of view of the requestor and the responder. They correspond to *Dialogue Rules* in the original model.
- *Focus Strategies*, the definition of the strategies to collect the concepts that can be discussed in a conversation. They correspond to the *focus strategies* in the *components* in the original model.A *strategy* can be described as semantics-based query over the (RDFS or OWL) ontology.
- *Scope Strategies*, the list of strategies used in this game to select between the concepts retrieved by the focus strategies. They correspond to the *scope strategies* in the *components* in the original model.

---

[9] http://www.ubisworld.org/

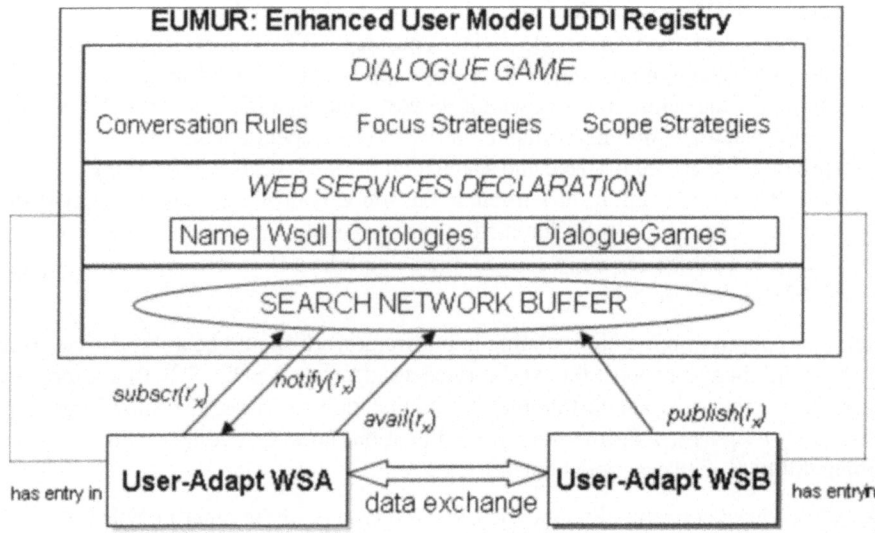

Fig. 1. Framework Architecture

Note that both *specifications* (i.e. preconditions) and *postconditions* of the original model are not considered in the framework, since we prefer to leave each dialogue participant free to implement her own strategies to decide whether to start a dialogue and what to do after the end of the game.

5.2   Web Services Declaration

It contains the list of Web Services available in the framework associated with the declaration of the supported *Dialogue Games*. For each Web Service we have the following fields:

- *Name*: the name of the service.
- *Wsdl*: the reference to the WSDL file describing the operations offered by the service.
- *Ontologies*: the list of all the ontology schemes the service refers to.
- *Dialogue Games*: the list of Dialogue Games the service is able to play.

By means of this central registry an application looking for partners to exchange user knowledge can immediately know which Web Service shares the same ontology, and which kind of Dialogue Games it supports.

5.3   Search Network Buffer

The Search Network Buffer (SNB) is a shared network space able to automatically match service requestors with service providers of specific UM knowledge. The interaction model is managed according to the *publish/subscribe* pattern and the data exchanged through this space represent requests of user features and responses of availability of values for the requested features. In details:

- all the services *subscribe* themselves to SNB asking to be notified (as providers) when a certain kind of request arrives into the buffer (*subscr(r'_x)* in figure 1);
- when a service (acting as a Requestor) looks for some user information, it *publishes* a request to the buffer describing the desired feature (*publish(r_x)* in figure 1);
- the SNB notifies (*notify(r_x)* in figure 1) all the subscribed services according to the requested features;
- all the notified services look at the received request, and, if able to satisfy it, they reply to the SNB declaring their availability, i.e. that they have the requested data ((*avail(r_x)* in figure 1);
- the requestor service *reads* from SNB which are the available services, checks the *Service Declaration* to know the features of those services, and it can directly contact each provider service to ask for the desired information.

In the SNB neither UM *dimensions* nor *values* are shared, since the buffer just hosts requests (and answers) of collaboration. The exchange of UM dimensions and values will take place in a peer-to-peer way. In this way, the requestor is free to select which tools to use for the interaction (according to its internal policies), while the provider can apply its own privacy policies for data access.

The format of a Search Network Buffer request is:

(Sender, Action, UM, Kind, Ontology, Object, User)

where

- *Sender* is the name of the requestor
- *Action* is the constant *inquiry*
- *UM* is a property (e.g. *hasInterest*) of the GUMO ontology,
- *Kind* is the typology of the request: *byUri* (if it refers to a specific ontology), or *byLabel* (if is expressed by means of a label)
- *Ontology* keeps a reference to the supported ontology
- *Object* the *URI* or the *Label* of the requested concept
- *User* refers to the user the request is referring to.

For instance, when iCITY needs information about the concept *conc#134* referring to the ontology *TourismTO*, it invokes the following operation on the Search Network Buffer

publish(iCITY,inquiry,hasInterest,byUri,TourismTO,conc#134,user456)

and in this case all the services previously subscribed by means of the operation *subscribe(MyName, inquiry, byUri, TourismTO)* will be notified by SNB.

6   The Framework in Action

In this section we illustrate how the framework can deal with the scenarios depicted in Section 2.

The hypothesis is that each service involved in the scenario respects the framework requirements:

– to provide a WSDL interface,
– to have an entry in the *Service Declaration* in EUMUR, where it declares the ontologies and the Dialogue Games it supports.
– to subscribe to SNB to be able to publish and read information from it.

Figure 2 illustrates the entries in the Web Services Declaration component in the registry for the discussed scenario.

NAME	WSDL	ONTOLOGIES	DIALOGUEGAMES
UbiquiTo	...	• ToursimTo	• clarifG
		• Art	
iCITY	...	• TourismTo	• exploG
		• Tour-guide	• clarifG

Fig. 2. Service Declaration in the scenario

6.1 Scenario 1

UbiquiTO, in order to provide personalized services to its user Mary (*us897*), needs her interest[10] in the concept *conc#345B* of the domain ontology *TourismTo*.

In order to verify which systems may provide it, UbiquiTO publishes a request into the SNB declaring that it is inquirying for the value of the interest of the user *us897* in the concept identified by the Uri *conc#345B*, referring to the ontology *TourismTo*

$$publish(UbiquiTO, inquiry, byUri, TourismTo, conc\#345B, us897).$$

iCITY, subscribed for this kind of request, is notified about the request. Since it has the value, it answers the call declaring that it has the requested value:

$$publish(iCITY, avail, conc\#345B, us897).$$

UbiquiTO, looking at the registry, retrieves the iCITY's WSDL reference, so it can directly ask it for the user feature, by means of the operation

$$getValue(byUri, conc\#345B).$$

Afterwards, UbiquiTO, since it has to suggest to Mary some relevant artistic places to visit, needs to know her preference about the concept labeled as *church*[11] in its ontology *Art*. By consulting the registry UbiquiTO sees that no application uses its ontology *Art*; thus, no answer can be obtained by a *byUri* request. Then, it decides to submit to the SNB a *byLabel* request with *church* as object:

$$publish(UbiquiTO, inquiry, byLabel, Art, church, us897).$$

iCITY, subscribed for this kind of request, answers offering its availability since it has the label *church* in its ontology *Tour-guide*. However in *Tour-guide* the label is associated to two different concepts: *church* as place to visit and *church* as place for religious celebration. Looking at the Service Declaration, iCITY finds that UbiquiTO is able to

---

[10] In these examples we consider requests for the user feature of *interest*, but the framework can be used also to exchange other domain-dependent features (e.g. knowledge, preferences).

[11] In this example we suppose that applications use a shared vocabulary of terms.

play the *Clarification Game* (Section 4) (clarifG in the Fig.2) that can be used to refine the request. Thus it asks UbiquiTO to start an instance of this game: iCITY, following the focus strategy prescribed by the game, inquires for the distinctive properties of the concept labeled as *church*, such as *priest_name*, *form_of_worship*, *celebration_time*. For instance, iCITY could produce the Speech Act

$$<iCity, UbiquiTO, inquiry, priest\_name>$$

since *priest_name* is a discriminating feature for religious places.
UbiquiTO replies with a

$$<UbiquiTO, iCITY, deny>$$

because it does not have this property associated to the concept *church* as place for religious celebration. The same answer is given for the other relevant properties.
Thus iCITY understands that they do no refer to the same concept and tries to investigate if UbiquiTO is actually referring to the concept of *church* as place to visit. Then it starts to ask for its discriminating features, for instance asking for:

$$<iCITY, UbiquiTO, inquiry, has\_style>$$

Since UbiquiTO has this feature and also a certain number of others features related to the concept, the two systems can agree that they are referring to same concept and iCITY can provide the correct information to UbiquiTO.

6.2   Scenario 2

A new personalization system ArtEvent is under development. In order to improve the interoperability capability of the new system it can be designed taking into account its integration in the framework. First of all the registry can be consulted in order to become aware of the main knowledge representations and Dialogue Games used by other systems: in fact, sharing the ontologies and the Dialogue Games with other systems increases the possibility of an effective future interoperability. In this case, for instance, ArtEvent decides to represent its domain knowledge by exploiting the most used ontology *TourismTo* and decides to implement the Clarification Game (*clarifG* in figure 2) since it is also implemented by a considerable number of other systems. Once all such aspects of the new system has been established, the integration in the framework is then trivial. The new service has only to:

– register to the EUMUR registry by filling an entry in the Web Services Declaration list providing all the requested features. This can be done using the API offered for this purpose by the EUMUR Registry passing as parameter the name of the new system (*Art*), the http address of its WSDL file (*Wsdl_Addr*), the list of the ontologies supported (just *TourismTo* in this case) and the list of the supported games (*clarifG* in this case):

$$< register(ArtEvent, Wsdl\_Addr, TourismTo, clarifG) >$$

– subscribe to the SNB in order to be notified for the requests it is potentially able to satisfy. First of all ArtEvent subscribes to the Search Network Buffer with the operation:

$$< subscribe(ArtEvent, inquiry, byUri, TourismTo) >$$

stating that it can understand and answer to specific query (*inquiry, byUri*) about concept referring to the ontology *TourismTo*.

Then, it can also subscribe to the Search Network Buffer in order to be notified in case of generic *byLabel* request. This can be quite useful since it is able to play the Clarification Game and then able to support a disambiguation dialogue.

$$< subscribe(ArtEvent, inquiry, byLabel) >$$

Right after these operations, ArtEvent becomes able to publish and read information on the EUMUR registry, and thereby it can start to collaborate with other systems. This has been achieved without any need of peer-to-peer agreement among systems.

7 Related Work

Two main kinds of UM interoperability solutions have been proposed in the literature: centralized [24] and decentralized [1]. While the centralized approach aims at collecting as many data about a user as possible in a central shared space, the decentralized approach focuses on the process of collecting and integrating information about the user at a particular time and with specific purposes, in a peer-to-peer way.

Our intention is to exploit the advantages of the distributed approach (such as flexibility in managing privacy) [1] providing a central shared point used as a warranted reference to cooperation. This is done by means of a SOA based framework, providing a solid and widely accepted environment for the integration and cooperation between services. Our proposal is based on the central registry EUMUR that stores information about services and communication protocols, and provides a Search Network Buffer that automatizes the discovery of the needed information.

The idea to enrich UDDI registry with semantic information is not new in Semantic Web community [25], but in general the goal is to describe the services provided by one application, in order to facilitate clients to discover available services. Our registry works in a more defined and bounded context where all the services exchange UM knowledge, and thus here the need is just to discover who maintains the needed user data and how to interact with it. In such a context the usage of our UDDI registry hosting semantic information combined with a discovery mechanisms can be efficiently used in order to reach interoperability.

A similar model to our discovery mechanisms (Search Network Buffer) has been proposed in [26] in order to share UM fragments by means of a central repository. In this work the broker component works on a central repository where the different user knowledge is shared between participants.

Other approaches propose a similar solution in a totally decentralized perspective, such as [27], applying agent-based technologies in ubiquitous environment.

We propose a mixed solution where the publish/subscribe pattern is just used as a central point for automatic user feature discovery, and where there is not a shared User Model description and the exchange of user knowledge takes place in a peer-to-peer way.

Ontologies as basis for interoperability are used in particular in the learning environment. We can mention [28], which proposes an ontology-based framework where the UM exchange among several UM Servers is realized by means of a set of Ontology Server. Each of them is a common central storage of knowledge about a student inferred by different UM Servers, related to a specific ontology. The usage of ontology is also exploited in [29], which presents an architecture where a central general repository (GUC) maintains user models described by means of different user application-views, i.e.UM instances associated with several schemes.

A similar approach is PersonisAD [30], a flexible framework which provides a support for distributed models and for the discovery of associated resource in ubiquitous environment. The work is an extension of Personis [31], originally conceived as a user model server which also makes adaptive systems scrutable, in the direction of decentralized user modelling.

The issue of semantic interoperability has been variously addressed in the literature. For example, in [29], it is reached by means of facilities offered to applications for the ontologies mapping. Instead in our approach, conversations are used as means of reaching an agreement over not shared concepts. However, a similar form of semantic agreement can be implemented in our framework as well: for instance, an ontologies-mapper Web Service can be easily integrated in the architecture by means of the publish/subscribe mechanism in order to provide an automatic translation service between ontologies concepts. In such a solution the mapper service could translate concepts between different schemes representation, and the result of its work (published by the mapper in the shared space) would be used by the requestor to correctly inquiry the service responder. This can be a possible future research direction to extend the interoperability capabilities of the framework.

Another approach for interoperability is the *mediation* of user models proposed by [2], who presents a framework for importing and integrating data collected by other recommender systems, making a sort of mediation among different representation modalities. In particular, the solution allows data interoperability from collaborative-filtering user models to feature-based user models.

8   Conclusion

In this paper we present a model to manage the interoperability among feature-based user-adaptive applications in order to exchange User Model knowledge. We describe how a framework can be set up in order to support the exchange of user model data between applications on the Web, proposing a framework architecture and analyzing the execution of some scenarios using our approach.

The main contribution of our work is the proposal of a solution for UM interoperability, that provides i) an environment based on Web Services and Semantic Web standards, ii) a powerful discovery mechanism, ii) the support of conversations as means of negotiation.

Our approach has been specifically conceived for interoperability of feature-based adaptive systems. A possible extension of the work could to investigate the possibility to apply it also to collaborative-based systems, and to use the mediation mechanism proposed by [2] to allow interoperability from collaborative-filtering user models to feature-based user models.

One of the problems not explicitly considered in our work regards security and reputation of the involved systems. However, in our model we can consider two different levels in which this problem can be managed: i) the central registry can play a role of warranter with respect the other system, making a first evaluation of the system which asks to join the framework; ii) each system can apply its own policy with respect to this problem.

Furthermore, a tool as the central registry EUMUR can be used as a shared space where all the systems can collect their opinions on the other systems. Some techniques for reputation evaluation could be implemented exploiting these opinions; this is a possible future evolution of this work.

One of the main advantages of the peer-to-peer interaction provided by the framework is the flexibility in managing privacy. How the propagation of user data among applications can be regulated with respect to the user privacy is a very relevant issue in UM interoperability. User Model data have to be exchanged according to some privacy policy [32], in order to fulfill both user preferences and legal requirements. The user can have her personal preferences on privacy dimensions, e.g. about which part of the User Model to make available to other applications; which applications can access, the purpose of the sharing of data, etc. The management of the privacy is not the core focus of our framework, anyway the framework takes into account these aspects and do not force the systems to share any user data information. The user data are not exchanged in the shared space (SNB) and each system can apply its privacy policy rules in each interaction with other systems, with respect both the involved user and the interacting systems.

Acknowledgment

We would like to thank Luca Console and Lora Aroyo for their support, suggestions and fruitful discussions during the years.

References

1. Vassileva, J.: Distributed user modelling for universal information access. Universal Access in Human - Computer Interaction 3, 122–126 (2001)
2. Berkovsky, S., Kuflik, T., Ricci, F.: Cross-representation mediation of user models. UMUAI User Modeling and User-Adapted Interaction 19(1-2), 35–63 (2009)
3. Cristea, A., Celik, I., Ashman, E., Stewart, C.: Interoperability between aeh user models. In: Conference on Hypertext and Hypermedia (2006)
4. Kobsa, A.: Generic User Modeling Systems. In: Brusilovsky, P., Kobsa, A., Nejdl, W. (eds.) Adaptive Web 2007. LNCS, vol. 4321, pp. 136–154. Springer, Heidelberg (2007)
5. Aroyo, L., Dolog, P., Houben, G., Kravcik, M., Naeve, A., Nilsson, M., Wild, F.: Interoperability in personalized adaptive learning. Educational Technology and Society 9(2) (2006)
6. Cena, F., Furnari, R.: A soa-based framework to support user model interoperability. In: Nejdl, W., Kay, J., Pu, P., Herder, E. (eds.) AH 2008. LNCS, vol. 5149, pp. 284–287. Springer, Heidelberg (2008)

7. Cena, F.: The role of semantic dialogue for adaptation in ubiquitous environment. PhD thesis, Department of Computer Science, Torino, Italy (March 2007)
8. Pazzani, M.: A framework for collaborative, content-based and demographic filtering. Artificial Intelligence Review 13(5-6), 393–408 (1999)
9. Cena, F., Console, L., Gena, C., Goy, A., Levi, G., Modeo, S., Torre, I.: Integrating heterogeneous adaptation techniques to build a flexible and usable mobile tourist guide. AI Commun. 19(4), 369–384 (2006)
10. Carmagnola, F., Cena, F., Console, L., Cortassa, O., Gena, C., Goy, A., Torre, I., Toso, A., Vernero, F.: Tag-based user modeling for social multi-device adaptive guides. UMUAI User Modeling and User-Adapted Interaction, Special Issue on Personalizing Cutural Heritage Exploration 18(3), 478–506 (2008)
11. Laera, L., Tamma, V., Euzenat, J.: Reaching agreement over ontology alignments. In: Cruz, I., Decker, S., Allemang, D., Preist, C., Schwabe, D., Mika, P., Uschold, M., Aroyo, L.M. (eds.) ISWC 2006. LNCS, vol. 4273, pp. 371–384. Springer, Heidelberg (2006)
12. Alonso, G., Casati, F., Kuno, H., Machiraju, V.: Web Services - Concepts, architectures and applications. Springer, Heidelberg (2004)
13. Ardissono, L., Petrone, G., Segnan, M.: A coversational approach to the interaction with web services. Computational Intelligence 20(4) (2004)
14. Hanson, J.E., Nandi, P., Levine, D.W.: Conversation-enabled web services for agents and e-business. In: International Conference on Internet Computing, pp. 791–796 (2002)
15. Berners-Lee, T., Hendler, J., Lassila, O.: The semantic web. Scientific American, 28–37 (2001)
16. Heckmann, D.: Ubiquitous User Modeling. PhD thesis, Department of Computer Science Saarbrucken, University of Saarlandes (2005)
17. Ahuja, S., Carriero, N., Gelernter, D.: Linda and friends. IEEE Computer 19(8), 26–34 (1986)
18. Dimitrova, V.: Interactive Open Learner Modelling. PhD thesis, Leeds University (2001)
19. Levin, J., Moore, J.: Dialogue games: meta-communication structures for natural language interaction. Cognitive Science 1(4), 395–420 (1977)
20. Searle, J.: What is a speech act. Language and Social Context (1972)
21. Rich, E.: Users are individuals: Individualizing user models. International Journal of Man-Machine Studies 18(3), 199–214 (1983)
22. Cena, F., Aroyo, L.: A semantics-based dialogue for interoperability of user-adaptive systems in a ubiquitous environment. In: Conati, C., McCoy, K., Paliouras, G. (eds.) UM 2007. LNCS (LNAI), vol. 4511, pp. 309–313. Springer, Heidelberg (2007)
23. Stojanovic, N.: On the role of a user's knowledge gap in an information retrieval process. In: k-CAP 2005 (2005)
24. Yimam, D., Kobsa, A.: Centralization vs. decentralization issues in internet-based knowledge management systems: experiences from expert recommender systems. In: TWIST 2000, Irvine, CA (2000)
25. Paolucci, M., Kawamura, T., Payne, T.R., Sycara, K.: Importing the Semantic Web in UDDI. In: Bussler, C.J., McIlraith, S.A., Orlowska, M.E., Pernici, B., Yang, J. (eds.) CAiSE 2002 and WES 2002. LNCS, vol. 2512, pp. 225–236. Springer, Heidelberg (2002)
26. Chepegin, V., Aroyo, L., De Bra, P.: Broker-based discovery service for user models in a multi-application context. In: ICALT 2005 (July 2005)
27. Specht, M., Lorenz, A., Zimmermann, A.: Towards a Framework for Distributed User Modelling for Ubiquitous Computing. In: DASUM 2005 at UM 2005 (July 2005)
28. Brusilovsky, P., Sosnovsky, S., Yudelson, M.: Ontology-based framework for user model interoperability in distributed learning environments. In: Proceedings of World Conference on E-Learning, pp. 2851–2855 (2005)

29. Houben, G.J., van der Sluijs, K.: Towards a generic user model component. In: Workshop on Personalisation on the Semantic Web (PerSWeb 2005) at the 10th International Conference on User Modeling (UM 2005), Edinburgh, UK (2005)
30. Assad, M., Carmichael, D.J., Kay, J., Kummerfeld, B.: PersonisAD: Distributed, active, scrutable model framework for context-aware services. In: LaMarca, A., Langheinrich, M., Truong, K.N. (eds.) Pervasive 2007. LNCS, vol. 4480, pp. 55–72. Springer, Heidelberg (2007)
31. Kay, J., Kummerfeld, B., Lauder, P.: Personis: A server for user models. In: De Bra, P., Brusilovsky, P., Conejo, R. (eds.) AH 2002. LNCS, vol. 2347, p. 203. Springer, Heidelberg (2002)
32. Kobsa, A., Schreck, J.: Privacy through pseudonymity in user-adaptive systems. ACM Transactions on Internet Technology 3(2), 149–183 (2003)

Open Policies for Decentralized User Modeling in Online Communities

Tariq Muhammad and Julita Vassileva

Department of Computer Science
The University of Saskatchewan
110 Science Place Saskatoon, SK S7N5A9
Canada
{tam706,jiv}@cs.usask.ca

Abstract. Online communities can benefit from communication across their borders. However, any such inter-community collaboration requires compatible policies for rights of access. Currently, the user models in online communities serve two main purposes: authentication of users and verification of their access rights. These user models focus on exclusion rather than inclusion. This paper describes how open (editable by users) polices can be used to develop open and interoperable user models and implement a purpose-based decentralized user modeling approach.

Keywords: Purpose-based user modeling, User policies, Online Communities.

1 Introduction

The basic purpose of online communities is to support social interactions and exchange of digital resources among people (Kimberly et al., 2003) (DeSouza and Preece, 2004), which requires a critical mass of users for sustainability. In the physical world, we see the movement of people from one place to another due to economic or social reasons. Such movement results in loss of population at one place and increase at another. Although also being susceptible to user migration, online communities should not fall victim to this phenomenon. In the virtual world, the availability of technological tools such as web services, make the "virtual merger" of online communities possible. Still, the current designs of online communities do not focus on allowing collaboration among large online groups. Most existing communities are independent from each other; allow no sharing and/or interaction across online community borders, thus losing the potential advantage that the virtual world has over the physical world in terms of sharing time and space. Inter-community collaboration can help resolve this issue of participation and sustainability. One of the main design problems to ensure inter-community collaboration is the transfer of the user data, including the user identity and user model, across online communities.

Most of the online communities manage user models for multiple reasons, varying from authentication to personalization. Users create individual accounts in different communities which prevents any cross-links or information sharing. Thus users have

T. Kuflik et al. (Eds.): Advances in Ubiquitous User Modelling, LNCS 5830, pp. 55–72, 2009.

to start from scratch building their reputation in each community. This results in a fragmented user models scattered across the communities. User data is shared frequently in social network applications. Facebook, for example, is evolving as a platform that provides user identity and allows third party applications to share user data. A number of other social platforms including those from Orkut, MySpace, Hi5, Bebo, Ning, LinkedIn, and Yahoo, use open standards such as OpenSocial, and OpenID to allow user identity to be established, third party applications to be added by users, and user data to be shared. Especially when using open standards, this sharing can happen in a decentralized way, in context, by exchanging partial profiles for a purpose, very much in line with the decentralized/ ubiquitous user modeling paradigm.

Normally user models are defined at design time according to the business process, functional roles and workflows of the application. In online communities, the roles and the status of the users evolve as they participate in community. Their trust relationship with other users also changes as they interact with each other. However, the roles and status in online community evolves through a far less authoritative process in online communities when compared to other applications. There are two reasons for this. First, the social mechanisms leading to this evolution aren't clearly understood and are hard to predict in advance (at design time). Second, in online communities the rules and policies to set status and roles have to be understandable for the users and democratic in nature, to be considered fair and acceptable. Communities (or their owners) learn from their past experience and change the rules for role- and status-definition frequently, dynamically adapting to the needs of the community. This requires a transparent and user-controlled way of doing user modeling in online communities. We propose to allow users (community owners or leaders) to create user modeling policies defining user status, roles, access rights and rules for joining in. These explicitly defined and user-readable policies allow community members to understand and appreciate the policies of their own and of other communities; policies can be "borrowed" across communities. They also facilitate the transfer of users across communities and their fair treatment according to agreed policies for interoperation among different communities, defining the transfer of the user model (the user's roles, privileges, status and reputation). In this paper we describe the user policy framework and the results of a study aimed at evaluating the usability of an interface designed to allow policy editing by users.

2 Related Work

One of the basic purposes of user models in multi-user applications, apart from personalization, is to ensure security of computer systems. The Role-Based Access Control (RBAC) system was created for the first multi-user computer environments and has been used widely in web-enabled applications. In role-based access control systems users are associated with a roles defined according to the operational needs of groups and organizations. Rights of access are defined at the role level. Users can work in one or more roles and can perform actions allowed to these roles (Mohammed and Dilts 1994, Sandhu and Park 1998, Park, Sandhu and von Ahn 2001). In many online communities, like Slashdot, or Wikipedia, users can be assigned roles, such as moderators, administrators etc.

The Comtella system is a web-based online community framework, which was created in the MADMUC lab to support resource sharing and discussion by students (Cheng and Vassileva 2005). The users in Comtella are assigned different *status* (e.g. bronze, silver, gold) to reward them for participation. The status is computed based on the number of desirable actions the users perform and is rewarded with certain privileges. More recently, users in Comtella can take also different *roles*. They can create new communities and become *owners* of communities. In the same time the architecture of Comtella has evolved from a single web-based system for one community sharing URLs for different topics (each topic being a focus of the entire community for a given time), to a single system hosting many communities created by different users (each focused on a different topic), and finally to a multi-node system, consisting of many systems at different websites, hosted by different organizations and administered by users in the roles of *administrators*. The new design of Comtella allows communities to be hosted in different web sites (nodes). Communities can collaborate within and across nodes. Members of one community can join other communities with the same user profile and maintain different roles and statuses (with their associated rights and privileges) in each community.

RBAC is insufficient to capture the complexity of user models required by reward-based and learning communities. These applications need to model user goals, capabilities, user attitudes and knowledge (Kass and Finn 1988). Kagal et al. (2001) proposed an ontology-based RBAC approach for pervasive computing environments. This approach allows not only defining user hierarchies but also representing user properties, which are expressed in XML language. Denaux et al. (2005) and many other authors, e.g. (Heckmann et al., 2005) have proposed ontology-based user modeling approaches to allow for interoperability and overcome the "cold start" problem.

Many applications keep their user model hidden from the user. However, applications such as learning environments need an open learner (user) model, so that both the system and learner can interact with each other to correct the user model (Bull and Pain 1995, Bull 1997, Vassileva et al., 1999). A user model framework that is based on user policies can open the user model both for the user and for other systems. Policies will not only communicate the current status of the user but also explain why she has gained this status.

Agent-based software environments, mobile applications and online communities can not work with monolithic user models as each point maintains a local profile of the user according to context. Distributed user modeling or decentralized user modeling is an option for such environments. In this approach user information is scattered around in independent and autonomous agents as user model fragments. Each agent develops these fragments according to its context and preferences. The properties and issues of these '*fragmented, relativized, local and often quite shallow*' user models is described by Vassileva et al. (1999, 2003). The active modeling approach is a decentralized user modeling for learning environment (McCalla et al, 2000). Active learner modeling can be combined with open user models to create small fragmented models just in time (Hansen and McCalla, 2003). Purpose-based user modeling (Niu et al, 2004) is an approach that involves computing distributed and fragmented user models from various decentralized sources for a specific purpose. The purpose consists of a process and the user data types it requires as input and output. The process computes new user model data type and/or provides a certain application-dependent adaptation.

Thus, a purpose is an independent processing unit, which can be applied to whatever user fragment data is available at the moment from distributed and possibly decentralized sources. The purposes can work together in an anytime manner in a hierarchy based on abstraction. More specific purposes positioned towards the leaf nodes are executed when more data from fragmented sources is available while more general purposes near the root typically demand less data or easier to access data. The purpose-based modeling approach has two advantages: speed and providing a local context for computing the model fragment and adaptation.

Purpose-based user modeling can be implemented using policies to compute user models on the fly in online communities. The policies define the rights and privileges of users in the new communities that they join, so they do not have to start from scratch as new users. The policy document, like a purpose in (Niu et al, 2004), describes a procedure, but it is human-readable and editable according to the wishes of the community owner or node administrator. A policy provides all the relevant information for computing a user model and adaptation of the functionality and interface to a given type of user in a given context, e.g. when visiting a community. This policy based approach allows for a smoother transition of users across communities and enables in this way collaboration of online communities. In the next section we explain how a policy driven framework can implement a purpose-based user modeling approach for collaborating online communities.

3 Policy-Driven Online Communities

The need for bridging across online communities is felt stronger recently, as shown by many recent popular publications, e.g. the Economist in 2008. Online communities need to interact with each other to maximize the participation of users. These interactions require the transfer of both community resources (discussion, shared articles and other digital artifacts) and user models (user identity, user status and roles). User policies represent the processes of defining and managing user models. They specify what user data is kept, when and how it is updated, and how it is interpreted for adaptation purposes to personalize the interface and/or functionality of the community to the individual user. The user policies need to be man/machine readable and transferable across communities. Therefore, the interface for editing a user policy should communicate to the user its purpose, the user actions/data it reflects and the corresponding adaptation actions (roles, status, rights awarded to the user).

Allowing users to move across communities results in a fragmented user profile in all of the visited communities and requires interoperability of their user modeling components and a trust relationship among the collaborating communities. A typical user joins one community according to her primary interest. However, the same user can visit other communities of temporary or marginal interest. In Comtella the user models are represented in a database which is updated according to user policies. These policies describe also the reason for the current state of the user model in a given context. The policies command also the transfer of user data along with the user's identity to any new community where a new user model can be established according to the context. The policies in Comtella determine the access rights, the status of users and user roles (and the privileges associated with roles and status) both in the home communities of the users and in new communities they are visiting. Policies can be created only by users in a particular role – the role of community owner (the user who created the community). The owner of a community creates and manages four types of policies: access control policies, status policies, role policies and transfer policies. Examples of these policies are shown in Figure 1.

1) Policy to update user participation		Description
Policy Type:	Status	This is a policy to control the parameters for calculation the user participation.
Effective Date	Jan 10, 2007	
Node	http://kardam.usask.ca	
Community id:	1	The community owner controls the rewards by changing the weight for the frequency and quality of each activity.
Community Title:	Pictures	
Wrq →Weight for Rating Quality	4	
Wrn →Weight for Rating Quantity	3	
Wpq →Weight for Paper Quality	4	
Wpn →Weight for Paper Quantity	3	
Action	UP=Wrq*rq+Wrn*rn+Wpq*pq+Wpn*pn	

2) Status level definition policy				Description
Level	Description	Start Value	End Value	This policy defines each status level by setting the range of participation points required for each level. The participation points are earned according to the policy for participation update.
1	Gold	700	1000	
2	Silver	500	699	
3	Bronze	300	499	
4	Plastic	0	299	
Action	If (Plastic(StartValue)<= UP <= Plastic(Endvalue)) →US=Plastic If(Bronze(StartValue)<=UP <=Bronze(Endvalue)) →US=Bronze If (Silver(StartValue)<= UP <= Silver(Endvalue)) →US=Silver If (Gold(StartValue)<= UP <= Gold(Endvalue)) →US=Gold			

3) Status Permissions policy	√ Action allowed × Action not allowed				Description
Level	Description	Share link	Share File	Post	Rate	The status level can be related to certain permissions.
1	Gold	√	√	√	√	These permissions are used for interface adaptation and access rights related to certain actions
2	Silver	√	√	√	√	
3	Bronze	√	√	√	√	
4	Plastic	√	×	√	√	
Action	If US=Plastic → disable "Share File" Interface widget				

4) Policy for Roles Permissions	√ Action allowed × Action not allowed				Description
Level	Description	Delete link	Create Community	Edit Policy	Edit Role	Based on role user can se access right for actions lik delete link create community, edit policy and edit roles.
1	Owner	√	√	√	√	
2	Expert	√	√	√	×	
3	Operator	√	√	×	×	
4	Member	×	√	×	×	
Action	If UR=Member → disable "delete link", "edit policy", "edit role" widgets from the user interface If UR=Operator → disable "edit policy", "edit role" If UR = Expert → disable "edit role"				

Fig. 1. Examples of different types of polices in Comtella

Access control policies implement rules and conditions under which users can perform actions on a resource, such as reading, rating, replying, commenting, or deleting a posting. Usually access control policies are the basic policies that are used by higher level policies, such as status-, role- and transfer-policies to express specific decisions, e.g. allowing or disallowing a user request.

Status policies implement the reward mechanism for desirable actions in the community. The objective of these policies in Comtella is to motivate the user participation in a community (Bretzke and Vassileva, 2003). The status policies define the participation metric that is used, the threshold values that are required for users to acquire a given status, and the associated privileges (access rights). The participation metric in Comtella is based on awarding points for frequency and quality of desirable activities, such as sharing and rating resources. Thus the participation update policy (see Figure 1-1) defines how the user model is updated to reflect the participation of the user. The status definition policy (Figure 1-2) states how the user status attribute in the user model is computed from the participation metric. By editing this policy, the community owner can define the status-levels (e.g. plastic, bronze, silver and gold in Comtella) and their point thresholds. The status access policy (Figure 1-3) defines the adaptations that are related to users belonging to each status level, thus defining the privileges of the status. For example, the gold status users in Comtella have access to the gold-coloured interface frame, while plastic status users have access to the green-coloured interface. In addition, gold status users in Comtella receive more ratings to give out (a different value of an attribute in the user model). They community owner can also link a given status with a policy of access control.

Role policies define the conditions under which users with given status can acquire a certain role and the accompanying rights and responsibilities. Like any organization online communities should manage a separation of duties. This requires the management of user roles in the community. Communities should devise policies to express the entitlements to these roles. Comtella uses role policies to allow community owners to share the burden of community management with deserving community members. A community owner may designate a few members through either individual policy (by naming individuals) or through a selection-based policy (e.g. all gold-status members) to special roles, such as operators and experts. The moderator can assign special access rights to these roles such as editing and deleting resources. (see Figure 1-4) Role-based policies result in defining user groups based on their functional responsibilities such as expert, community moderator, and operator.

The three types of polices presented above define how to update the user model and what access rights to grant the user when she is working *within the boundary of her community*. Each user in Comtella has a home community, which she can select from all communities hosted on the user's node when she starts using the system. It is expected that the user will contribute and participate mostly in her home community. Their user participation metrics are used to update her main user model, and identity which are linked to the home community.

Users can search freely and find resources shared in other communities. In order to access and read these resources, they have to "visit" the other community. When a user moves from one community to another, for example, by requesting access to a resource in a new community, there is a question what rights and privileges, role and

Comtella

Hello Tariq! You are in "picture" community

| Display Policy | Operator | House Keeping | Community Administration | Transfer Policy | Logout |
| Welcome | Select Community | Search | Create Community | Share Link | Upload File | Discussion | Community Help |

Edit a transfer policy from "Gardening" to "picture" Community

Policy of Points for Activity and Quality of Contributions

Weight for Rating Quality 3 [3]   Weight for Rating Quantity 3 [3]   Cpoint per Rating 6 [6]

Weight for Paper Quality 4 [4]   Weight for Paper Quantity 3 [3]

When a member of "Gardening" community visits "picture" community
<Editing existing trasnfer policy>

| "Gardening" Community | | | | | | | | Transfer policy: "picture" Community | | | | | | | |
| Policy of Status in Community | | | Policy of Access Rights | | | | | Policy of Status in Community | | | Policy of Access Rights | | | | |
Description	Start	End	Share Link	Share File	Post Message	Rate	Level	Description	Start	End	Share Link	Share File	Post Message	Rate	Level
GOLD	70	100	☑	☑	☑	☑	1	GOLD	700	1000	☑	☑	☑	☑	1
SILVER	50	69	☑	☑	☑	☑	2	SILVER	500	699	☑	☑	☑	☑	2
BRONZE	30	59	☑	☑	☑	☑	3	BRONZE	300	499	☑	☑	☑	☑	3
PLASTIC	0	29	☑	☑	☑	☑	4	PLASTIC	100	299	☑	☑	☑	☑	4
			☐	☐	☐	☐	5	START	0	99	☐	☐	☐	☐	5
			☐	☐	☐	☐	6				☐	☐	☐	☐	6
			☐	☐	☐	☐	7				☐	☐	☐	☐	7
			☐	☐	☐	☐	8				☐	☐	☐	☐	8
			☐	☐	☐	☐	9				☐	☐	☐	☐	9
			☐	☐	☐	☐	10				☐	☐	☐	☐	10

[Use policy of "Gardening" community]   [Save] [Reset]

* To enforce current policy Save without change
* To use the same policy as in previous community of the user click "Use policy of Gardening community" button and click "Save"
* To change policy, edit policy and click "Save" button

Comtella 2005 MADMUC Lab
Department of Computer Science University of Saskatchewan

Fig. 2. Editing a transfer policy in Comtella

status this user should have in the new community. To govern movement of users across two communities, the communities must have a contract/agreement about the status, role and access rights of visiting users. These contracts are called **transfer policies** and can be *unilateral* (e.g. the owner of the receiving community defines the policy according to which to treat visitors from other specific communities or in general) or *bilateral* (e.g. the two owners agree about mutual recognition of status, roles and rights). For example, the community owners may decide that visitors from the other community will be given automatically the same status in the new community or status with one level lower than the status they enjoy in their home community.

In Comtella these policies are unilateral. If a user wants to visit a new community (e.g. to read an article posted in this community), she has to send a request to the owner of the destination community. The community owner sets a transfer policy after reading the policy under which user was working in her home community. Comtella allows three options for transfer policy to community owner: (I) enforce the current policy; (II) allow the policy of the previous community from where the user is coming; and (III) define a new policy for visiting users. The definition of a new policy can be achieved by using different approaches. One may be to show the community owner the policy of both communities and to create a new policy, as shown in Figure 2. In this approach community owners can define new statuses and their respective thresholds. Another approach may be to declare one of the status slots of the community equal to one or more slots of the other community from where a user is coming. We have used the former approach as it provides finer grained control to community owners.

One problem in many learning communities is the *'cold start'* (Denaux et al. 2004), (Sun and Vassileva, 2006) where the system fails to provide adaptation due to the lack of information about users when they first visit a community. With transfer policies the community does not have to wait for the accumulation of user information to offer customization and adaptation. Transfer policies can help in acquiring user model data about the previous experience of the user from other communities. These transfer policies provide a guideline whenever a user may visit a community for the first time. It will give the user a starting point to participate in the community instead of starting from scratch. The subsequent visits of the user will follow the same policy and update profile on every visit. Yet, through transferring back and forth across communities, users may find ways of increasing their status due to the inconsistencies between the policies in each community and too generous transfer policies. Therefore, the transfer policies for temporary visitors are different from the transfer policies for users who want to make the community their new home community and are usually quite conservative.

4 Policies Implementing Purposes

Each community has a policy framework, which consists of (see Figure 3):

- *shared view* used for all context and user data, both raw data as well as calculated user attributes;
- a set of user policies governing the community, each specifying the input data (about the user and context), the process and the output data
- an execution mechanism running in a loop which selects an appropriate policy for the current user request and context and executes its process.

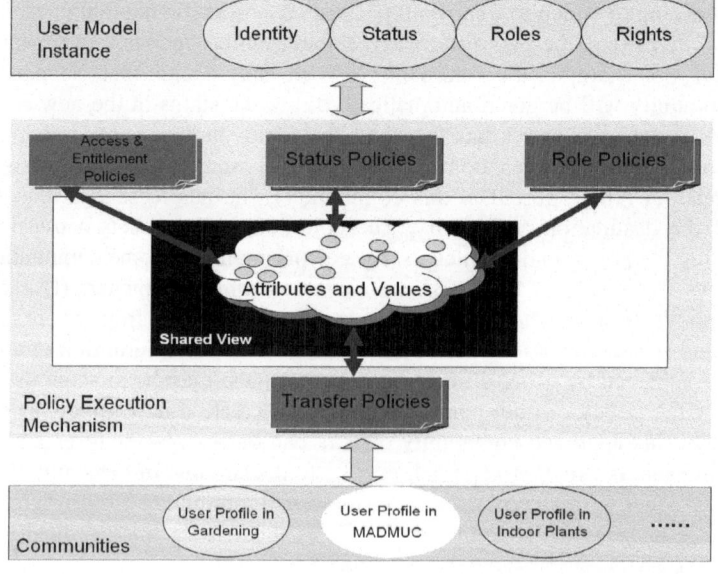

Fig. 3. The Policy Execution framework

The Policy Execution framework is responsible for the calculation, discovery and security on reading and writing of user attributes on a *shared view* , similar to a "blackboard" in systems like Hearsay (Hayes-Roth, 1985). The Policy Execution Framework fetches fragmented profile (user activity) from communities, establishes the role and status of the user as per policy, determines the access rights and creates a user model just in time. The policy framework ensures that the relevant policy is selected depending on the user request (which arrives on the *shared view*). The invoked policy in turn picks the required user data items (either raw data or user model data computed as output by other policies, in the same community or requested from other communities). There are many different policies in the set, which can be seen as managing different levels of decisions. For example, there are high-level policies that compute the role and status of the user in the community, using data received from other communities (which is either raw participation data or computed by other policies). Lower-level policies control the user access rights using data about the user role or status computed by the higher-level policies. In this way, the framework provides both personalization and a simple security layer to protect against unauthorized users and actions.

Just like purposes in purpose-based user modeling a policy has three components: input, process and output. The input is either raw user data or data computed as output by other policies. For example, the input of a policy controlling user access to a community can be a user action attempting to access an item shared in the community. As another example, the input of a policy controlling user actions on community resources can be an action of a user attempting to rate a posting in the community. We call such raw data indicating user intentions a user request. A request consists of three parts: the subject, action and resource (Merrells, 2004) (OASIS, 2005) (Seth, 2004). Here "subject" does not mean the complete user model, but just a primary identity key hosted at either a shared identity provider to which the collaborating communities have access or one of a federation of identify providers. This identity can be used to fetch the user attributes hosted in the user database from both the current community (that is receiving request) and from any other community which has data about this user. These user attributes can be inputs of another policy, for example, one that decides what status to grant the user in the community.

The process of a policy involves the algorithm that computes in context the output user model data or makes an adaptation decision. The process is executed by execution mechanism of the policy framework which retrieves the local and remote user profile, data required by the policy as input and places it in the *shared view*. The policy framework execution mechanism then computes the policy output data using the available input and current context data from the *shared view* and makes a decision, for example to allow / disallow the request or to adapt functionality or interface. For example, the process of an access control policy distinguishes between new users and local users (whose profiles are stored at the community). For a local user it retrieves the location of her user model, which becomes the output of the purpose and either grants or denies access depending on the role of the user. For new visitors it calls the appropriate transfer policy whose inputs match the user request and the current context and produces its output. The process of the transfer policy (using the user id as input) requests information from all other collaborating communities that have stored a model of this user and according to the mapping algorithm assigned by the community owner generates a local user model for the new user, which contains her status and role. This data will then be used as input by the community's rights and the status policies that decide about the user's rights and privileges.

5 Usability Evaluation of Policies

Ideally, a full evaluation of the viability of this approach would consider the following aspects: the usability of the interface for policy editing, the perceived need for such policies by the users, and the real use of an implementation of the policy framework. For this we need to implement the policy framework in a setting where users can create and manage their own communities. We have implemented such a setting - a community-building framework based on the Comtella bookmark and file sharing system. It allows users to create their own communities. The user policy framework implemented in the community-building Comtella framework, allows users who create new communities to decide all aspects of users modeling that will be used in their community to define user status and roles. This implementation allows us to study the user acceptance of the policy-based user modeling approach and the usability issues of the interface required for this.

However, it is difficult to attract a sufficient number of users for a large scale real-use study. Establishing successful new communities is hard, since a "critical mass" of active users has to be reached to have a self-sustained community. Moreover the focus of the Comtella framework is on the ability to create many communities, and each of them implies different focus of interest of the participating users, and will have to reach a critical mass on its own to become sustained. Therefore achieving a thriving multi-community system that would allow studying the real usage of user-modeling policies as it would occur in real setting would be harder than creating a successful single community, which by itself is hard enough.

Therefore we limited our evaluation to a small scale user-acceptance and usability study. This kind of study allows to collect both subjective (through questionnaires and interviews) and objective feedback (through observation of user actions as they go through a scenario) from the users. Our study aimed to evaluate the following:

1. **GUI usability:** To evaluate the effectiveness and usability of the graphic user interface to create and edit the user status/transfer/role policies in Comtella, the usability study focuses on the screens used for editing policies and the user's ability to read and edit policies using Comtella GUI.

2. *Acceptability of policies:* To evaluate the user acceptability of the concept of polices to express different purposes for user modeling and adaptation in the context of online communities and moving user data across communities the study includes observations of users playing the role of community owners completing scenarios with different tasks using the policy editing tools of Comtella GUI, as well as de-briefing sessions where they explain the policies they have created and reflect on the process and how it met their intentions.

3. ***Overall reaction to Comtella as online community framework:*** We installed and test Comtella as a research tool that allows creating small communities and the transfer of users between these communities. Comtella can be used as a test application by which we can study the interaction between communities/groups

with a decentralized user model. The readable, editable and transferable policies can express processes to manage user model. To evaluate the overall satisfaction of the users about the functionality and usability of the multi-community Comtella framework system we used a questionnaire (The QUIS™).

We selected participants with various backgrounds and asked them to go through the same scenarios of creating a community, defining user policies of different kinds and modifying the policies. There were twelve participants in the study; each was paid a $10 to participate in a one-hour experiment. Participants (7 males and 5 females) ranged from 23 to 29 year old. Six participants were graduate students in the Computer Science Department of the University of Saskatchewan. Four participants were graduate students from the School of Engineering, Veterinary Sciences, Soil Sciences, and Chemistry. Two participants were undergraduate students at College of Arts and Science, and College of Commerce. Fig. 4 shows the memberships of the participants in different online communities. It shows that all of them had accounts in more than one online community. Nine participants had more than four accounts and seven participants have five or more accounts. This reflects the fact that many of our subjects were young people.

We used a questionnaire to find out the users' backgrounds, experience with online communities and their willingness to create their own community, define user policies and their overall evaluation of the Comtella framework. We gave a 15 minute introduction of the notion of policies, Comtella and the interface screens related to editing policies before the start of experiment. We observed the users' performance in performing four pre-defined tasks related to creating different kinds of policies with the GUI. We checked afterwards their understanding of the created user policies by asking them to write down the defined community polices in their own words to determine their comprehension of these policies. After each task in the scenario, we asked specific and general questions regarding the task, for example, feedback concerning the usability of the web page, details of the form/web page widgets, ease of use, the user's comprehension of screen contents (policy) and overall experience. We also

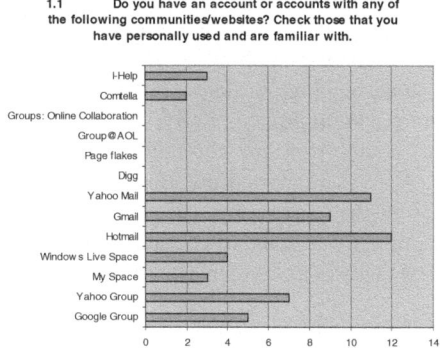
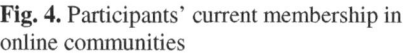
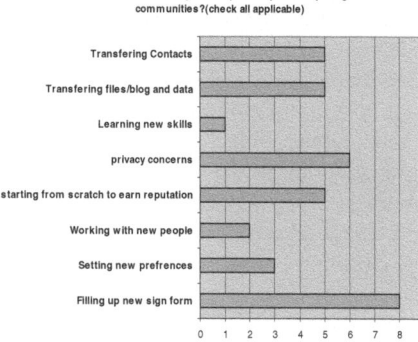

Fig. 4. Participants' current membership in online communities

Fig. 5. Factors preventing participants from joining a new community

recorded the degree of successful completion of each task (without help or with help, and what kind of help). The study provided us with information about the readability of policies, usability of the policy-editing interface, the users' conception of open user policies, their preferences for tools to author community policies and the learning curve of system.

So, to summarize: our hypothesis in this evaluation was that the editable and readable user policies for communities were easy to comprehend and acceptable by users. To prove or disprove the hypothesis we used the Comtella multi-community framework, which supports users in creating and editing policies for managing, transferring and adapting user models between the communities existing within the Comtella framework. We used both objective and subjective measures including the error rate, readability and understanding of the community policies, user satisfaction and comprehension of the Comtella user policy editing GUI.

6 Results

When we asked what are the factors that prevent them from joining a new community (see Fig. 5), the request to setup a new account appeared the most frequent factor preventing participant in joining new communities. Privacy, transfer of data, contacts and starting from scratch and earning reputation were other important factors. These statistics show that there is a need for transferable, open user model that may act as vehicle to transport user identity (role, access rights and system privileges), social status, trust and reputation in a community.

After the experiment we administered a questionnaire to the participants. We asked two types of questions to evaluate the acceptability of user policies. The first type asked users about their opinions of the overall importance of policies in an online community. The second type of questions tested the acceptability, comprehension and readability of the policies in the current implementation of the Comtella framework. We asked about the overall reaction of the user to the system.

The questionnaire asked participants if they supported the idea that communities may set their own policies for reward rules. One third (33.33 %) of the participants agreed strongly and 58.33% agreed with the idea. The rest were neutral or moderately negative. Probably the reason is that transfer of status is appropriate across communities that share something (common interest, goal, ideology or demographics), but may not be appropriate in general, for two random communities. Similarly, 58.33% participants agreed with the idea of the transfer of status from one community to another, probably due to the same reason. However, 91.67% supported the idea that the community owner may set the reward mechanism of the community. All participants supported the idea of limiting user access based in their status and role in a community.

During the study the participants performed tasks in three scenarios.

1) **The first scenario** was where the participants performed just one task - to create a new community.

2) In **the second scenario** the participants were asked to perform two tasks regarding the status policy of the community.

Table 1. Examples of some questions about user *status policy* and *transfer policies*

	Do not agree at all	Not agree	Somewhat agree	Agree	Strongly agree
The community owner should be able to set reward rules for his/her community members.	0	0	0	1	11
Would you support the idea of limiting users' actions in the community based on their status (for example limiting who can read, share and comment)?	0	0	0	9	3
Do you agree with the statement, "Communities may have their own set of reward rules for participation"?	0	1	0	7	4
If you find a policy of some other community suitable for your community, would you request the policy from that community owner?	0	1	0	10	1
When a user moves from one community to another, do you think his/her status should be transferred to the second community?	0	2	3	7	0
Do you think the community owner should be able to set rules for transfer of user from one community to another?	0	0	0	7	5
If you found a Role Policy of some other community appropriate for your community, would you like to request the XML based role policy document from that community owner?	0	1	1	7	4

- task (2.1) was to "create a status policy of the new community" and
- task (2.2.) was to "edit/change the status policy".

3) The **third scenario** focused on transfer policies. Assuming that the user is in the role of a community owner of the new created community, and another user, coming from the "gardening community" requests to see materials from the new community, the user has to create a suitable transfer policy for users coming from the "gardening" community. In this scenario, the participants performed three tasks.

- task (3.1) was to "allow visiting users to use the status policy of the community they come from – the 'gardening community' – as a transfer policy";
- task (3.2) was to "allow visiting users to use the status policy of the new community as a transfer policy", and
- task (3.3.) was to "create a new transfer policy from the 'Gardening Community' to the new community".

4) The **fourth scenario** required the participants to perform one task - to "edit the role policy of the community".

Table 2. Tasks performed with some help versus no help (further distinction between different kinds of help is provided in Figure 6)

Create Community		Create and Edit a Status Policy				Create Different Types of Transfer Policies						Create Role Policy	
Task 1		Task 2.1		Task 2.2		Task 3.1		Task 3.2		Task 3.3		Task 4	
Help	No Help	Help	No Help	Help	No Help	Help	No Help	Help	No Help	Help	No Help	Help	No Help
0	12	4	8	5	7	5	6	2	9	1	11	1	10

Our observations show that most of the users performed the tasks successfully (Table 2). While the tasks related to creating policies (Task 2.1 and 2.2) created difficulties to some of the users, the performance generally improved as the users progressed through the sequence of tasks and there was only one user who needed help in creating a new Role Policy in the last scenario. The number of requests for help decreased as user progressed through each scenario (from task 3.1 to 3.3) and over the course of the experiment (from task 2 to 5). In Table 2, by "help" we mean that the observer had to either verbally explain the functionality of the interface (the screen) or the meaning of the task.

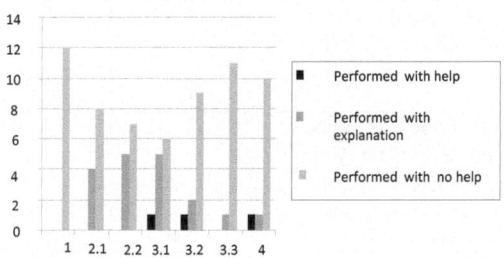

Fig. 6. Tasks performed with explanation, with help, and with no help

Figure 6 shows that the observer intervened only three times to partially perform the task for a user. The trend of reduced needs for help shows that participants quickly learnt the system. They were able to edit and explain the default policies from Comtella screens in their own words. These results are encouraging, but there is room for improvement in some of the screens e.g. editing a transfer policy.

After performing all the tasks the participants were asked to give their overall impression about the interface (screens), ease of learning and capabilities of the Comtella system on a Likert scale from 1 to 9, where 1 means bad/ difficult and 9 means good/easy. The users responses are summarized graphically in Fig. 7-A, 7-B and 7-C. The users' impression of the interface (screen layout) is overall positive. Learning the system and performing tasks was judged as easy by most of the users. However, it wasn't so easy for some users to remember the names and use of commands; yet the lowest rating on this question is 5, given by only one user. This problem can be rectified by providing in context help by a popup screen and making screens across the system more uniform. Users also found the Comtella system reliable, with a good response time.

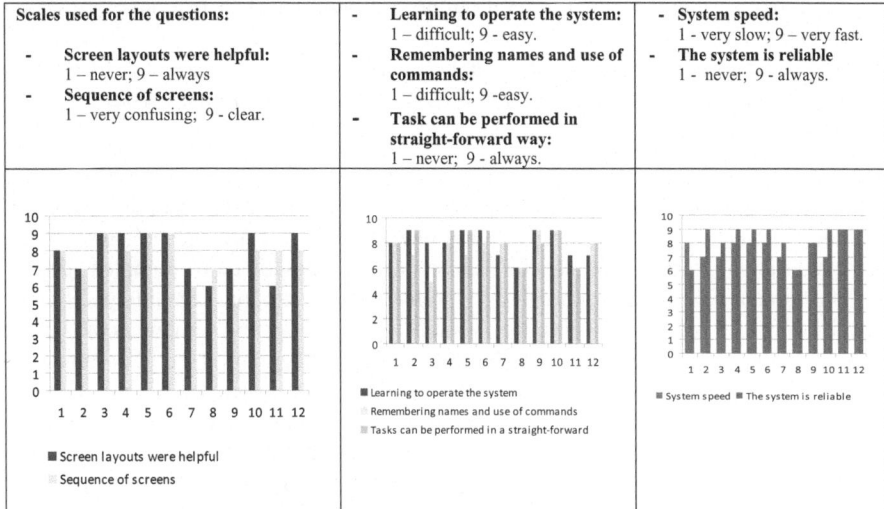

Fig. 7-A. User impression about the Comtella interface (screens)

Fig. 7-B. User impression about Comtella learnability

Fig. 7-C. User impression about Comtella capabilities

7 Discussion and Future Work

Collaborating online communities have to deal with fragmented user models. These environments need interoperable, context and purpose-sensitive user models. Online communities need a shared framework to express, discover, transfer and secure user models. User policies can be used to define purposes for user modeling and compute the required user model just in time. We propose a policy framework with the following advantages:

- Interactions between different communities will result in exchange of both users and contents, which otherwise is not possible due to island nature of online communities (Harth et al., 2005), (Breslin et al., 2005). In this way there will be no necessity for each community to gain a critical mass of participation to be sustainable by itself.

- Transfer policies provide a starting point for customization for the user across communities without '*cold start*'.

- Explicitly assigned roles for users lead to a more sophisticated user model, representing the context, purpose, and reputation of users within and across communities.

- User policies are readable for the community members, and in this way they know the consequences of their actions and activity. Community owners can change the policies according to the changing needs of the communities.

- People in other communities will feel more comfortable since 'strangers' will be allowed only after policy negotiation with their trusted domain/community.
- The availability of policy documents for a community system, owner and user work helps establish trust between online communities. This can have further implications for privacy.
- The evaluation of the usability of policies showed that user have no difficulty in understanding the notion of policies and using the provided interface to create policies.

The current implementation of the proposed approach has limitations. The system only considers a simple user model approach, mostly related to the user authentication and verification of their access rights. Only the transfer of simple participation metric and status is supported. The transfer across communities of more complex, domain specific models that involve knowledge, preferences to support domain-specific personalization, will require ensuring interoperability of syntax and semantics of the user models. In our Comtella framework the user models created in different communities are hosted by one engine, in one database with the same structure. We are currently working on generalizing this approach for user model interoperability across existing social networks (Wang & Vassileva, to appear). Yet the user models in these social networks are rather simple and tend to follow standards like OpenSocial, so the problem is not so different than in Comtella. Bridging across completely different domain specific user models is may not be possible in the near future and may not be even desirable, since the interpretation of the semantic differences and integration of the data may prove to be too complex and the advantages for adaptation, questionable.

The Comtella community framework with the policy-based user models provides a platform to study the dynamics of online communities. We can envisage several interesting studies that can be done in the future.

Study of single community: Comtella has been used for the study of reward mechanisms and its effects on the participation in communities. The flexible reward mechanism of the current implementation provides an opportunity to observe the effects of different reward strategies. For example what should be the parameter values at the start of the community to attract users and how the reward mechanism may be adjusted to achieve the quality in contributions of users in the later stages of community's life? This information will be useful for defining the reward policies in the current and future deployments of Comtella and other reward based communities.

Study of interaction between communities: Previous Comtella studies were focused on a single group and its dynamics. This implementation can be used to study both interactions within one community and interactions between communities. Studying the transfer of users between communities will point out what factors trigger the transfer of user. The composition of local and visiting users in a community and actual community of visiting users will help to highlight the relationship between communities. The knowledge about the movement of users between communities and contributing factors for the direction of movement will be useful for both attracting and retaining users in future communities.

***Study of user activity and sustainability*:** The study of contributions by local and visiting community members will help to appreciate the effects of collaboration between communities on their sustainability. This study will visualize the activities such as *sharing* and *rating* of by local and visiting community members. It would be interesting also to study the effects of policy-based user modeling on the *cold start* problem by comparing the time taken by local and visiting users to attain the top status in the community.

Acknowledgement. This work has been supported by NSERC and Cameco with a research grant for the Prairie Chair for Women in Science and Engineering.

References

1. Anderson, J.R.: The expert module. In: Polson, M., Richardson, J. (eds.) Hand-book of Intelligent Training Systems, pp. 21–53. Erlbaum, Hillsdale (1988)
2. Breslin, J.G.: Towards Semantically-Interlinked Online Communities. In: Gómez-Pérez, A., Euzenat, J. (eds.) ESWC 2005. LNCS, vol. 3532, pp. 500–514. Springer, Heidelberg (2005)
3. Bretzke, H., Vassileva, J.: Motivating Cooperation in Peer to Peer Networks. In: Brusilovsky, P., Corbett, A.T., de Rosis, F. (eds.) UM 2003. LNCS, vol. 2702, pp. 218–227. Springer, Heidelberg (2003)
4. Bull, S., Nghiem, T.: Helping Learners to Understand Themselves with a Learner Model Open to Students, Peers, and Instructors. In: Proceedings of Workshop on Individual and Group Modeling Methods that Help Learners Understand Themselves, International Conference on Intelligent Tutoring Systems 2002, pp. 5–13 (2002)
5. Bull, S., Pain, H.: Did I say what I think I said and do you agree with me?: Inspecting and Questioning the Student Model. In: Proceedings of World Conference on Artificial Intelligence and Education (ACCE), Charlottesville, VA, pp. 501–508 (1995)
6. Cheng, R., Vassileva, J.: Design and Evaluation of an Adaptive Incentive Mechanism for Sustained Educational Online Communities. User Modeling and User-Adapted Interaction, special issue on User Modeling Supporting Collaboration and Online Communities 16(3/4), 321–348 (2006)
7. DeSouza, C.S., Preece, J.: A framework for analyzing and understanding online communities. Interacting with Computers 16, 579–610 (2004)
8. Denaux, R., Dimitrova, V., Aroyo, L.: Interactive ontology-based user modeling for personalized learning content management. In: AH 2004: Workshop Proceedings Part II, pp. 338–347 (2004)
9. Denaux, R., Aroyo, L., Dimitrova, V.: An approach for ontology-based elicitation of user models to enable personalization on the semantic web. In: Special interest Tracks and Posters of the 14th international Conference on World Wide Web, WWW 2005, Chiba, Japan, May 10 - 14, pp. 1170–1171. ACM Press, New York (2005), http://doi.acm.org/10.1145/1062745.1062923
10. Hansen, c., McCalla, G.: Active Open Learner Modelling. In: Proceedings of AIED 2003, Sydney, Australia, July 20-24 (2003)
11. Harth, A., Breslin, J.G., O'Murchu, I., Decker, S.: Linking Semantically-Enabled Online Community The Semantic Web: Research and Applications. In: Gómez-Pérez, A., Euzenat, J. (eds.) ESWC 2005. LNCS, vol. 3532, pp. 500–514. Springer, Heidelberg (2005)
12. Hayes-Roth, B.: A blackboard architecture for control. Artificial Intelligence 26, 251–321 (1985)

13. Heckmann, D., Schwartz, T., Brandherm, B., Kroener, A.: Decentralized User Modeling with UserML and GUMO. In: Proceedings of Workshop on Decentralized, Agent-based, Social User Modeling (DASUM 2005), with User Modeling 2005, Edinburgh, Scotland (2005)
14. Kagal, L., Finin, T., Joshi, A.: Trust-Based Security in Pervasive Computing Environments. Computer 34(12), 154–157 (2001), http://dx.doi.org/10.1109/2.970591
15. Kass, R., Finin, T.: Modeling the user in natural language systems. Compute. Linguist. 14(3), 5–22 (1988)
16. Kimberly, R.S., Farnham, D.S., Davis, P.: Sharing personal information in online community member profiles (2003), http://research.microsoft.com/scg/#papers (04-13-2005)
17. McCalla, G., Vassileva, G., Greer, J., Bull, S.: Active Learner Modelling. In: Gauthier, G., VanLehn, K., Frasson, C. (eds.) ITS 2000. LNCS, vol. 1839, pp. 53–62. Springer, Heidelberg (2000)
18. Merrells, J.: XACML: XML Access Control (2004), http://www.idealliance.org/papers/dx_xmle04/papers/ 04-01-04/04-01-04.pdf (last Visited: October 2006)
19. Mohammed, I., Dilts, D.M.: Design for dynamic user-role-based security. Compute. Secure. 13(9), 661–671 (1994)
20. Niu, X., McCalla, G.I., Vassileva, J.: Purpose-based Expert Finding in a Portfolio Management System. Computational Intelligence Journal 20(4), 548–561 (2004)
21. OASIS (2005) eXtensible Access Control Markup Language 2 (XACML) Version 2.0 OASIS Standard, February 1 (2005), http://docs.oasis-open.org/xacml/2.0/ access_control-xacml-2.0-core-spec-os.pdf (visited: October 2006)
22. Park, J.S., Sandhu, R., Ahn, G.: Role-based access control on the web. ACM Trans. Inf. Syst. Secur. 4(1), 37–71 (2001), http://doi.acm.org/10.1145/383775.383777
23. The QUISTM 7.0 The Questionnaire for User Interaction Satisfaction (QUIS) Office of Technology Commercialization The University of Maryland
24. Sandhu, R., Park, J.S.: Decentralized user-role assignment for Web-based intranets. In: Proceedings of the Third ACM Workshop on Role-Based Access Control Fairfax, Virginia, United States (October 1998), http://doi.acm.org/10.1145/286884.286887
25. Seth, P.: Sun's XACML Implementation. Programmer's guide for version 1.2 (April 2006)
26. Sun, L., Vassileva, J.: Social Visualization Encouraging Participation in Online Communities. In: Dimitriadis, Y.A., Zigurs, I., Gómez-Sánchez, E. (eds.) CRIWG 2006. LNCS, vol. 4154, pp. 349–363. Springer, Heidelberg (2006)
27. The Economist, Online Social Networks Everywhere and Nowhere March 2008 From The Economist print edition (2008), http://www.economist.com/business/ displaystory.cfm?story_id=10880936 (visited: December 2008)
28. Vassileva, J., McCalla, G., Greer, J.: Multi-Agent Multi-User Modeling. User Modeling and User Adapted Interaction 13(1), 1–31 (2003)
29. Vassileva, J., Greer, J., McCalla, G.: Openness and Disclosure in Multi-Agent Learner Models. In: Workshop on Open, Interactive, and Other Overt Approaches to Learner Modeling (Proceedings from 9th International Conference, AIED 1999), pp. 43–49 (1999)
30. Wang, Y., Vassileva, J.: A User-Centric Authentication and Privacy Control Mechanism for User Model Interoperability in Social Networking Sites. In: Proceedings of the International Workshop on Personalization in Web 2.0, with UMAP 2009, Trento, Italy, June 22-26 (to appear, 2009)

Automatic Generation of Semantic Metadata as Basis for User Modeling and Adaptation

Kees van der Sluijs[1] and Geert-Jan Houben[1,2]

[1] Technische Universiteit Eindhoven
PO Box 513, 5600 MB, Eindhoven, The Netherlands
{k.a.m.sluijs,g.j.houben}@tue.nl
[2] Technische Universiteit Delft
PO Box 5031, 2600 GA, Delft, The Netherlands
g.j.p.m.houben@tudelft.nl

Abstract. With the help of the simple and world-wide accepted technique of tagging, users can help to collaboratively provide metadata over previously uncharted collections of multimedia documents. However, the semantics of tags are rather limited and not always as helpful in disclosing a dataset as a proper ontology can be. In this paper we introduce the Relco framework that applies syntactic, semantic and collaborative techniques to connect tags to ontological concepts, which helps to quickly get more semantics about a tag. We demonstrate the applicability of our techniques in two concrete Web applications: one in the educational domain and one in the cultural heritage domain. For the former we describe how students are better able to find the information in socially tagged videos and in the latter we also show how the used techniques allow building a faceted browser over the previously uncharted multimedia objects and we show which techniques could be applied to control the quality of user driven annotation.

Keywords: Tag, Ontology Alignment, Semantic Web, String Matching, Semantic Expansion, Faceted Browsing.

1 Introduction

With the ongoing Webification most users expect to be able to fill in their entire information need from the Web and its Web applications. To answer this demand, most companies and institutes try to open up their information collections to their users. However, this massive amount of information directly leads to a massive information overload problem, as it becomes a problem for single human users to find the right information. Therefore it is essential that companies and institutes provide metadata for the information in their collections, such that subsequently knowledge management and semantic web techniques can help to retrieve relevant information. It means that the content is annotated with metadata that allows the systems to store, manage, find and personalize the content to support their users. By now it has been established that using metadata like this is indeed effective. However, acquiring the

T. Kuflik et al. (Eds.): Advances in Ubiquitous User Modelling, LNCS 5830, pp. 73–93, 2009.

metadata is a big problem for the collection owners. This is most apparent with information sources such as collections of multimedia resources.

Knowledge acquisition in the light of these collections means obtaining metadata that is rich enough to facilitate the proper retrieval of relevant content for the users. These users can play a very important role also in this knowledge acquisition process. In this paper we look at how users can help the systems to obtain metadata and how they co do this in a collaborative community-based fashion. In the paper we share the experience from several applications that use the user-involvement in providing the metadata, and we focus on techniques that help to turn user-generated metadata into useful knowledge for both the disclosure of the collections and personalization for the user. In section 2 we explain how we have applied a simple approach for tagging in different scenarios and we present the problems that it introduces for the metadata acquisition. In section 3 we describe Relco: a component that we have created to relate user tags to ontological data utilizing Semantic Web techniques. This component uses syntactic, semantic and collaborative techniques to find these relationships. Then in sections 4 and 5 we describe two applications in which we applied that component for acquiring more metadata on the tagged objects, but also about the users that are tagging. There, we also show how we can capitalize on the result of our techniques in different ways, for example for providing better personalization and faceted navigation for the user. In section 6 we specifically discuss some techniques we applied to help detecting which tags are most probably correct and which tags are controversial. We end the paper with conclusions in section 7.

2 Tagging

New Web applications with tagging functionality appear everyday. Tagging is the process of a user assigning a simple keyword or a short sentence fragment to a resource (e.g. a multimedia document). It is therefore a special kind of annotation process. An inherent property of tagging is that it is schemaless. This means that the user does not need any prior knowledge of the domain for annotating resources, in the sense that the user does not need to know a given conceptual (knowledge) structure from which a concept needs to be chosen to annotate the resource. This simplicity is what makes tagging inherently easy to do for regular users.

Some very well known tagging systems are for instance Del.icio.us [1], Flickr and Youtube: these are systems that exploit collaborative tagging for web bookmarks, photos and videos resp. In [1] and [2] it is observed that based on user behavior different kinds of tags can be distinguished. Tags that identify what (or who) the content is about are used the most by far. On the other hand, also tags that identify the kind of content, the owner, qualities or characteristics (for example regarding the photos or the cameras with which they were taken), and refinements are used. Moreover, users sometimes use unique tags for their own bookmarking purposes. Also in the research community tagging has received quite some attention, e.g., refer to [3], [4]. In [3] a formal basis for collaborative tagging systems is laid out and both [3] and [4] describe how tagging can help in the search process.

Even though tagging is a very simple and accessible mechanism for the regular user, it also poses some problems, especially in its semantics. One problem with tagging is that it is not always clear what is exactly meant with a tag. Perhaps it is not known what the purpose of the tagging was for the user, the user could have made spelling mistakes, there could have been disambiguation concerns (e.g. "Pluto": god, planet or cartoon character), words that have more than one common spelling (e.g. "modeling" versus "modelling") or morphology, etc. Another problem is that it is not always clear what property of a resource is actually described or how specific tags are. For example, the picture in Figure 1 could be tagged with "Building", "Church" or "Catharinachurch". This granularity of tags plays a role in the subsequent retrieval of resources. In this example, if you would know that "Catharinachurch" is of the type "Church" and that "Church" is a kind of "Building", this information could be used such that in a search for buildings also resources are provided that are only labeled with "Catharinachurch". As an example of so-called property confusion consider that the tag "old" is given to the picture in Figure 1. Does it mean that the building on the picture or the photo itself is old, or maybe both?

Fig. 1. Example Picture[1]

For these problems related to the quality and structure of the annotations from the regular users, the Semantic Web initiative can come to the rescue by offering ways to describe metadata more structurally. Furthermore, it allows defining ontologies that can be used for (limited) reasoning capabilities. An ontology is considered here as a knowledge or data structure that in a carefully constructed (hierarchical) manner lists all the relevant concepts and their relationships, thus representing the semantics of the domain for that knowledge or data.

To obtain richer semantic annotations the user has to (know more and) provide more information. However, this might seem too complex or too time-consuming for the users. Therefore, the central issue in this work is that we try to maintain the simplicity of tagging while unlocking the potential of Semantic Web metadata by

---

[1] Taken from the RHCe dataset, see section 5.

relating the user tags to ontological information. Our research differs from others, e.g. [5], which points towards building a structured ontology based on user tags, where we try to use existing (well crafted) ontologies and look at techniques to relate the user tags to concepts in those ontologies.

3 Relco

To exploit available ontological information in a tagging system, one wants to relate the user tags to concepts in the ontology. For this purpose, we developed a matching component that is named Relco. The goal of Relco is to support the process of relating user tags to concepts in a structured ontology, so that we can use the ontology as a basis for the user experience in browsing and searching the object domain. Relco is constructed to be a general library that is useable by several specific applications. Therefore, the general functionality should be configurable for deployment in a specific application.

A simplified diagram of the main input/output behavior of Relco is depicted in Figure 2. Note that Relco is based on the underlying assumption that professionals use structured ontologies to describe the content of data and that regular users do the same (in some degree) using tags. We are looking for relations between input tags and ontological concepts that might exist. Tags might exist which are not relatable to ontology concepts because no syntactical or semantic equivalent of it exists in the ontology (e.g. consider tags like "2009" or "great"). In this case Relco will (and should) not find any matching concepts from the target ontology.

The input of Relco is a set of tags. Typically, this is just a single tag, the one just entered by the user. However, it is possible that users attach several tags to a resource. In that case we might use these other tags for disambiguation purposes (as will be detailed later). The set of tags is compared with a set of ontologies or other domain data like previously accepted (consolidated) tags. After analyzing this comparison, then a suggestion for tags that match the input tags is produced as output. Every tag suggestion has a certainty attached to it, which represents the system's confidence that the tag suggestion matches the input. These tag suggestions are essentially tags, but they can also have a set of concepts (i.e. URIs) associated with it consisting of concepts that have the tag suggestion as a label. It is a set because several concepts may share the same label.

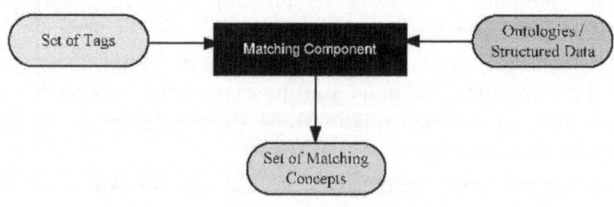

Fig. 2. Relco

At the centre of Relco is the actual intelligence of what suggestions to return to the user given an input tag. This process of analyzing the input tags in the light of the ontological information is divided in four steps: string matching, semantic expansion, context disambiguation, and user feedback. These four steps make up the matching process and we will discuss each of them next.

First, though, we describe the way the data is represented. As a data model we focus on the use of RDF[2] and later on we will use some typical RDF properties. For efficient access to our structured data we store it in a database. Because of our use of the RDF data model we chose Sesame[3] as our data store. As a query language we currently chose the Sesame SeRQL[4] query language, because its current implementation is quite mature and has some handy query features. However, in the future we might as well switch to W3C recommendation SPARQL[5] when a mature implementation becomes available (for Sesame).

Step 1: String Matching

The first step in our analysis is string matching: searching for similarities in strings.

The user input, the set of tags, consists basically of strings. The ontological concepts are given in RDF and are denoted by URIs: the syntax of those URIs typically don't need to mean anything, so we have to find the labels associated with those concepts. A typical way to model a label is with the aid of the rdfs:label property, however this might differ per source. An often used alternative would be for instance using SKOS[6], i.e. skos:altLabel and skos:prefLabel, for more fine-grained control. For this reason, in the Relco configuration, for each source a graph pattern is defined that states how to find the labels that should be compared with the input tags. This pattern definition includes a variable representing the label and a variable representing the original concept. An example would look like:

```
Source.0.GraphPattern = {x}rdfs:label{y}

Source.0.ConceptVar = x

Source.0.LabelVar = y
```

This configuration specifies that every concept 'x' in the ontology is textually represented by label 'y'. This implies that if the string matching process matches a tag 't' with a label 'y', we than consider 'x' as a conceptual match with 't'.

We implemented several algorithms for string matching. The simplest matching algorithm is exact matching. We have two versions of exact matching: strict and non-strict. In strict the whole tag has to match the whole label. In non-strict also substrings are considered.

Other matching algorithms are fuzzier and consider spelling mistakes by calculating word-distances, i.e. expressed in the number of symbol transformations (like deletions, insertions and substitutions). In Relco we use the open source Simmetrics library[7] for our fuzzy matching needs, as it contains implementations for

[2] http://www.w3.org/RDF/
[3] http://www.openrdf.org/
[4] http://*www.openrdf.org/doc/SeRQLmanual.html*
[5] http://www.w3.org/TR/rdf-sparql-query/
[6] http://www.w3.org/TR/swbp-skos-core-spec/
[7] http://sourceforge.net/projects/simmetrics/

many of the well-known string matching algorithms. In practice there are three algorithms that we use most often, namely Levenshtein distance [6], Jaro-Winkler distance [7] and Soundex [8]. Levenshtein is a very well-known metric for calculating word distances. It calculates the minimum number of edits to transform one word into another (the fewer edits the more alike the words are). Jaro-Winkler is an alternative in which matching characters in two words are compared based on the position of the character in the words. Words that share many similar characters on similar positions in the word are considered more similar than words that do not. The Soundex algorithm is based on the phonetics of words. Words are considered more similar to each other the more they sound alike.

Relco needs to be configured to define which matching algorithm to use. The algorithm derives that a tag and a label match if the word distance calculated by the algorithm is equal or greater than a (configurable) threshold. The result of this string matching step in the matching process is a set of (tag) suggestions, each with a certainty that reflects the calculated word distance. The result of this string matching step is then input for the next steps of the matching analysis.

Step 2: Semantic Expansion

After the first step we find a set of syntactic matches between tags and the textual representations of concepts. In our next step we want to exploit the semantic structure of the ontology we use. The underlying assumption is that an ontology connects semantically related concepts and that such related concepts might be a good alternative for the matches we computed after step 1. Making semantically related suggestions might be convenient if the user who is tagging cannot come up with the exact concept he tries to describe and therefore uses a related concept.

We can for instance think of exploiting the rdfs:subClassOf property. This property can be used to find more specific concepts, more generic concepts or sibling concepts. Suppose we have a tag "church" that matches with the concept that has the label "church" in our ontology. By following the rdfs:subClassOf relationship we can now extend this initial match with the concept "religious building" (more general) or "cathedral" (more specific) as semantically related matches. We could even consider to follow a longer path in the graph instead of a single property, e.g. by also considering the subclasses of "religious building" we would find "mosque" or "synagogue", i.e. sibling concepts of "church".

Which property or path of properties to follow must be specified in the configuration, as it is ontology (and application) dependent which property or path of properties is the most appropriate one. We allow two ways to define which path of properties to follow. One way, in the singular case, is to simply define the property, good examples being the often used properties "rdfs:subClassOf" and "skos:related". It is also possible to specify in which direction the property should be followed. For example, to find the more general concept in an ontology that uses the rdfs:subClassOf property we need to follow it inversely.

Sometimes this simple schema is too simple however, i.e. if we want to follow a path of properties (e.g. the sibling example we used earlier). Therefore the second way to specify semantic expansion is by specifying an explicit query (using SeRQL). In case of our previous sibling example we require to follow two properties (the inverse rdfs:subClassOf and then the regular rdfs:subClassOf). A bit more complex example can be found in the query of Figure 3, where we look for the synonyms of a word by using WordNet[8] as our target ontology. The %inputTerm% variable in the query will be substituted for every matching concept label we have thus far. The words that will result from this query are specified in the SELECT clause.

```
SELECT DISTINCT wordForm
FROM {Synset} ws:containsWordSense {aWordSense} ws:word {aWord}
     ws:lexicalForm {"%inputTerm%"@en-us},
     {Synset} ws:containsWordSense {bWordSense} ws:word {bWord}
     ws:lexicalForm {wordForm}
WHERE NOT wordForm = "%inputTerm%"@en-us
LIMIT 5
WHERE NAMESPACE ws=http://www.w3.org/2006/03/wn/wn20/schema/
```

Fig. 3. SeRQL query for finding synonyms in WordNet

It is possible to define more than one semantic expansion query per ontology if in that specific ontology more than one path of properties are interesting for expansion. Note that an ontology (or thesaurus) like WordNet can also be used as a helper ontology. This helps finding concepts in the ontology that are not syntactically related to the input tag, but might have semantic relationship because a synonym is used in the ontology. In this case also context disambiguation is important, which will be discussed in more detail in step 3.

The second, semantic expansion step of the process thus moves from a set of concept matches to an extended set of concept matches (each with a certainty value and a set of associated concepts). The certainty value of the extending concepts is derived from the certainty of the original matching concepts' certainty values, where the derived certainties have a configurable decrease factor based on how certain the designer judges a specific property path to be semantically relevant to the input concept. For our "church" example the designer could for instance define a decrease of 0.2, meaning that if the concept for "church" was originally matched with a certainty of 0.9, the certainty for sibling concept "mosque" would be $(1-0.2)*0.9=0.72$.

Step 3: Context Disambiguation

In the third step in Relco we go for context disambiguation. There we exploit that the input for Relco is a set of tags instead of a single tag (i.e. the current user tag for an object, and all previous tags for that object). The underlying assumption is that some of these previous tags can provide insights in what the user meant with the input tag. The idea is, as illustrated by Figure 4, that if two or more tags have a match in the same neighborhood of an ontology (defined by a maximum distance in the length of the property path between concepts) then the chance is probably higher that the suggestions are better. For example, suppose that in our ontology there is a property "skos:related" between "christianity" and "church". If the user then inputs the tag

---

[8] Refer to: http://www.w3.org/2006/03/wn/wn20/

"religious building" and we already have a previous tag "christianity", the suggestions "chapel" and "church" could be regarded more relevant than "mosque" or "synagogue". We could conclude this based on the path length between "christianity and "church", which is of length 1, while the path length between "christianity" and "mosque" is 3 (given that we follow inverse relationships). "christianity" and "mosque" might still be in each other's neighborhood (there is still a weak link of semantic relatedness), but in this case the path length determines which alternative is considered the most appropriate.

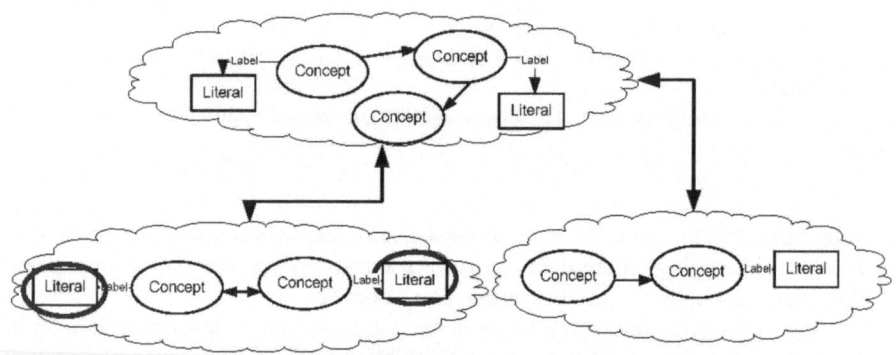

Fig. 4. Two matches in one region of an ontology

Determining the path length between all concepts that are matched with a set of input tags is very costly if this is determined during runtime only. To do this efficiently we pre-compute the neighborhood of every concept in the ontology, i.e. we compute for every concept all the concepts that are within the maximum path distance. This maximum path distance is typically rather small, especially for well-connected graphs, but a good value depends on the structure of the ontology.

The certainty-increase for tag suggestions that are found in the same region (in function of the path length) is configurable, as is the maximum path length. We could for instance configure to decrease uncertainty with a maximum factor of 0.5. If the matching concepts have distance 1, as with our "church" and "christianity" example, where "church" has an initial certainty of 0.7, then the new certainty would be ($(1-0.7)*(0.5/1)+0.7=0.85$. For "mosque" (e.g. also initial certainty of 0.7) and "christianity" in this example would compute the new certainty value of $((1-0.7)*(0.5/3)+0.7=0.75$.

Step 4: User Feedback

After the first three steps we have for an input tag obtained a set of matching concept-certainty value pairs. We can now consider what to do with these matches. One scenario is to now automatically use the matches and make relationships between the input tag and matching concepts provided that the certainty value is above a certain threshold. We will however mainly look at the scenario that we present the matches to the user and ask for feedback: the user already provided an input tag and we can now use his mental semantic model to validate our matches.

To present these concepts to the user a good textual representation of the concept needs to be chosen, especially in the case a concept has more then one textual representation. This process is illustrated in Figure 5. Suppose we have a concept with several labels where we can discern between labels, e.g. preferred labels and alternative labels. If the input of the users matches with an alternative label we might want to show the preferred label instead of the alternative one. For instance suppose we have a concept with a preferred label "Building" and an alternative label "Construction". Now if a user tag matches with "Construction", we might want to give "Building" as the alternative and not "Construction".

Relco provides three configuration options for choosing the best textual representation of a concept. Once can choose to define a preferred label and present that to the user. Another possibility is to present only the labels that were matched during the string matching process in step 1. The third option is presenting the user all string representations of a concept.

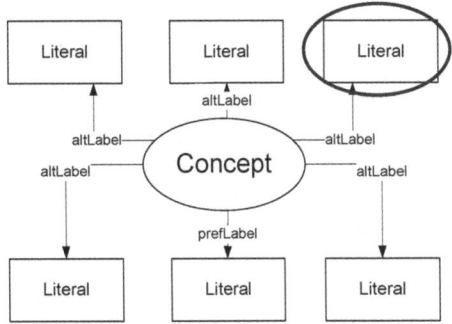

Fig. 5. Example of Concept with multiple labels

The user can now be presented with the best matching concepts for his input tag. The former processes for finding concept matches for tags were user-independent. Given the input tags, the ontology, and its configuration, the concept matches would always be the same. By utilizing user feedback we want to improve the process of computing concept matches.

Relco has a feedback channel, for both simple and extensive feedback input. In the simple case, the user is presented with the concept matches and is asked if one of them is a good alternative description for the current object. If the user does select one of the concept matches we consider this as implicit feedback that indicates that the selected concept is a good match to the input tag. We also provide a more explicit feedback channel by allowing the user to explicitly value concept matches for his given input tag.

We store the feedback using an RDF data format. Figure 6 represents the (simplified) schema for the feedback instances that we store in our datastore. If supplied (i.e. logged in), we record the involved user (for the moment simply identified by a URI), the original tag (or tags) and also which suggestion the user chose. Similarly with concrete feedback, we store per input tag and suggestion the feedback of the specific user.

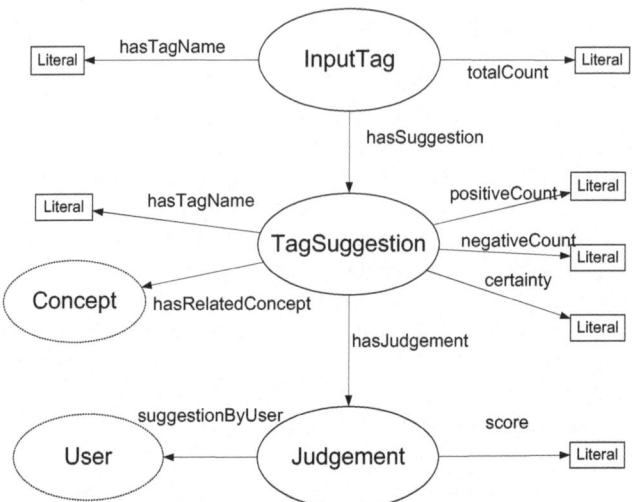

Fig. 6. Feedback data model

The feedback information that we keep in the store is in the first place used to change the certainty value, and make it more fitting with the user's opinion. The first thing Relco checks (before the start of string matching) is to see if the tag is already in the feedback store. If so, we are able to immediately output the result, namely the concept matches we already presented to a user before (which for a fixed tag is always the same), where we update the certainty given the user feedback. The exact way in which the result is adapted by that feedback is configurable.

Consider for instance the input tag "religion". Concept matches for religion might include "church", "mosque" and "synagogue". From previous user feedback we might have recorded that "church" is chosen much more often as final concept for "religion" than the other religious buildings (e.g. because the object database could mainly contain images about churches instead of the other religious buildings). The certainty of the "church" concept is then promoted based on this user behavior as we find it more likely that "church" will be again be chosen instead of the other alternative concepts.

A side effect of storing user feedback data is that we can build a user profile. Based on the feedback database we have information on the tags that are used by a user, the objects that are tagged by the user and the concepts that a user links tags to. This user profile is used in two ways. First it helps us as further input for the disambiguation function. As users typically use certain parts of the underlying ontology more often than other parts, it becomes more likely that a concept in that part is a good concept match for a new user tag. Second, during the tagging process the user gets to see his most frequently used tags. In this way we speed up the tagging process and if these tags are related to ontological concepts also the concept matching process. The user profile is also exposed to the application that integrates Relco. It can use the user profile for personalization purposes, which we for instance have applied in [9].

Implementation

Relco was implemented in Java. It depends on the Sesame[9] RDF store library, the Simmetrics[10] library (for string matching purposes) and the Apache Lucene[11] library. Apache Lucene is used for performance reasons as string matching does not scale well. In principle, the string matching algorithms as described earlier need to compare every tag suggestion by the user with every label in the reference ontology. Tests on a reasonable large representative ontology with about 3800 concepts showed us that it would take about 7 seconds on a standard modern computer to match the input tag with the string representations of those concepts. To avoid this and improve on this performance, Relco uses Apache Lucene to build a 'fuzzy' index. The principle behind this index is to compute n-grams of words, meaning that strings are broken up into all subsequences of length n. These subsequences are put in an inverted index. Using the heuristic that two strings that are only slightly different share many common subsequences, the n-grams of an input tag can be quickly compared with the labels in the ontology by decomposing the tag into an n-gram and compare that n-gram with the ones in the index to find labels similar to the tags.

As such the Lucene index can itself also be used as a string matching algorithm. However, experiments showed that the accuracy of Lucene as a string matching algorithm is generally worse than that of the previously discussed algorithms. Therefore, in our case Lucene is used with a low accuracy setting in order to quickly pre-select all candidate strings that might match, and afterwards the string similarity algorithms from the Simmetrics library are used for higher-quality string comparisons on the relatively small set of candidates (i.e. compared with the original set of 3800 labels). Using this method on the same test ontology with 3800 concepts reduced the computation time from the original 7 seconds to less than a second.

Relco can be deployed in two ways. It can be deployed as a library. In this mode external applications can easily embed Relco. This has the disadvantage that Relco has to initialize its datastores for every concept matching process, which will give it a slight but perceivable slowdown. Relco can also be deployed as a web service. It then has to be deployed in a Java servlet container like Apache Tomcat and can then be called by SOAP messages. Relco then only has to be initialized once to be ready for operation. Its setup is slightly more complex, but it is faster (especially when using the in-memory store) and can be used by more Web applications at once.

Figure 7 represents the class diagram of the Relco component.

The class MCProperties is used by other classes to retrieve properties of the configuration. It can return individual properties or a list of properties, for example all source files for a specific repository. The properties are read from the configuration file. The classes Lucene and Sesame support the storage information. In this case Sesame stores semantical ontologies in repositories and Lucene creates indexes of tag names, their related concepts and n-grams of tag names. An index is always based on a repository. The class TagExtendManager contains the method Execute(). This method instantiates the models, invokes the algorithms and keeps track of the

---

[9] http://openrdf.org/
[10] http://sourceforge.net/projects/simmetrics/
[11] http://lucene.apache.org/

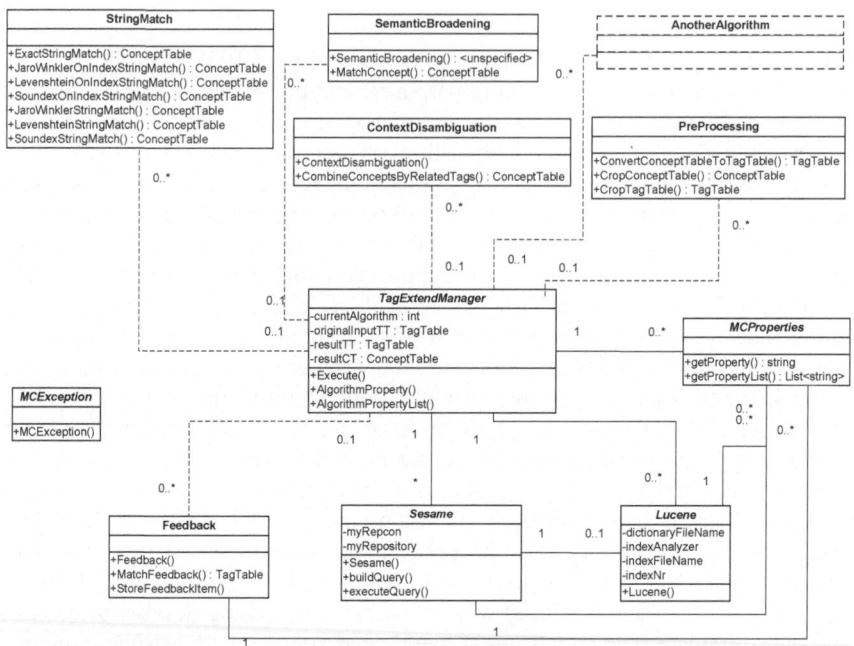

Fig. 7. Relco Class diagram

intermediate tag and concept suggestions and eventually returns the suggestions. A TagTable and ConceptTable object are instantiated to store the intermediate results and are updated after the execution of each algorithm. The actual behavior depends on the configuration as defined in the configuration file. The configuration specifies which algorithms are used and it specifies the parameters for each algorithm.

4   ViTa Use Case

The facility offered by Relco to match tags with other tags or concepts has been applied in the context of two applications that we discuss in this and the next section. In both cases the objective is to improve the retrieval process by exploiting easy tagging for regular users. The subject application in this section is called ViTa, which is constructed in a project with the same name. ViTa is a Video Tagging system for educational videos. The system provides access to a collection of video clips that are supplied with professional metadata such as keywords, title and description. The metadata were provided by Teleblik[12], a Dutch organization that provides access to multimedia sources for students in secondary education. The goal of the project was to research and review techniques that allow to find more relevant information by its users. Two other stakeholders in this project are SURFnet[13] and Kennisnet[14].

---

[12] http://www.teleblik.nl/
[13] http://www.surfnet.nl/
[14] http://www.kennisnetictopschool.nl/

SURFnet is a Dutch national non-profit organization that provides internet access and internet-related services to most higher education institutes (like universities) and research centers. Kennisnet is a Dutch public organization dedicated to providing IT-services for primary, secondary education and vocational training. Both have a videoportal[15] with many educational videos, but with also very little known metadata about most videos.

4.1 Goal

The goal of the ViTa project is to study and review the amount of relevant videos that students can find via keyword search by using various types of metadata. The video collection that is used in ViTa has professional metadata. However, as many videos in the collections of Teleblik, Kennisnet and SURFnet do not have this professional metadata (yet) other alternatives were considered as well. The idea was to experiment with different metadata sets on the same video collection and to compare the different types of metadata in a user test with students to see how the different metadata approaches help the user to find the videos they are looking for.

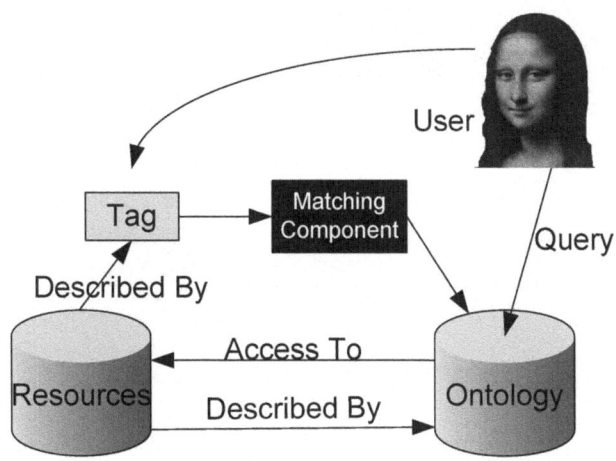

Fig. 8. "Relating tags to ontology (concepts)" scenario

One way to acquire this metadata is user tagging. In this setup we first let a group of students watch the videos and asked them to provide tags. Relco was used to help the students providing those tags. We tried different scenarios in extending the tags. The typical scenario in which Relco is used is depicted in Figure 8.

The user provides a tag for a video and Relco is used to match the tag with concepts in an ontology. The user then gets a list of textual representations of concepts as suggestions. If such a suggestion is used, the video is effectively annotated with a concept from the ontology and a link is established between the particular tag and the chosen concept. This approach is based on the assumption that using the structured ontology provides an effective way to browse and search the

---

[15] http://video.surfnet.nl/ and http://videoportal.kennisnet.nl/

ontology. That using ontologies in browsing and searching can be effective has been demonstrated in various faceted browser solutions, e.g. [10] and [11].

Another approach that we tried in this study is depicted in Figure 9. Users provide tags and Relco is configured to use the existing set of user tags to come up with suggestions from amongst previous user tags. In order to use Relco effectively in this domain we configured it to use the GTAA ontology (an extensive Dutch ontology, e.g. described in [12]) to find semantic relations between tags. This approach helps us in two ways. First, we can find relations between tags and thus build a structured ontology based on the user tags (which also has been tried in [5]) Second, it allows consolidating the tag set where only the most popular tags are shown and the less frequently related tags will be hidden as alternative for the more popular ones, i.e. we hide unpopular tags and show the more popular related tags as alternative.

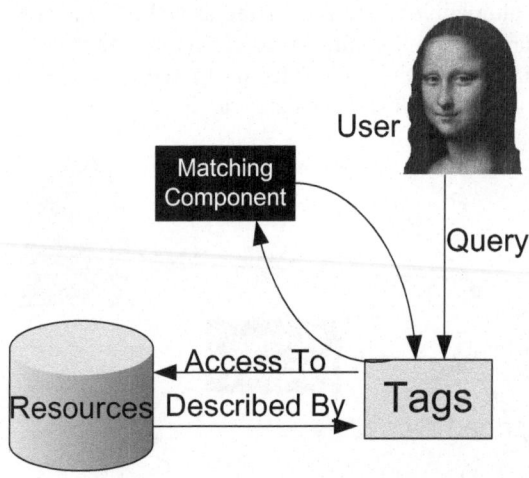

Fig. 9. "Suggesting previous tags" scenario

A third way to acquire metadata that has been used in ViTa was automatic extraction of relevant tags based on documents that described a video. The videos in the ViTa dataset were described in short documents that contained a natural language description of the video (between half a page and a page long). With a keyword clustering technique the keywords that best describe the topic are detected; the technique is described in [13]. Next, Relco was used to automatically extend this set of keywords with semantically related terms. We used again the GTAA ontology for this. Together these keywords and their semantic extension provide a sufficient description for the video over which the user can search.

4.2 ViTa Evaluation

These various scenarios have been evaluated with 153 students. The students all got the same eight assignments (in random order) that required them to answers questions for which the answer could always be found in a particular video. The variable condition for the students was the metadata that was available to search over the videos. The metadata collections were based on one of the previously described metadata acquisition scenarios or a combination of them, i.e. professionally annotated, user annotated, automatically generated annotation, and combinations of these scenarios. Note that the goal of the evaluation was to review the use of several different sources of metadata and not reviewing solely the efficiency of Relco.

The perhaps surprising result of this evaluation is that students obtain better results by using social tagging by fellow students than by the metadata of professional annotators. The reason could be that students have a shared vocabulary that slightly differs form the vocabulary of the professional annotators. This supports that social tagging techniques might be the best choice to acquire metadata in this particular domain. Automatically generated tag metadata based on automatic extraction techniques performed by far the worst, which suggests that automatic extraction techniques might not be suitable in this domain. A more extensive description of the ViTa application, the applied scenarios and result analysis can be found in [14].

5   Chi Framework Use Case

A second application using Relco that we present in this section is Chi. The main stakeholder for the Chi application is RHCe. RHCe (Regional Historic Center Eindhoven) is an institute that governs all historic information that is related to the cities in the region around Eindhoven in the Netherlands. The information is gathered from local government agencies or private persons and groups. This includes collections like birth, marriage and death certificates, but also posters, drawings, pictures, videos, city counsel minutes, etc. The amount of information they store is huge: physical archives are quantified in kilometers.

5.1   Goal

Chi wants to expose these collections to the general public. However, especially for the videos and pictures very little metadata is available which makes indexing this data for the sake of navigation or searching hard. RHCe spends parts of their financial resources on obtaining high-quality metadata on their collections, which allows finding specific objects in their archives (both online and offline, and both for the general public and for the officials of the local government). To this end RHCe employs a number of domain experts whose full-time job is to provide high quality metadata over multimedia documents. However, in spite of all their efforts by far most of their collections have no metadata at all.

The goal of Chi is twofold. First, it has to disclose the RHCe-dataset to the users for searching and browsing. Second, it wants to involve the (end) users, often lay users, into a process where they suggest metadata, and then subsequently use that metadata easily but with the appropriate level of quality: it means that the professional domain experts get the most promising metadata first and then can simply agree with a suggestion or not to make that metadata available widely for the end users.

In order to accomplish this, Chi also uses a tagging mechanism for the users to overcome the sparseness of the metadata, similar to ViTa, because of its simplicity and time effectiveness. Characteristically, within Chi we discern three types of tags based on the three dimensions that are applicable to practically all items in the collection: time, location and keywords. Users can make suggestions for all three dimensions. Relco uses specific ontologies for those dimensions, which are crafted in collaboration with RHCe. Relco will then look in these ontologies if there are concepts that relate to the input tags.

5.2 Faceted Navigation

We use these ontologies that we just mentioned for navigation purposes. We constructed a specialized navigation view for all of them, i.e. faceted navigation (for an example of a similar approach refer to [15]). If a user searches in Chi the results can be visualized in one or more of those views. The views can also be used to start browsing the collection or to browse collection items that are related according to the relations from one of the ontologies.

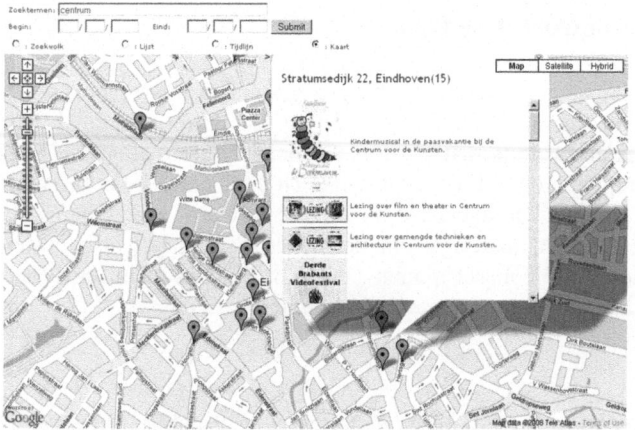

Fig. 10. Screenshot of the map view in Chi

For a location perspective on the collections we implemented a map view (screenshot in Figure 10). To enable the map view we first built the location ontology. The RDF location ontology is based on a location hierarchy that RHCe maintained in a relational database. This ontology contains a hierarchy of city, district, street and addresses. It also contains buildings related to some of the concrete addresses (like churches, town halls, etc). This hierarchy was coupled to another database that contains coordinates for many addresses in and around Eindhoven that RHCe obtained from the city of Eindhoven. Here we had a nice example of the benfits of Relco. We could use the string matching part of Relco to couple these databases to overcome small differences in street and building naming. The Map view was implemented by using Google maps[16].

---

[16] Via de Google Maps API, refer for more information to: http://www.google.com/apis/maps/

Keywords, that constitute a second perspective, are visualized in a graph visualization (see a screenshot in Figure 11). This visualization is based on the GraphViz graph library[17]. This graph visualization is built upon RHCe's domain ontology that is created in collaboration with other regional historic centers. This ontology was constructed for a structured annotation of the objects in the collection. This ontology was translated into RDF and allows a basic structure for annotation of most of the objects in the collection (i.e. most objects in the collection can be classified by at least one of the concepts in the ontology). The ontology is regularly extended if new concepts are found that can be used to describe a proportional part of RHCe's collection.

To keep the graph view simple, the user is shown one central concept and all its related concepts. If a user selects one of the related concepts, that concept becomes the central concept and its related concepts become the related concepts in the view. Different kinds of relationships are visualized by using different colors in the graph. The user can also view the set of objects (the resources behind the concepts) that are annotated with the current concept (i.e. by double clicking it).

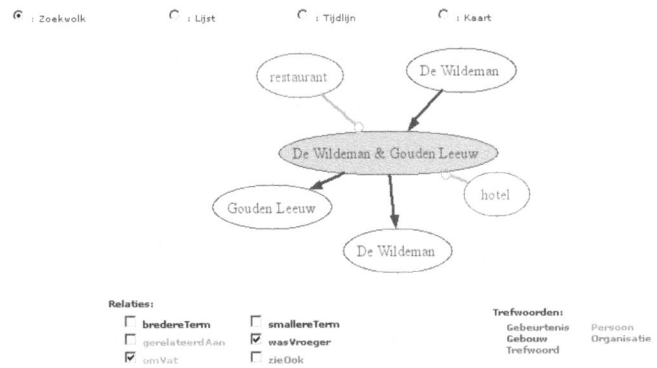

Fig. 11. Screenshot of the graph view in Chi

For the time perspective we implemented a timeline view (screenshot in Figure 12), by using Simile Timeline[18]. Time is generally used to indicate the creation date of the objects in the collection. To represent the time dimension in Chi we reused the OWL Time ontology. OWL time allows us to represent time at different granularities, which is for instance needed because we do not know all object creation dates to the same detail. For recent photographs we sometimes know the creation date with a second precision based on the digital camera-generated metadata. For old drawings we sometimes know only the age or century it is created. By extending concepts in the domain ontology that represent events with duration information (e.g. World War 2 -> 1940-1945), we can display all objects that are tagged with World War 2 in the timeline and also allow to query for all objects that are dated during that war or are dated before or after the war.

---

[17] cf. http://www.graphviz.org/
[18] cf. http://code.google.com/p/simile-widgets/

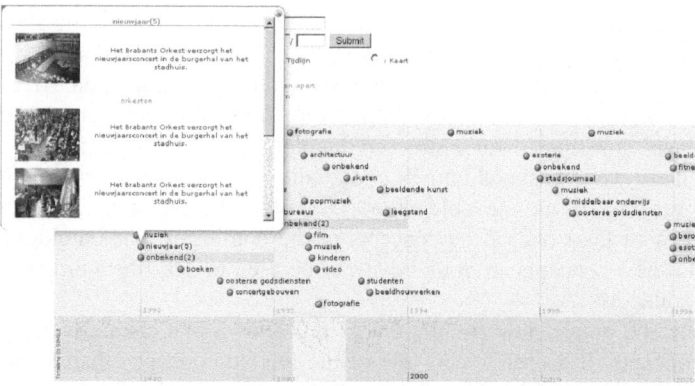

Fig. 12. Screenshot of the timeline view in Chi

6   Additional Tagging Concerns

User tagging provides Web applications in different domains a great platform for obtaining metadata. However, our experience in some concrete domains showed some typical tagging concerns. In this section we briefly discuss some of these concerns, and we outline our solutions to these concerns as they are generally applicable in tagging applications.

Tag quality assessment
Especially in the RHCe use case, quality control in user tagging system is extremely important. In their case they are not only obliged (by law) to preserve the objects themselves as good as possible, they have to guard the quality of the metadata describing the objects as well. This is the main reason to employ professional expert annotators. Annotation by end-users (tagging) is a great additional opportunity to easily gather metadata and especially exploits the possibility that specific information is known within the regular user group that the professional experts do not know (yet). However, obtaining metadata from outsiders is also a threat: people might have good intensions but provide sub-par information or even have bad intentions. So, we considered ways to ensure the quality of user annotations while at the same time not increasing the overhead and costs for the professional annotators.

One way is to use the self-cleaning capabilities of the user community. In Chi the users can vote for or against tags of other users, to express whether they think that a tag accurately describes the content of an object. The assumption is obviously that if more people favor a tag for an object, it is more likely that this tag correctly describes the content of that object. The RHCe administrators of Chi Explorer can from the positive, negative and accumulated (amount of positive minus amount of negative votes) votes, quickly find the most likely tags for an object for them to use in their professional annotation process.

In this way every multimedia document has a set of user tags and a set of tags approved by the professionals. Users can vote for tag suggestions of others if they agree with a tag or not (see screenshot Figure 13). System administrators have an overview of the most approved tags and they can simply decide to officially accept a tag or to reject it. They can also see a list of the tags that are used the most, but are not (as concepts) in the initial ontologies. This information can for instance be used to extend the initial ontologies.

Fig. 13. Current Location Tags for an Object (in Dutch)

User reputation

Votes for tags are also used to compute the reputation of users. A vote for a tag is interpreted as an indirect vote for the user that suggested that tag. A positive or negative vote will increase or decrease the user reputation weighted by the voter's reputation. So a user's reputation gets higher the more users with high reputation (indirectly) vote for that user, where the system administrators by default have the highest (unchangeable) reputation.

The users' reputation value is also used during the tag quality assessment, as votes are weighed by the user reputation.

In this way we can detect the most valuable taggers and assign additional rights to users with high reputation values. Additionally these users can get access to more advanced annotation tools (e.g. by using ontological annotation directly instead of tagging). These trusted "power users" could then be used to cost-effectively maintain the quality of the metadata content. Showing leader boards of the most valuable users could even provide competition and in this way motivation to voluntarily do this work.

Tagging previously un-annotated objects

In the current system, mainly the well-annotated objects can be easily found because of their annotations. However, many objects will have no (or very little) metadata at all when they are added to the system. Therefore, a mechanism is needed to make users look at previously uncharted objects and annotate them. Users will not find these objects through the metadata-based search, so motivation strategies are envisioned to make them willing to explore these objects. We are currently studying how to introduce a competition element, for instance inspired by Google's Image labeler[19].

---

[19] cf. http://images.google.com/imagelabeler

7 Conclusion

In this paper we concentrated on multimedia Web information systems that use collaborative tagging to acquire metadata for their data collection, while at the same time they benefit from structured ontologies based on Semantic Web technologies to disclose their datasets. We explained how these two techniques can be brought together. We introduced Relco, a framework that allows relating user tags to concepts in an RDF ontology. Relco uses syntactic and semantic techniques to achieve that. We also show how collaborative user involvement can help to better fine-tune that process by utilizing their feedback.

The paper illustrates how Relco has been applied in two concrete application scenarios: one in the educational domain and one in the cultural heritage domain. We show in which ways Relco can help these applications to improve the user experience, e.g. by improving search and personalized faceted browsing. We also considered some typical additional tagging-related issues that this kind of applications face and an outline of our solutions for those issues.

Acknowledgments

This work was carried out within the ViTa project and the Chi project. ViTa is part of the MultimediaN[20] program, which is sponsored by the Dutch government. ViTa participants are the Telematica Instituut, SURFnet, Kennisnet, FabChannel, Roessingh Research and Development, and Eindhoven University of Technology. The Chi project is a joint effort of RHCe (Regionaal Historisch Centrum Eindhoven) and Eindhoven University of Technology.

References

1. Golder, S., Huberman, B.A.: Usage Patterns of Collaborative Tagging Systems. Journal of Information Science 32(2), 198–208 (2006)
2. van Setten, M., Brussee, R., van Vliet, H., Gazendam, L., van Houten, Y., Veenstra, M.: On the Importance of "Who Tagged What". In: Workshop on the Social Navigation and Community-Based Adaptation Technologies, held in conjunction with Adaptive Hypermedia and Adaptive Web-Based Systems (AH 2006), Dublin, Ireland (2006)
3. Mika, P.: Ontologies Are Us: A Unified Model of Social Networks and Semantics. In: Gil, Y., Motta, E., Benjamins, V.R., Musen, M.A. (eds.) ISWC 2005. LNCS, vol. 3729, pp. 522–536. Springer, Heidelberg (2005)
4. Choy, S.-O., Lui, A.K.: Web Information Retrieval in Collaborative Tagging Systems. In: Proceedings of the International Conference on Web Intelligence, pp. 352–355. IEEE Press, New York (2006)
5. Specia, L., Motta, E.: Integrating Folksomonies with the Semantic Web. In: Franconi, E., Kifer, M., May, W. (eds.) ESWC 2007. LNCS, vol. 4519, pp. 624–639. Springer, Heidelberg (2007)

---

[20] http://www.multimedian.nl

6. Damerau, F.J.: A Technique for Computer Detection and Correction of Spelling Errors. Communications of the ACM 7(3), 171–176 (1964)
7. Jaro, M.A.: Advances in Record Linking Methodology as Applied to the 1985 Census of Tampa Florida. Journal of the American Statistical Society 84(406), 414–420 (1989)
8. Knuth, D.E.: The Art of Computer Programming: Sorting and Searching, vol. 3, pp. 394–395. Addison-Wesley, Reading (1973)
9. van der Sluijs, K., Houben, G.-J.: A Generic Component for Exchanging User Models between Web-based Systems. International Journal of Continuing Engineering Education and Life-Long Learning (IJCEELL), Inderscience 16(1/2), 64–76 (2006)
10. Schraefel, M.M.C., Smith, D.A., Owens, A., Russell, A., Harris, C., Wilson, M.L.: The evolving mSpace platform: leveraging the semantic web on the trail of the memex. In: Proceedings of the sixteenth ACM conference on Hypertext and hypermedia, pp. 174–183. ACM, New York (2005)
11. Hildebrand, M., van Ossenbruggen, J., Hardman, L.: /facet: A Browser for Heterogeneous Semantic Web Repositories. In: Cruz, I., Decker, S., Allemang, D., Preist, C., Schwabe, D., Mika, P., Uschold, M., Aroyo, L.M. (eds.) ISWC 2006. LNCS, vol. 4273, pp. 272–285. Springer, Heidelberg (2006)
12. Brugman, H., Malaisé, V., Gazendam, L.: A Web Based General Thesaurus Browser to Support Indexing of Television and Radio Programs. In: Proceedings of the 5th international conference on Language Resources and Evaluation, LREC 2006 (2006)
13. Wartena, C., Brussee, R.: Topic detection by clustering keywords. In: DEXA Workshops. IEEE Computer Society, Los Alamitos (2008)
14. Melenhorst, M., Grootveld, M., van Setten, M., Veenstra, M.: Tag-based information retrieval of video content. In: Proceeding of the 1st international conference on Designing interactive user experiences for TV and video, Silicon Valley, California, USA, pp. 31–40
15. Mäkelä, E., Hyvönen, E., Saarela, S.: Ontogator - A Semantic View-Based Search Engine Service for Web Applications. In: Cruz, I., Decker, S., Allemang, D., Preist, C., Schwabe, D., Mika, P., Uschold, M., Aroyo, L.M. (eds.) ISWC 2006. LNCS, vol. 4273, pp. 847–860. Springer, Heidelberg (2006)

AUGUR: Interface Adaptation for Small Screen Devices

Melanie Hartmann and Daniel Schreiber

Telecooperation Group
Technische Universität Darmstadt
Hochschulstraße 10
D-64289 Darmstadt, Germany
{melanie,schreiber}@tk.informatik.tu-darmstadt.de

Abstract. The amount of functionality offered by nowadays applications is constantly growing, mostly leading to more and more complex user interfaces. This decreases their usability especially in settings with limited input and output capabilities like in mobile or ubiquitous computing. In these settings the interaction costs are much higher than for traditional desktop applications. Adapting the interface to the available devices as well as to the user's preferences and tasks is the key to reducing interaction costs and increasing usability of applications. In this paper, we present the AUGUR system that can automatically generate user- and device-adapted interfaces. For that purpose, we developed the FxL* algorithm which is introduced in this paper. FxL* is the first algorithm that considers the individual user as well as her current situation to determine which user interface elements should be presented. We show that it clearly outperforms algorithms that do not take the user's situation into account.

1 Introduction

Current mobile or ubiquitous computing devices provide enough computing power, battery lifetime, and network connectivity to run standard desktop applications. They can be easily carried around, but are hence restricted in size and have limited input and output capabilities. This causes many difficulties for the user interface (UI) of applications running on them. The UI for a mobile or ubiquitous application has to cope with more device constraints and restrictions than a UI for a desktop application. Further, mobility often also leads to limited attention of the user [1]. Users cannot always direct their full attention towards the UI, as this might be socially unacceptable, e.g., in a restaurant, or even dangerous, e.g. while crossing a busy street. These factors make usability an even more important issue in these settings compared to standard desktop settings.

One possibility to increase usability is to decrease the required amount of interactions, i.e., key presses or scroll movements to fulfill a task with the application [2]. This can be achieved by reducing the UI to the most important parts. Thereby, we must take into account (i) the capabilities of the device it runs on, and (ii) the tasks and desires of the user. Both adaptation problems cannot be solved by manual optimization, as the amount of different devices is ever increasing, and there is a great diversity in the user population.

The first contribution in this paper is the intelligent UI system AUGUR that can automatically generate user- and device-adapted interfaces by considering user models that

T. Kuflik et al. (Eds.): Advances in Ubiquitous User Modelling, LNCS 5830, pp. 94–110, 2009.

are created from the users' interaction history. The second contribution is the novel algorithm FxL* that we developed for this purpose. FxL* is to our knowledge the first algorithm that is able to consider device constraints and the individual user in a concrete situation for determining the most relevant interaction elements. However, adaptive UIs face the problem that it is difficult to infer from observing the user which non-interactive elements (texts, images etc.) are relevant for her. For that reason, AUGUR provides a graphical editing environment, so that this information can be added by the user or the application developer by annotating application models with additional information about the UI.

In the remainder of the paper, we first inroduce the AUGUR system and how it can support the interaction. We describe how the interface adaptation feature is described. For adapting the UI of an application to the user's needs, AUGUR requires knowledge about the application as well as about the user. The models that are used for that purpose, are presented in Section 3. The overall architecture of AUGUR is described in the succeeding Section 4. Next, the FxL* algorithm underlying the UI adaptation process is presented. In Section 6 we describe how this algorithm is then applied to generate an adapted UI. In the evaluation, we show that the interaction costs for a user- and device adapted UI applying FxL* is significantly smaller than for UIs that do not consider the user or her current working context. In Section 8, we relate AUGUR to existing approaches. Finally, we conclude the paper and give some perspectives for future research.

2   Interaction Support

The objective of the intelligent UI system AUGUR is to facilitate the users' interaction as much as possible. For that purpose, we can support (i) the navigation and (ii) the input of data. We identified four ways of supporting these two tasks:

- **Interface Adaptation** *(Navigation Support)*: adapt the provided UI, i.e., the input elements as well as the content - to the available devices and the user's needs and preferences.
- **Support Mechanisms** *(Navigation Support)*: explain the interaction with the UI to the user. This is realized by highlighting the element the user should interact with next or by displaying explanations for elements.
- **Content Suggestion** *(Input Support)*: suggest content for interaction elements, i.e., data to enter in input fields or which data to select from a list. This data is inferred from the user's context and from previous interactions.
- **Task Automation** *(Navigation and Input Support)*: recognize usage patterns to allow automation of repetitive tasks, i.e., to automatically enter data or navigate on behalf of the user.

We realized all these features in AUGUR for the usage with any form-based web application. In this paper, we focus on the *Interface Adaptation* feature of AUGUR, i.e., how knowledge about the user's behavior and the device is used for rendering user-adapted UIs of web applications, especially for devices with limited screen space (see Figure 1). For that purpose, AUGUR observes the user's interactions with the application. This data is used to learn the structure of the application (application models)

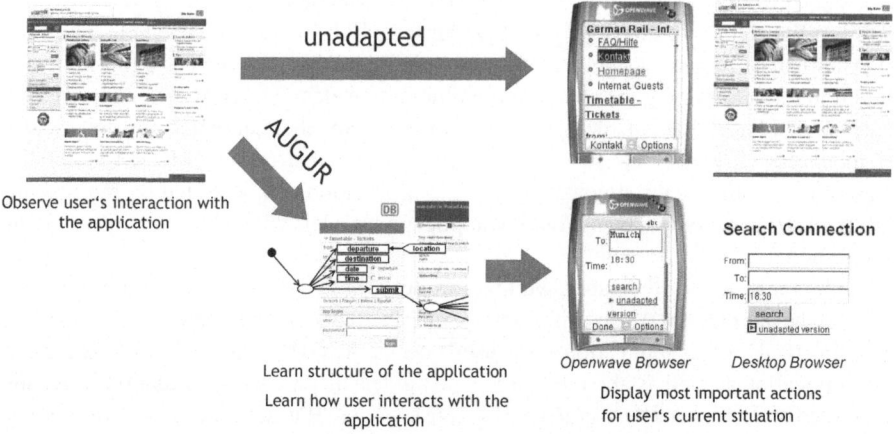

Fig. 1. Interface Adaptation process of AUGUR

and the way the user usually interacts with it (user model). We assume that the user's behavior can be inferred from her interaction history, which is supported by the analysis of our datasets (see Section 7). Both models are used to predict which interaction elements and which information are currently most relevant to the user. AUGUR determines which of this information is displayed depending on the available screen space. This adapted UI also contains a link to the unadapted UI, thus still providing access to the whole functionality. If the user wants to access new functionality which is not yet present in the application model of the application, she can always fall back and use the unadapted UI. AUGUR thus does not reduce the functionality of the application, but provides more efficient access to the elements that are really relevant to the user. In the following, we illustrate this with the example of looking up a train connection on the Deutsche Bahn (German railways) web site. The original web interface of this application is shown in the upper part of Figure 1, as it is displayed in in an emulator for mobile devices and in a normal desktop browser. The lower part shows how the AUGUR system has tailored the UI of this application to the needs of an example user.

3   Knowledge Representation

In this section, we describe how we model the knowledge of the application and the user which is needed for effectively adapting UIs. Using the example of the Deutsche Bahn (the relevant part of the website is shown in Figure 2), we explain how these models are either created automatically by AUGUR or manually by using the editing tools provided by AUGUR.

3.1   Application Model

AUGUR stores knowledge about an application in the corresponding application model. For that purpose AUGUR uses a modeling language called ATML (Application Task

Fig. 2. Detail of the Deutsche Bahn website

Modeling Language) based on statecharts. ATML models have an intuitive representation, enabling the end-user to extend and modify them. In the following, we present the main components of ATML that are relevant for automatically generating user-adapted UIs. For a more detailed description of ATML, we refer to [3].

In ATML applications are modeled as directed graphs where the nodes represent states (visualized as ellipses) and activities (visualized as rectangles). Each node can be referred to with its unique ID. ATML distinguishes between states and activities, because this maps naturally to the user's view of a web application where states represent web pages, and activities the different interactors on a page. Figure 3 illustrates the application model for the train booking example.

A *State node* is associated with a webpage via an ID that is stored as attribute of this node. The URL itself is not a good choice for identifying a webpage as the URL often contains many additional parameters (e.g., a session key) that change from one usage of the application to the next. Therefore, we cut off all the parameters of the URL. However, this sometimes generalizes too much when applications offer different

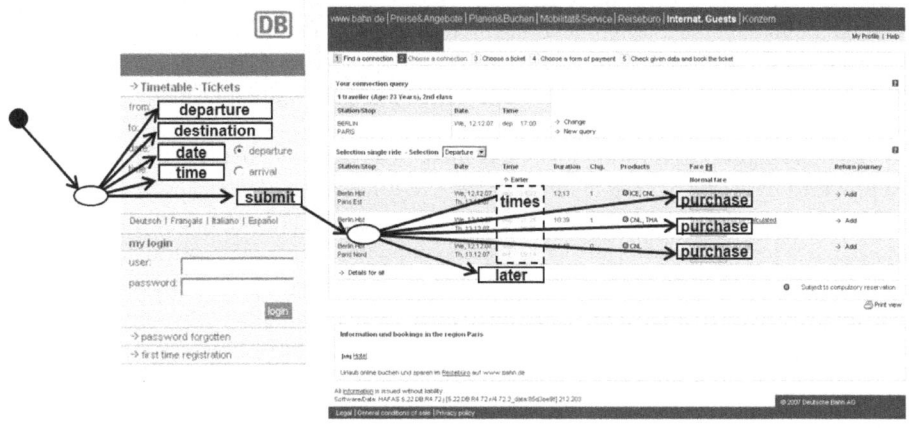

Fig. 3. Example application model for the train booking application

functionality that is just determined by a parameter. Hence, we add the title of the webpage to the URL which describes the current webpage better. For example, the webpage with the URL www.bahn.de/sth?sessionid=13&... and the title Your timetable results in the id www.bahn.de/sth[Your timetable].

Each *Activity node* is coupled to a UI element via an XPath expression that unambiguously identifies the corresponding interaction element on the webpage. We found that the following three different activity types suffice to describe the interaction with a form-based web application: (i) *Fillout Activities* refer to an input field for arbitrary text (in our example this are the "from", "to", "date" and "time" element), (ii) *Select Activities* represent elements for selecting from a set of predefined items, i.e., select elements, checkboxes and radiobuttons (in our example "departure" and "arrival"), and (iii) *Click Activities* refer to navigational elements, i.e., buttons or links (in our example the "search" button). Besides this type and the XPath expression, each activity node contains a label for the interaction element. This label is inferred from the visual representation [4], but can be modified manually.

The State nodes are linked via *control flow relations* to Activity nodes which correspond to the interaction elements on the webpage. Activity nodes again are linked to the state that the user reaches when performing the activity. For example, Click Activities usually lead to a new webpage and thus to a new state in the application model. However, for Fillout and Select Activities this is the same state as before. For ease of readability the transition from the Activity to the State node is then omitted in the graphical representation.

In order to generate an adapted UI for an application, AUGUR needs to know which information provided by the application is of interest to the user. This comprises the most relevant interaction elements (Activities) as well as non-interactive information, e.g., the departure times of trains if the user is searching for a train connection. The non-interactive parts of the interface can be modeled in ATML with *UIContent nodes*. Such nodes are coupled to a specific UI element via an XPath expression and linked to the corresponding state with a *content relation*. Unfortunately, this introduces some modeling effort as it is very difficult to automatically identify the relevant non-interactive elements. However, this may be less important in mobile and ubiquitous computing settings as the feedback of applications in these settings is often conveyed through the environment. For example interacting with a home control system for changing the lighting condition gives implicit feedback by dimming the light, thus making explicitly displayed feedback redundant.

The more additional information is specified for an application, the better support can be provided by AUGUR. For that reason, AUGUR has an integrated application model editor (see Figure 4) which allows the end-user to modify and augment the application models. It is implemented as an overlay to the original UI to ease the identification of the different elements of the ATML model. Ideally, an initial application model is provided by the application developer as not all details can be learned reliably by only observing the user's actions. The initial application model can also be automatically created by monitoring the user's interaction with the application. This ensures that the application model only contains the interaction elements the user really needs, in contrast to adding all interaction elements that are presented on a web page.

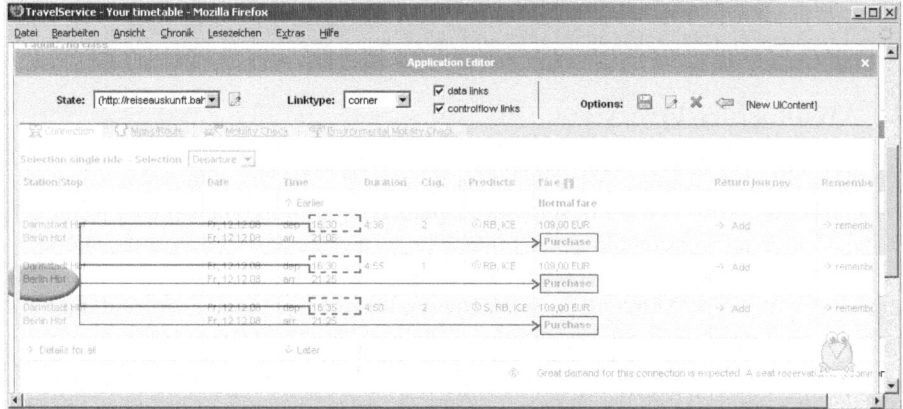

Fig. 4. ATML Editor

```
                    ┌──────────────┐  ┌──────────────┐       ┌──────────────┐
                    │ departure, 24│  │destination, 24│       │  submit, 24  │
                    └──────────────┘  └──────────────┘       └──────────────┘
           ┌──────────────┐ ┌──────────────┐ ┌──────────────┐ ┌──────────────┐
           │destination, 20│ │  submit, 4  │ │ departure, 4 │ │  submit, 20  │
           └──────────────┘ └──────────────┘ └──────────────┘ └──────────────┘
           ┌──────────────┐                  ┌──────────────┐
           │  submit, 20  │                  │  submit, 4   │
           └──────────────┘                  └──────────────┘
```

Fig. 5. Example usage sequences for the train booking application

3.2 User Model

We assume that the user's behaviour can be inferred, at least to some degree, from her interaction history. This assumption is also supported by the analysis of our datasets (see Section 7). Each action in the interaction history refers to an activity in an application model (via its ID). In the example application model in Figure 3, a typical sequence may be to type in the place of departure, the destination and then submit the form. We do not store the entire user history, but only the frequency of observed sequences up to a certain length in a trie structure (for more details see [5]). Each sequence is represented by a node in the trie. The elements of the sequence correspond to the symbols on the path from root to the node. The value stored in the node besides the actual action represents the absolute frequency of this sequence in the interaction history. Figure 5 shows an interaction history of the example after 24 usages, e.g., the highlighted sequence "departure, submit" occurred 4 times in the interaction history.

For determining the next actions the user will most likely perform, we use the FxL* algorithm as described in the next section. Considering the train booking example, we see that the user frequently accessed the input fields for the point of departure, the destination and the submit button in that order. Thus, AUGUR can automatically reduce the UI to these elements as can be seen in Figure 1.

4 Architecture Overview

The AUGUR system augments existing form-based HTML UIs with features for supporting the interaction. In contrast to the adaptation algorithms employed by [6] or [7], AUGUR does not work on the model of the UI, i.e., a static description of the interface, but on its actual visual representation. This visual representation is taken from the interpretation of the DOM tree in the web browser. It can thus also augment and interpret highly dynamic web pages using AJAX etc.

We, rely on a proxy architecture for implementing the support features in AUGUR. AUGUR fetches the UI of the application from the webserver and hosts it in an internal web browser. Depending on the application scenario, AUGUR either shares the internal web browser with the user and augments the UI with proactive features or provides a newly generated UI. The latter is used for realizing interface adaptation on which we focus in this paper. The generated UI is a reduced version of the original UI. It can be designed for a completely different modality than the original UI, e.g., using VoiceXML. AUGUR integrates scripts in the UI that is delivered to the user, e.g., JavaScript files for HTML output. These scripts are responsible for reporting all user actions to AUGUR, e.g., by using Bayeux[1], so that AUGUR can track the user's behavior. This enables AUGUR to build a more accurate user model that contains in which order the interaction elements are usually used. AUGUR forwards the events invoked by the user on the generated UI to the original UI hosted in the internal web browser. Changes in the original UI are in turn reflected back to the generated UI. The application on the web server cannot distinguish between input coming from AUGUR and input coming from the user.

The architecture of AUGUR consists of two major tiers: The *Support Tier* and the *Knowledge Base* as shown in Figure 6. The *Support Tier* is responsible for handling the communication between user and application. The *Knowledge Base* provides all the knowledge that is required for that purpose.

The **Support Tier** intercepts the user's input, forwards it to the application, interprets the result returned by the application and adapts the output accordingly. The components that are needed for that purpose are (i) an interpreter for the events invoked by the user and the application (*Interpreter*), (ii) a component that generates the required support information (*Support Generator*), and (iii) a component to decide which parts of the application should be presented to the user (*Representation Manager*).

At first, the *Interpreter* handles incoming user events with the help of the Knowledge Base. It possibly updates the user model and the application model of the current application by adding new elements or new relations. Further, it transforms the events into appropriate actions on the DOM tree of the internal web browser. Most events do not invoke a response of the web application, e.g. entering text in input fields. If the event is forwareded to the web application, the response returned by the application is then

---

[1] Bayeux is a protocol for transporting asynchronous messages (primarily over HTTP) with low latency, see http://svn.cometd.org/trunk/bayeux/bayeux.html

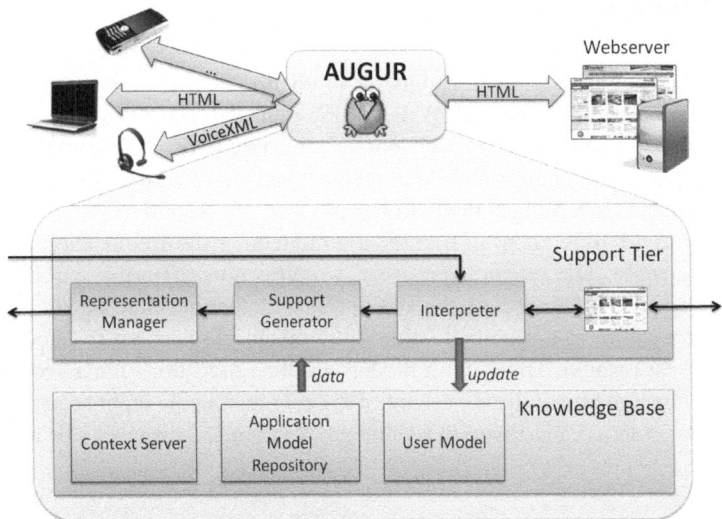

Fig. 6. Architecture of AUGUR

again processed by the *Interpreter*, e.g., to update the application model, and sent to the *Support Generator*.

The *Support Generator* takes information about the current UI from the *Interpreter* (e.g., which UI elements are displayed) and generates support information. This information comprises which interaction elements of the UI the user will most probably use next, along with confidence values. For example, a user mostly fills out the destination and time after entering the departure information in the train booking example. These predictions are provided by the FxL* algorithm described in detail in Section 5. Furthermore, the *Support Generator* predicts content for input fields depending on the user's interaction history and the current context (also with corresponding confidence values), which can be used to further save interaction costs for the user (for more details see [8]).

Next, the *Representation Manager* takes the support information and information about the available devices to decide which information and which interaction elements should be presented to the user. Thus, AUGUR can automatically generate an adapted UI version, e.g., as can be seen in Figure 1.

The **Knowledge Base** provides the information needed by the Support Tier. It holds a repository of application models, the user model and knowledge about the user's current context. The *Application Model Repository* stores knowledge about the applications the user interacted with via AUGUR (as described in Section 3.1). This comprises knowledge about the structure of the application as well as semantic information like labels. The *User Model* contains information about how the user interacted with the applications. This is used as basis for predicting how the user will interact with the application in the future. The *Context Server* provides information about the various interaction devices used, i.e., how much screen space is available or whether an interaction device supports VoiceXML.

5   Prediction Algorithm

In [5] we evaluated different algorithms for predicting the next user action, so-called sequence prediction algorithms (SPAs). A SPA returns for a given sequence $a_1...a_i$ the probability distribution P over all possible next actions. We found that the FxL algorithm [5] is best suited for mobile usage as it has the best prediction accuracy and very little demands regarding computational and memory resources.

The algorithm builds upon an n-gram trie containing the frequencies of different input subsequences. The function $fr(a_1...a_i)$ returns how often the sequence $a_1...a_i$ has already been seen. To reduce the amount of data that needs to be stored, only n-grams of a length up to a specified value k are taken into account (we found $k = 4$ to yield the best results). The n-gram models are then used to assign a score to every symbol denoting the probability of a symbol to occur next in the input sequence. As the scores for the symbols can sum up to a value greater than 1, they have to be normalized. Thus

$$P(x|a_1...a_i) = \frac{score(x)}{\sum_{y \in \Sigma} score(y)}$$

where $score(x)$ is calculated by adding the absolute frequencies of x succeeding any suffix (up to length $k - 1$) of $a_1...a_i$. As the longer suffixes yield more reliable results than the shorter ones, the frequencies are assigned a weight $w(j)$ depending on the length j of the suffix that is considered. Thus, the score is computed as follows with $\circ$ being the concatenation:

$$score(x) = \sum_{j=1}^{k-1} w(j) fr(a_{i+1-j}...a_i \circ x)$$

FxL uses the suffix-length as weight, $w(j) = j$. We call this approach FxL as the score for a symbol is calculated by multiplying the frequency (F) of the symbols with the length (L) of the suffix they succeed.

The predictions of FxL are based on the interaction history of a user which is stored in the user model in the Knowledge Base. However, for reducing the UI to the most relevant functionality it is not sufficient to predict only the next action, we need to know the next n actions the user will most probably perform. Thereby, n depends on the available display size and on how much additional information is presented, i.e., how many interaction elements can be displayed. For that purpose, we use the FxL algorithm and extend it as described in the following (resulting in **FxL***). We illustrate its behaviour with a simple example: The original UI of the web application displays the interaction elements a,b,c and d, the user only has a very small screen device for displaying $n = 2$ elements. Her user trace is efeffd (e and f are interaction elements of the preceding UI state). This example is shown in Figure 7.

To determine which interaction elements should be displayed to the user, we at first use FxL to compute the most probable next actions $x_1, ..., x_n$ for the recent interaction history $a_1..a_i$. In our example, the most probable next actions are a (70%), c (20%) and b (10%). For every possible next action x_j, we apply FxL again on every sequence

$a_1...a_i x_j$. The resulting probabilities are multiplied by $P(x_j|a_1...a_i)$, i.e., the probability for x_j succeeding $a_1...a_i$, as the probability of an action cannot exceed the probability of its preceding action. In our example, we apply FxL for the sequence efeffda returning a with probability 30% and b with a probability of 70%. The probability that action a is performed as second activity thus is 30%·70%=21% and for b 49%. Further, the resulting probabilities are merged with the probabilities calculated so far: If a probability was calculated for an action that is already stored, the maximum probability of both actions is taken. In our example, we do not update the probability of a as 21%<70% but we update the probability of b to 49%. This process is repeated until no action with a higher probability than the elements that would be currently displayed can be found. In our example, the elements we would display are a and b. As no action with a higher probability can be found, the algorithm terminates.

The following pseudo-code again illustrates the algorithm:

Algorithm 1. FxL*

Purpose: Calculates the probabilities for all possible actions in the global P_n, if n actions can be displayed
   The global variable p_{min} thereby denotes the probability of the nth probable action, i.e., the action that is displayed with the minimal probability.
Input: $a_1...a_i$ Sequence of most recent actions
   p parent probability (initialized with 1)

 1: **procedure** FxL* $(a_1...a_n, p)$:
 2:     $P(x|a_1...a_j) \Leftarrow$ FxL$(a_1...a_j)$
 3:     **for all** x **do**
 4:         $q(x) \Leftarrow P(x|a_1...a_j) \cdot p$
 5:         $P_n(x) \Leftarrow \mathbf{max}(P_n(x), q(x))$
 6:         update p_{min}
 7:         **if** $q(x) > p_{min}$ **then**
 8:             FxL*$(a_1...a_j x, q(x))$
 9:         **end if**
10:     **end for**
11: **end** FxL*

The n actions with the highest probabilities are then presented to the user. To further reduce interaction costs and to support the user in his familiar workflow, they are ordered by the sequences in which they will most probably occur.

6 Generating the Adapted UI

In this section, we describe how our developed prediction algorihtm is applied for generating adapted UIs. If the user accesses a UI with a small screen device via AUGUR, AUGUR at first determines the size of the screen. This information is provided by the integrated Context Server. If the UI to be shown contains relevant non-interactive elements, i.e., elements that are modeled as UIContent nodes in the corresponding application model, these elements are integrated in the adapted UI. The size of these elements

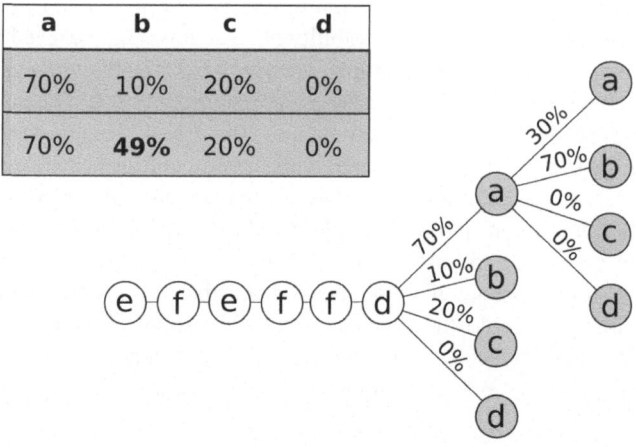

Fig. 7. Example calculation of FxL* if two elements can be displayed. As result the interaction elements a and b are presented.

is deducted from the available screen size. How many interaction elements can be displayed is computed by dividing the remaining screen space by the average interaction element size. Which interaction elements of the current UI are finally displayed is computed with the FxL* algorithm. Finally, links are inserted at the end of the adapted UI: a link for switching to the unadapted version ("unadapted version") to provide access to the whole functionality of the original UI and optionally a link for displaying the next relevant interaction elements ("next") if more relevant elements were found than fit on a screen. For example, if the UI consists of six relevant elements and only three can be displayed at once on a screen, the UI is split into two pages showing three elements each.

Thus, our approach using FxL* can be used to adapt the UI (i) to the device used, by incorporating the display size, as well as (ii) to the user and her current situation, by relying on her interaction history.

7 Evaluation

To evaluate our adaptation strategy we compared it to other strategies, which do not adapt to individual users or to their current situation. We thereby focused only on interactive elements, as it is hard to automatically judge whether the relevant non-interactive elements were displayed. We applied every strategy to three sets of real usage data: The Greenberg dataset [9] containing UNIX commands, the CrossDesktop log data from a web application for managing files and emails[2] and the Word dataset with logs of MS Word usage[3]. Device constraints were modeled by varying the amount of elements n that can be displayed at the same time (corresponding to different display sizes). As dependent variable we counted how often the action that was actually performed next (given

---

[2] http://www.crossdesktop.com
[3] http://www.cs.rutgers.edu/ml4um/datasets/

by the usage log), was found among the elements that were currently displayed according to the adaptation strategy applied. The elements that are displayed were recalculated whenever an action was requested that was not present among the current elements.

We compared four adaptation strategies:

- The *static* strategy presents the interaction elements most frequently used averaged over all users. We chose this strategy because it represents the best result reachable by a non user-adapted interface, as this has to optimize for the average user for all situations.
- The *user-adapted* strategy takes the individual user into account, presenting the actions the user has used most often so far. However, the user's current situation reflected by the immediate interaction history is not considered.
- The *situation-adapted* strategy in contrast, considers only the interaction history ignoring the individual user. In this strategy we compute a single user model for all users and apply the FxL* algorithm to predict the next actions for each user.
- The *FxL** strategy combines user- and situation-awareness by applying FxL* on the interaction model learned for each individual user. All strategies operate incrementally and update their user model after each observed action.

In Figure 8 the macro averaged results over all user traces of the three different datasets are shown. In the Word dataset, the *static* strategy performs only slightly worse than the *user-adapted* and *situation-adapted* strategy. In the other two datasets even no difference could be detected. This indicates that the frequently used actions for the given datasets are the same for most users and that there are no global usage patterns which are valid for all users. For that reason we omit the results for the *situation-adapted* strategy for the ease of readability in the graphs. The user- and situation-adapted *FxL** strategy clearly outperforms the three other strategies (the difference in the hit ratio ranges for $n \in [2, 10]$ from 6.0% to 27.1% for the Word dataset, from 25.3% to 30.2% for the Greenberg dataset, and from 3.2% to 15.2% for the CrossDesktop data). The hit ratio for the *FxL** strategy ranges from about 47% to 86% for all datasets (Word: 48% to 83%, Greenberg: 47% to 83% and CrossDesktop: 50% to 86%). This shows that it is important to take the user and her recent interactions into account in order to gain a good user model.

The actual benefit of user-adapted UIs can be estimated by determining the interaction costs for an unadapted UI with an adapted UI. If the next action is part of the currently displayed elements in p percent of all cases, the user has to switch to the unadapted UI in $1 - p$ percent of all cases. We now assume that the costs for using one of the n elements in the adapted UI or for switching to the unadapted UI is c_a and that the average costs for selecting an action in the unadapted version is c_u. Thereby, the interaction costs comprise the amount of clicks, navigational movements and keys that need to be pressed in order to interact with this element. The value of c_u and c_a depend on the individual user. The benefit b of using the adapted UI can be calculated as difference between the average costs for interacting with the unadapted UI (c_u) and the average costs for the adapted UI. Thereby, the average costs for interacting with the adapted UI is c_a in p percent of all cases, and $c_a + c_u$ in all other cases, i.e., c_a for selecting the link to the unadapted version and c_u for performing the operation in the unadapted UI:

$$b = c_u - [p \cdot c_a + (1 - p)(c_a + c_u)] = p \cdot c_u - c_a$$

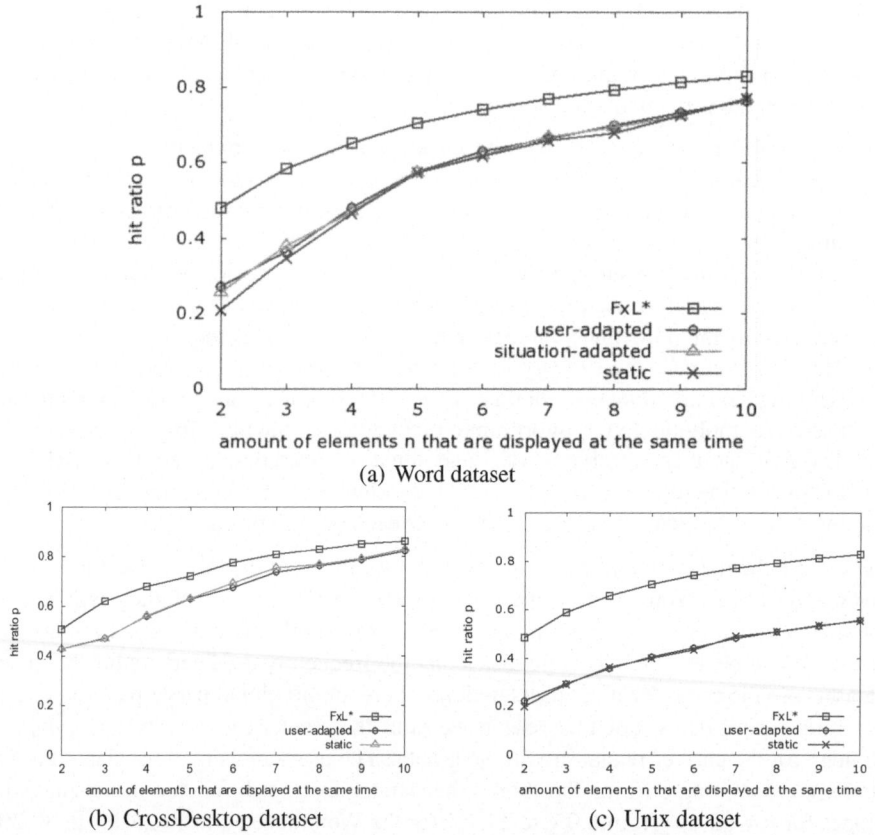

(a) Word dataset

(b) CrossDesktop dataset   (c) Unix dataset

Fig. 8. The evaluation results for the (a) Word, (b) CrossDesktop and (c) Unix dataset. For the ease of readability, we omit the results for the *situation-adapted* strategy in (b) and (c) as they run very similar to the *static* strategy. The y-axis represents the ratio of how often the next user action was currently displayed on the adapted UI with the given adaptation strategy.

Thus, using an adapted UI is beneficial if $c_a/c_u \leq p$. For example the adaptation with FxL* in the Word dataset is beneficial for displaying four elements, if $c_a/c_u \leq 0.62$, i.e., if $c_u \geq 1.61 \cdot c_a$. This value can easily be reached, as the average interaction costs c_a for interacting with one of four elements is much lower than the average costs c_u for interacting with one of more than 100 elements (or even 1000 for the Greenberg dataset).

8   Related Work

Existing approaches for Interface Adaptation adapt the UI to the device or the user. Thereby, we refer to user adaptation as the online adaptation of the UI to the current user situation as opposed to adapting to static user properties, e.g., motor skill level or short sightedness. In the following, we give an overview of approaches that adapt the UI either to the user or to the device. In contrast, AUGUR combines the two dimensions into a single system.

8.1   Device Adaptation

The goal of automatic device adaptation is to save development costs by transforming a single UI description automatically into concrete UIs on a multitude of platforms. The UI is described in a platform independent, often XML-based, language like [10,11] or [12]. See [13] for a more detailed survey of such languages. These UI descriptions do not contain any state information, e.g., which data was currently entered in a field, and need to be instantiated into a concrete UI for each targeted platform. XWeb [14] introduces an device independent representation for UI instances, including state information. In addition to device independence, [15] aims at modality independence and thereby introduces further layers of abstraction. The generation of a device specific UI from the abstract description can be parameterized, e.g., to incorporate static user preferences like motor skills. However, adaptation to dynamic user features like goals and intends is not supported. In contrast to these systems, AUGUR does not only provide device independency for UIs but also adapts UIs automatically to the user at runtime. We believe that adapting to the user is at least as important as to adapt to device constraints. Especially for small screen devices, adaptation to the user is beneficial as was shown by [16].

A drawback of single authoring is that UIs have to be designed without seeing the final result. To compensate for this [6] and [17] propose ways for creating the needed abstract models from concrete UIs. This allows the designer to build a concrete UI using visual tools, and to infer the abstract model from it. The same approach is taken by AUGUR, where the part of the concrete UI is played by the HTML front-end of a web application and the part of the corresponding abstract model by the ATML model of the web page (see Section 3.1). In contrast to other modeling languages like CTT [7], ATML models have a graphical representation that can be visualized as overlay to the UI used to generate it. This makes the ATML models easy to understand and edit by the end-user with minimal technical knowledge (see Figure 4). Allowing the end-user to control and participate in the adaptation process is an important feature for adaptive UIs as it induces trust in the UI.

8.2   User Adaptation

For desktop applications many user adaptation (also called personalization) techniques have been explored, leading to mixed results. An overview of studies on the subject can be found in [18]. It shows that correctly applied automatic adaptation can be beneficial in a desktop setting. This indicates that user adaptation is even more valuable in mobile or ubiquitous computing settings where we have to deal with much higher interaction costs. This assumption is also supported by the findings of [16].

A mixed-initiative approach on user adaptation is presented by Bunt et al. [19]. It relies on an algorithm to suggest customizations of the UI based on an automatic analysis of interaction costs. The idea of reducing interaction costs is also one of the main goals of the AUGUR approach. However, unlike Bunt et al. the adaptation in AUGUR also incorporates device constraints, e.g. in the form of screen size. Further, mixed-initiative approaches have the drawback of inducing additional interaction costs. In contrast, AUGUR relies on implicit user feedback, i.e. it observes the user's interactions and uses machine learning techniques to infer knowledge from it. As stated for example by [20] such approaches are mostly preferable to approaches that require explicit user feedback.

User adaptive mobile systems have been proposed for example by [21], where cards in a WAP deck are reordered to match navigational patterns. In contrast AUGUR can reorder at the level of single interaction elements. Similar to the goals of AUGUR is the approach of [22], it however restricts itself to hierarchical applications, where every point in the application can only be reached in a single way.

The SUPPLE [23] system employs an integrated device and user model for adaptation. The adaptation is performed by optimizing a cost function, which is based on the predicted average cost for interacting with a UI on a device. Online adaptation to a user specific cost model is not considered as part of SUPPLE. In contrast, AUGUR updates the user model as well as the interface online.

9   Conclusion

In this paper, we presented the AUGUR system that can automatically adapt existing form-based web applications to the needs of an individual user and device constraints. This is especially important in settings where the interaction costs are high as often found in ubiquitous or mobile computing settings. Hence, the first contribution of the paper is the AUGUR system that is to our knowledge the first system for adaptive interfaces that combines device adaptation and dynamic adaptation to the user and her situation. In addition the adaptation works on visual user interface instances in the browser as opposed to abstract models employed in other approaches.

The second contribution of this paper is the FxL* algorithm for predicting the next actions a user will perform depending on her past interactions and the number of interaction elements that can be displayed on the screen of the device used. We showed that this adaptation strategy is superior to strategies that do not take the user or her current situation into account by evaluating the algorithm on three sets of real usage data.

An open issue is the automatic identification of the (non-interactive) information that is relevant for the user. Although we often have to deal with implicit feedback in ubiquitous computing, there are still a multitude of applications that require to explicitly display feedback (e.g., the train departure times in the train booking example). For that purpose, we want to target this issue in our future work. Towards the adaptation to devices we aim at providing the user with the ability to use different devices concurrently at her discretion and automatically fusioning the input data. We suppose that this further reduces the user's interaction cost by liberating her from switching devices.

Acknowledgements

We would like to thank SAP Research Darmstadt for supporting our research in the AUGUR project.

References

1. Satyanarayanan, M.: Pervasive computing: Vision and challenges. IEEE Personal Communications (2001)
2. Buchanan, G., Farrant, S., Jones, M., Thimbleby, H., Marsden, G., Pazzani, M.: Improving mobile internet usability. In: Proceedings of WWW 2001, pp. 673–680. ACM, New York (2001)
3. Hartmann, M., Schreiber, D., Kaiser, M.: Task Models for Proactive Web Applications. In: Proceedings of WEBIST 2007, March 2007, pp. 150–155. INSTICC Press (2007)
4. Hartmann, M., Zesch, T., Mühlhäuser, M., Gurevych, I.: Using similarity measures for context-aware user interfaces. In: Proceedings of 2nd International Conference on Semantic Computing, pp. 190–197. IEEE, Los Alamitos (2008)
5. Hartmann, M., Schreiber, D.: Prediction algorithms for user actions. In: Hinneburg, A. (ed.) Proceedings of Lernen Wissen Adaption, ABIS 2007, September 2007, pp. 349–354 (2007)
6. Florins, M., Vanderdonckt, J.: Graceful degradation of user interfaces as a design method for multiplatform systems. In: Proceedings of IUI 2004, pp. 140–147. ACM Press, New York (2004)
7. Paterno, F., Mancini, C., Meniconi, S.: Engineering task models. In: Proceedings of ICECCS 1997, Washington, DC, USA, p. 69. IEEE Computer Society, Los Alamitos (1997)
8. Hartmann, M., Schreiber, D., Mühlhäuser, M.: Providing context-aware interaction support. In: Proceedings of Engineering Interactive Computing Systems (EICS). ACM, New York (to appear, 2009)
9. Greenberg, S.: Using unix: Collected traces of 168 users. Research report 88/333/45 (1988)
10. Ziegert, T., Lauff, M., Heuser, L.: Device independent web applications - the author once - display everywhere approach. In: Koch, N., Fraternali, P., Wirsing, M. (eds.) ICWE 2004. LNCS, vol. 3140, pp. 244–255. Springer, Heidelberg (2004)
11. Puerta, A., Eisenstein, J.: Ximl: A common representation for interaction data. In: Proceedings of the 7th international conference on Intelligent user interfaces, San Francisco, California, USA, pp. 214–215. ACM, New York (2002)
12. Abrams, M., Phanouriou, C., Batongbacal, A.L., Williams, S.M., Shuster, J.E.: UIML: An appliance-independent XML user interface language. In: Proceedings of the eighth international conference on World Wide Web, Toronto, Canada, pp. 1695–1708. Elsevier North-Holland, Inc., Amsterdam (1999)
13. Souchon, N., Vanderdonckt, J.: A review of XML-compliant user interface description languages. In: Jorge, J.A., Jardim Nunes, N., Falcão e Cunha, J. (eds.) DSV-IS 2003. LNCS, vol. 2844, pp. 377–391. Springer, Heidelberg (2003)
14. Olsen Jr., D.R., Jefferies, S., Nielsen, T., Moyes, W., Fredrickson, P.: Cross-Modal Interaction Using XWeb. In: Proceedings of UIST 2000, pp. 191–200. ACM, New York (2000)
15. Calvary, G., Coutaz, J., Thevenin, D., Limbourg, Q., Bouillon, L., Vanderdonckt, J.: A unifying reference framework for multi-target user interfaces. Interacting with Computers 15(20), 289–308 (2003)
16. Findlater, L., McGrenere, J.: Impact of screen size on performance, awareness, and user satisfaction with adaptive graphical user interfaces. In: Proceeding of the twenty-sixth annual SIGCHI conference on Human factors in computing systems, Florence, Italy, pp. 1247–1256. ACM, New York (2008)
17. Bouillon, L., Vanderdonckt, J.: Retargeting of Web Pages to Other Computing Platforms with VAQUITA. In: Proceedings of WCRE 2002, p. 339 (2002)

18. Gajos, K.Z., Czerwinski, M., Tan, D.S., Weld, D.S.: Exploring the design space for adaptive graphical user interfaces. In: Proceedings of AVI 2006, pp. 201–208. ACM Press, New York (2006)
19. Bunt, A., Conati, C., McGrenere, J.: Supporting interface customization using a mixed-initiative approach. In: Proceedings of IUI 2007, pp. 92–101. ACM, New York (2007)
20. Langley, P.: Machine learning for intelligent systems. In: AAAI/IAAI, pp. 763–769 (1997)
21. Anderson, C.R., Domingos, P., Weld, D.S.: Adaptive web navigation for wireless devices. In: IJCAI, pp. 879–884 (2001)
22. Smyth, B., Cotter, P.: The plight of the navigator: Solving the navigation problem for wireless portals. In: De Bra, P., Brusilovsky, P., Conejo, R. (eds.) AH 2002. LNCS, vol. 2347, pp. 328–337. Springer, Heidelberg (2002)
23. Gajos, K., Weld, D.S.: Supple: automatically generating user interfaces. In: Proceedings of IUI 2004, pp. 93–100. ACM Press, New York (2004)

User Modeling for Pedestrian Navigation Services

Panayotis Kikiras[1], Vassileios Tsetsos[2], Vassilis Papataxiarhis[2],
Thanassis Katsikas[2], and Stathes Hadjiefthymiades[2]

[1] Dept of Computer and Networks Engineering, University of Thessaly,
37 Glavani - 28th October Str, 382 21 Volos – Greece
kikirasp@inf.uth.gr
[2] Pervasive Computing Research Group, Dept of Informatics and Telecommunications,
National and Kapodistrian University of Athens, Panepistimiopolis, 15784, Ilissia, Greece
{b.tsetsos,vpap,std02040,shadj}@di.uoa.gr

Abstract. Human-centered and user-adaptive systems are at the heart of the
Design for All and Ambient Intelligence concepts. Evidently, user models are
necessary "ingredients" of such systems. We present a user model for
navigation systems (mainly pedestrian), which is based on relevant human
wayfinding and navigation theories. We represent this model through a
Semantic Web ontology and show how it can be incorporated in an indoor
navigation system called MNISIKLIS, which enables personalized path
selection. Moreover, we propose a method for learning rules for the
classification of users based on Inductive Logic Programming.

Keywords: personalization, user model, ontologies, location based services.

1 Introduction

Gluck [1] defines wayfinding as "the procedure that is used for the orientation and
navigating, in order an individual to navigate from one place to another, especially in
very huge and complex environments indoors or outdoors". In general, it is a
particularly demanding process, which requires the mobilization of a number of
cognitive/mental processes, besides the kinetic ones. Such process is, naturally,
executed unconsciously for the majority of people. However, for certain categories of
individuals, with certain abilities/disabilities in their cognitive and/or physical status,
wayfinding and navigating may be an extremely cumbersome process. Hence, a "one-
size-fits-all" approach does not apply to pedestrian navigation. Personalization of
navigation is required in cases where an advanced user experience should be provided
or an inclusive design approach [47] is adopted. Since personalization is based on a
user description (profile), the establishment of some appropriate user model is
necessary. Such model will be taken into consideration when a) computing possible
navigation paths, b) selecting the "best" path for the user and c) guiding the user
through it by giving her appropriate instructions. Moreover, the more expressive this
model is, the more advanced the application logic that can be implemented.

In this paper we present the main theories regarding navigation and their relevance
to user models. We exploit such knowledge in order to build a User Navigation

T. Kuflik et al. (Eds.): Advances in Ubiquitous User Modelling, LNCS 5830, pp. 111–133, 2009.

Ontology (UNO) that can be used in a navigation system for personalized path selection. Specifically, UNO is an ontology that was developed for modeling users based on their individual characteristics that influence a) navigational decisions (i.e., selection of the optimum path), and b) the form and the means that these navigational decisions are communicated/presented to them. Such ontology is necessary for developing a knowledge-based system for personalization and thus, supports service intelligence in a declarative way. In order to put the presented model in the context of a navigation system we briefly describe MNISIKLIS, an indoor navigation system implemented with Semantic Web technologies.

One of the most challenging parts in user modeling is the automation of the user profile creation process. Data mining and other machine learning techniques can be used as potential solutions. In this paper we introduce a novel technique for learning user models that is fully compatible with the symbolic representation of UNO. This technique is heavily based on Inductive Logic Programming (ILP), a rather old, but not widely explored, field of machine learning.

The organization of the rest of the paper is as follows. In Section 2 we present some theoretical foundations on pedestrian wayfinding, navigation and user modeling in general. Section 3 serves also as an introductory section that describes the basic concepts and technologies of knowledge-based user modeling and personalization. In Section 4, we outline the basic principles and concepts of a navigation-oriented user model. A more formal specification of these concepts is also provided, where the core of the UNO ontology is presented. Section 5 provides basic information on ILP and how it can be used in the context of user model creation, updating and refinement. In Section 6 we present the basic functionality of MNISIKLIS platform, focusing on the modeling components. Additionally, some related systems are presented. The paper concludes with directions for future research.

2   Background on Pedestrian User Modeling Human Navigation and Wayfinding Theories

Wayfinding is a fundamental human activity and an integral part of everyday life. Individuals are mainly using their knowledge and previous experience with geographic spaces in order to navigate from one location to another. As a result, a huge amount of research literature from the fields of cognitive science, psychology and artificial intelligence examines the mechanisms that enable humans to find their way in unknown and complex environments. In the following paragraphs we discuss the main theoretical approaches to human wayfinding and navigation that have influenced our work.

Wayfinding

Downs and Stea [2] suggested that wayfinding involves the following four steps:

1. Orientation: Finding out where someone is with respect to nearby landmarks and the navigation destination.

2. Route Selection: Selecting a route, under certain criteria, that will eventually lead the individual to the desired destination.

3. Routing Control: Constant control and confirmation that the individual follows the selected route.

4. Recognition of destination: The ability of an individual to realize that she has reached the destination or is located in a nearby area.

In general, the wayfinding ability of individuals is greatly influenced by a number of factors, based on findings from research in human neurophysiology [3]. The most important of these are:

1. Individual Characteristics (e.g., age, sex, cognitive development, perceptual capability, mental and physical condition).

2 Characteristics of the environment (e.g., size, luminosity, signage, utilization, structure, familiarization with it).

3. Learning Processes (e.g., learning strategies, learning conditions, learning abilities).

Furthermore, the wayfinding ability of individuals is mainly affected by the following four factors: spatial ability, fundamental information processing capabilities, prior knowledge of the environment and motor capabilities. *Spatial ability* can be defined as the ability of every individual to perceive the surrounding environment with its sensing and cognitive mechanisms. This ability includes all cognitive procedures that are used whenever we are learning our environment and comprehend correlations among its elements. This leads to *spatial consciousness*, which describes the degree to which an individual understands/reacts with the environment using her spatial ability. Thus, wayfinding is a dynamic and demanding cognitive procedure, which involves many spatial and navigational abilities. Moreover, similarly to every other human activities, not every individual has the same navigational skills [4]. This fact calls for a classification of potential users of a navigation system so that it could provide its services in a way tailored to their specific cognitive and physical abilities/disabilities.

Finally, we should mention that an interesting attempt to identify and represent some semantic cognitive concepts of pedestrian wayfinding is described in [35].

Navigational Awareness

Navigational awareness is defined as the wayfinding task which takes place when the individual who navigates in an area has complete knowledge of the navigation environment. There are two distinct types of navigating through an environment, with significant differences between them. The first navigation type is based on what is called *procedural* or *route knowledge*. The procedural knowledge is human centered (ego-referenced) and is mainly acquired through personal exploration of an unknown environment. The main characteristic of the procedural knowledge is that, while an individual can navigate from one landmark to another in a known route, she has no other knowledge about alternatives routes (fastest, quickest, etc.). The second type of navigation is based on the *survey knowledge*. Such knowledge is acquired through iterative multiple explorations of an area following different path each time. This type of survey knowledge is characterized by its ability to support distinctive places of the environment (landmarks) as reference points and, thus, is called world-referenced.

Research in this area has shown that acquiring complete knowledge of unknown, big and complex areas is a dynamic process, which involves four distinct steps [5]:

1. Recognition of landmarks: Objects may constitute landmarks for two reasons a) for their distinctive characteristics, and b) due to their individual significance [6]. Objects can be distinguishable because of their architectural style, size, or color [7]. Moreover, objects can become significant landmarks whenever they provide navigational information (e.g., when they are positioned at a crossroad or junction, at big interior halls that connect different corridors, etc.).

2. Correlation of routes or connections with landmarks: Routes and connections are formed while navigating between two landmarks. Acquiring route knowledge is highly correlated with the process of recognizing landmarks, which can be recalled with the same cognitive mechanism that is used to recall a route at a future time. This step is the cognitive procedure of matching routes with landmarks.

3. Primary Survey Knowledge: This type of knowledge is acquired after a thorough survey and exploration of the navigation environment. When acquired, it provides the means to calculate different routes and to estimate the distance between landmarks.

4. Area–Route Segmentation: This step provides the mechanisms to decompose a huge area to smaller segments/regions. Such smaller regions are parts of bigger regions, which in turn form other bigger ones and so on. This "segmentation procedure" enables the individual to mentally focus on regions relevant to its navigation task, to discover relations between different spaces, and, thus, by minimizing the amount of information to be processed optimizes the navigating performance of an individual.

User Modeling in General

To our knowledge there is no other user model for describing user characteristics from the perspective of navigation. On the other hand, there are some generic, user modeling efforts that try to cover a wide range of application domains and to adopt open technologies for enabling interoperability between systems. The most relevant work of this category is the General User Model Ontology (GUMO) [16]. GUMO has means of representing several "user dimensions" such as user demographics, user abilities, user emotional and psychological status, etc. In addition, it supports the specification of some auxiliary information such as the preferences, interests, and knowledge of the users. The main advantage of GUMO is that it is implemented in OWL, which has become very popular in the Semantic Web [12] community. This language not only provides a well-defined syntax for user models but is also capable of describing the semantics that are implied by a model. As already mentioned, we have tried to align UNO with GUMO by reusing and extending all suitable concepts and attributes.

GUMO has been partly influenced by the UserML language [17]. UserML's objective was to provide a commonly accepted syntax, based on the XML standard, for representing user models in Web applications. UserML is quite generic and, thus, can be used as a syntax layer for any semantic user model.

Another attempt to represent certain functioning and disability issues of an individual is the International Classification of Functioning, Disability and Health (ICF) of World Health Organization (WHO) [19]. This classification scheme concerns the body structure (e.g., body parts and relationships among them) and functions (e.g., sensory functions, mental functions, etc.) while it takes into account several environmental factors that refer to the context where a disability occurs (e.g., environmental changes, attitudes, etc.). For example, an elderly person that has difficulty in covering long distances, experiences some degree of disability in a huge navigation environment. In this context, ICF constitutes a generic framework able to provide the appropriate terminology for capturing features and characteristics of 'health'.

3   Background on Knowledge Representation

There are various ways to represent a user model. The final decision should depend on how the user model elements are going to be captured and used. In our case we focus on knowledge-based formalisms, due to their symbolic nature, their support for several levels of expressiveness and the availability of a great variety of related tools. The main categories of such formalisms could be distinguished into ontology languages and rules languages.

Ontologies, mainly written through Semantic Web technologies, constitute a well-established paradigm for representing knowledge in the Web. Specifically, ontologies are used to describe the vocabulary of a domain of interest by defining the concepts and the relationships among them. Nowadays, ontologies have reached a sufficient degree of maturity through RDF(S) [20] and Web Ontology Language (OWL) [21], both being W3C recommendations.

Resource Description Framework (RDF) is a language for modeling and representing knowledge about Web resources. It is a data model for writing simple statements about objects (resources) and defining relations between them. Specifically, RDF identifies things through Web identifiers (Universal Resource Identifiers - URIs) and describes resources through properties and values. Generally, these statements constitute triples of the form *<subject, predicate, object>*. In a more human-friendly context, the aforementioned triples can be considered to compose a directed graph where every arc (*predicate*) is directed from a resource (*subject*) to a value (*object*) which can either be a resource or a literal. Furthermore, RDF Schema (RDFS) is a language able to define the vocabulary (i.e. concepts and properties) to be used in RDF graphs.

OWL extends RDF(S) expressiveness by providing more complex constructs (e.g., axioms, complex concept descriptions, transitivity of properties etc.). OWL is based on Description Logics [38] that are subsets of First-Order-Logic (FOL) and comes in three species: OWL-Lite, OWL-DL and OWL-Full. OWL-DL is the most common OWL formalism, OWL-Full is the most expressive, but undecidable, version of OWL, while OWL-Lite is a sublanguage of OWL-DL. Moreover, a number of efficient reasoning modules are capable of handling RDFS/OWL ontologies and reasoning over them (e.g., Pellet [22] and RacerPro [23]).

In contrast to ontologies, the rules layer of the Semantic Web is still a topic that needs further research efforts to be devoted. Although several approaches have been proposed to extend the expressiveness provided by ontologies through the addition of rules, none of them has led to a standard. Semantic Web Rule Language (SWRL) [15] is probably the most popular formalism in Web community for expressing knowledge in the form of rules. Specifically, it extends OWL with a specific form of Horn-like rules and has been proposed as a W3C candidate standard. The main advantages of SWRL are its simplicity and its compatibility with OWL syntax and semantics. A rather simple example of a rule expressed in terms of SWRL could be the following:

$$has\_parent(?a,?b) \land has\_brother(?b,?c) \rightarrow has\_uncle(?a,?c). \tag{1}$$

Finally, there are efficient rule engines that support the execution of SWRL rules such as Jess [24] and Bossam [25].

There are several other approaches that allow for declarative (symbolic) representation and programming of personalized systems. These approaches differ in expressiveness (e.g., some of them support uncertain and fuzzy knowledge to be modelled), in reasoning performance and in support of mature tools. Further information on such approaches and the way they can be used in personalized systems and services can be found in [26] and [27], respectively.

4 Navigation-Oriented User Modeling

According to the previously presented theoretical findings, a navigation-oriented User Profile (UP) is based on attributes from the following categories/components (see Fig. 1):

1. General User Demographics: This category captures all the basic user information such as name (required only for user identification and profile indexing, thus it can simply be a nickname), age, gender, as well as a series of optional information, e.g., communication details, etc. (if required by the application for billing, statistical or other reasons).

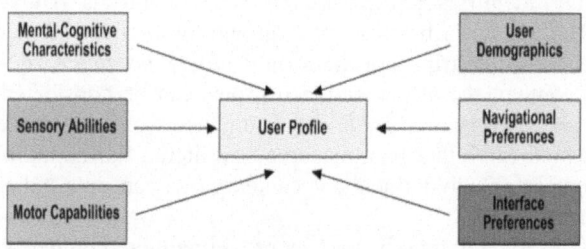

Fig. 1. Components of a navigation-oriented User Profile

2. Mental/Cognitive Characteristics: This category captures all information considering user's mental/cognitive abilities as follows:

   i. *Consciousness functions*: in this Boolean attribute the system captures the existence of possible malfunctions in the user consciousness abilities. Such abilities correspond to general mental functions which control user's state of awareness and alertness.

   ii. *Orientation disability*: This Boolean attribute captures user's orientation ability, which corresponds to knowing and ascertaining her relation to oneself, to others, to time and to the surrounding environment. This ability describes the cognitive abilities that an individual must possess in order to be able to navigate in a geographical space. Hence, potential malfunctions in this ability significantly hinder the navigation procedure.

iii. *Mental disabilities*: This Boolean attribute holds true if the user has disabilities considering her mental functions (mental impairment, Alzheimer disease, etc.).

iv. *Mental functions considering user's behavior and personality*: In this subcategory the system captures behavioral and personality characteristics such as introversion–extroversion, social abilities, psychic and emotional stability. These characteristics differentiate one person from another and this knowledge is used for the personalization of the routing instructions. As discussed in [9], such information affects the way that an individual comprehends and follows routing instructions.

v. *Concentration to an objective*: The World Health Organization defines this mental function as *"the mental ability of an individual to remain focused on an external stimuli or an internal experience for a certain period of time"*. Difficulty on this function is more often met in elderly people, teenagers and children.

vi. *High level cognitive functions*: this category considers difficulties in high level cognitive functions, such as decision making, planning and execution of actions and plans, degradation of memory functions, etc. Potential malfunction of any of these cognitive functions may lead to difficulties for the users to understand and execute complex instructions in a timely manner. Therefore, a navigation system should be able to correspond to such information by selecting proper paths and customizing the routing instructions in a way suitable for a user suffering from such impairments.

3. User's Sensory Abilities: Sensory impairments affect the way a user exploits her sensing abilities (especially viewing and hearing) during wayfinding. This category is further divided to two subcategories: visual and audile abilities. The visual abilities of users can be categorized using the following main criteria:

i. Visual Sharpness: A: perfect, -B: good, -C: medium, -D: bad.

ii. Visual Quality: Impairment in this ability affects the way an individual perceives light, color, texture, contrast and, in general, the quality of user's vision. Possible quality values are – A: perfect, -B: good, -C: medium, -D: bad.

The audile abilities of users are divided in four categories – A: perfect, -B: good, -C: medium, -D: bad, (where A means that the user has full hearing ability and D that she cannot hear at all).

4. User's Motor Abilities: This category captures a user's ability to move from one place to another with respect to the way she controls and coordinates her movement. Motor abilities refer to all kinetic abilities of users and not only to those associated to their mobility, although the latter are more important from the perspective of navigation. Users are categorized as having:

i. Autonomous mobility without assistive devices

ii. Mobility supported by an escort (with or without assistive devices).

iii. Autonomous mobility with wheelchair.

iv. Autonomous mobility with assistive devices (other than wheelchair)

Note that the user profile of a user supported by an escort should be the profile of the escort, since the latter is responsible for the navigation of the disabled user.

5. Navigational Preferences: This category captures user's navigational preferences. Typical preferences are:

    i. No specific preferences.

    ii. Selection of the shortest route first.

    iii. Selection of the fastest route first.

    iv. Preference in most "popular" path elements (e.g., main corridors and stairs).

    v. Avoidance of stairs.

    vi. Avoidance of crowded areas (e.g., for blind users).

    vii. Selection of the most/less popular path among all users.

    viii. Existence of landmarks in computed paths.

    ix. Dynamic tracking during navigation and provision of routing corrections.

6. Interface Preferences: This category captures user's preferences considering the means and the media in which user will receive routing instructions:

    i. Type of user's device (e.g., PDA, mobile/smart phone, mobile computer, information kiosk).

    ii. Modality of instructions' presentation:

        a. Only textual information

        b. Both textual and visual information

        c. Only visual information

        d. Both textual and audio information

        e. Both visual and audio information

        f. Only audio information.

4.1 User Navigation Ontology

The model described in the previous section has to be specified in a suitable form in order to be used in modern applications. Hence, we have decided to represent it through a Semantic Web ontology. For that purpose we have used the Web Ontology Language (OWL) [12] for describing the user classes and their properties. Ontology-based systems are becoming more and more popular due to the inference and reasoning capabilities that ontological knowledge representation provides. Moreover, Semantic Web standards, and technologies in general, provide a solid basis for open and interoperable information systems.

For the development of the UNO ontology we followed the directives of ontology engineering that promote ontology reuse and alignment between existing ontologies. Specifically, during ontology development we have tried to extend some of the concepts specified in the GUMO ontology (see section "Related Work"). Moreover, the International Classification of Functioning, Disability and Health (ICF) of World Health Organization (WHO) [19] was adopted for representing certain functioning and disability issues of an individual.

An extract of the UNO concept hierarchy is shown in Fig. 2, while Fig. 3 illustrates the basic UNO properties. Informal definitions of the top-level UNO concepts follow (the definitions of properties are regarded straightforward):

Fig. 2. The basic UNO taxonomy

Fig. 3. The basic UNO hierarchy of properties (the object properties are presented in the left while the datatype properties in the right part of the figure)

Ability: the super-class of the various abilities of a user with regard to the navigation procedure. A user may have many abilities. Disabilities may be defined through the use of the Quality class values (see below).

Demographics: value classes for user demographics (age, gender). Its subclasses are implemented as value partitions as dictated by the W3C Semantic Web Best Practices Group [18].

Quality: another class representing a value set for describing the degree/quality of the various abilities. Its values are {bad, medium, good, perfect}. A bad quality value for an ability denotes a disability.

User: an abstract class that subsumes the more specific defined user classes.

The main difference between UNO and GUMO, apart from their scope, is that UNO can be used actively in inference procedures, while GUMO provides a core knowledge base (i.e., taxonomy and assertions of individuals) for basic classification of users and their characteristics. Hence, a key feature of UNO lies in the formal definition (through restrictions, and necessary and sufficient conditions) of user classes. In the current version of UNO we have included a minimal set with some possible classes. Each specific navigation application should extend this set appropriately. The use of the OWL-DL language enables very expressive user definitions. Indicative definitions (in mixed OWL and first-order-logic-like notation, for readers unfamiliar with Description Logics notation) of such *defined concepts* are:

YoungWheelchairedUser ≡
∃ hasAbility AutonomousWheelchairedMobility ∧
∃ hasAge LessThan18

VisuallyImpairedMaleAdultUser ≡
∃ hasAbility (AbilityToSee ∧ hasValue(hasQuality, bad)) ∧ ∃ hasAge Between18and60 ∧ hasValue(hasGender, male)

(Note: *hasValue* is a reserved OWL term)

After performing reasoning on an ontology with such defined user classes, these will be classified under the generic User class and the various user instances will be classified accordingly.

Regarding alignment with GUMO, some UNO classes can be declared as equivalent to GUMO classes (e.g., Preference, Person, etc.). Moreover, some individuals of GUMO have been transformed to primitive classes in UNO (e.g., individual AbilityToTalk of GUMO class AbilityAndProficiency has been asserted as class AbilityToTalk in UNO). Such transformation enables fine-grained class definitions and advanced reasoning. Regarding demographics information, we have modeled some relevant GUMO instances as binary properties, since otherwise we would have to create a different instance of such information for each separate user. The aforementioned transformations (instances to classes and instances to binary relations) have been performed in order to enable more complex concept expressions for describing user class. Finally, we should note that there are GUMO classes that have not incorporated/aligned to the current version of UNO, although they are relevant to the domain of navigation. For example, the class Motion could be used for supporting dynamic tracking and route corrections and the class PhysicalEnvironment could support the context-aware adaptation of navigation instructions (e.g., high noise level could trigger increase in the volume level of audio instructions).

UNO was also aligned with a number of concepts described by the ICF standard. Specifically, all the concepts of UNO that concern the user capabilities (e.g., body functions, mobility etc.) were connected to the respective ICF descriptions. For instance, the UNO class AbilityToSeeInColor was aligned to the ICF description "Colour Vision" (seeing functions of differentiating and matching colors) which is defined by the ICF unique code b21021. In this example, the prefix "b" of the ICF code denotes that the description concerns a sensory ability of a human being. Another example is the alignment of the UNO class AbilityToPush to the ICF description "Pushing" (i.e. using fingers, hands and arms to move something from oneself, or to move it from place to place) given by the "d4451" ICF code. In this case, the prefix "d4" denotes that the description refers to a mobility activity.

5 Learning User Profiles

The automatic creation of user models is still an open research issue. Specification of explicit rules that represent implicit (and usually not trivial and obvious) dependencies between user model entities seem to be a desired feature for all systems, although hard to implement. For example, the ability of a user to concentrate on an objective may be automatically inferred by her age. Other cases of rules, from the LBS domain, that imply relationships between the UP elements or can classify the user status are the following:

- Learning whether a user moves around the building alone or if she is part of a team and, thus, moving along with that team.
- Learning when a door is locked in the building when no other sensing element is present.
- Learning when someone is lost in a building. Connecting locations of map hotspots with the time that someone stayed on that spot.

Towards the direction of UP learning, it seems reasonable to apply well-known machine learning techniques. Since, we are dealing with logic-based ontology languages for user modeling, a natural choice is Inductive Logic Programming (ILP), which belongs to the category of relational learning techniques (in contrast to most typical data mining algorithms that belong in the propositional learning category). By adopting ILP we have two advantages:

- the learning framework supports the knowledge representation language we used for describing the user model, and
- relational learning results in more expressive rules and captures more complex relationships between the model elements.

In the following sections we try to introduce the main concepts of ILP and demonstrate how it can apply to user profile learning, in the context of LBS. However, we should note that this is still work in progress and hence, no experimental results that prove the effectiveness of the method are presented in this paper.

To our knowledge, regarding the use of ILP in location-based systems and user modeling, only a few works have been done and published. In [41] the author applies ILP to build a user model that monitors and predicts user behavior (successive user entries in a diary). The author concludes that ILP can be used for accurate, usable, and understandable learning of user models. The authors in [39] have extensively analyzed ILP techniques that facilitate learning from multiple relations, applying it to an ILP system, called SPADA, that collected spatial data from an Italian province and identified spatial association rules. Finally, the authors in [40] showed that an inductive learning approach can result to a successful problem solving of path-finding and planning using distributed systems, implementing it in a system with several agents that combine their knowledge in an effective way (i.e., reduced communication cost).

5.1 Background Knowledge on Inductive Logic Programming

ILP is a subfield of machine learning, which provides means for multi-relational learning. It generally uses Horn clauses (similar to those used in logic programming) to represent all its elements. These elements are:

- Background knowledge: definitions of domain concepts and their relationships
- Examples: facts that are asserted by domain experts and are taken as a basis for the induction performed.
- Hypotheses: domain concepts for which formal definitions (i.e., rules describing them) are missing and should be learnt. In general, such definitions are built from the elements of the background knowledge.

In contrast to data mining, ILP:

- Copes with structured, complex and multi-relational data and not just with attributes of classes like typical data mining techniques do. Hence, it is much more powerful, in terms of expressiveness of the induced rules
- Takes into consideration also background knowledge in addition to training examples.
- Relies on logic-based knowledge representation that makes it compatible with platforms such as the Semantic Web.

Obviously, what makes an ILP system (and any other learning system) successful, is the accuracy of classifying unseen "objects", based on rules and training examples. ILP exploits sets of both positive and negative examples (E+ and E-, respectively). For an induced rule (a.k.a., hypothesis) H to be consistent it must hold that:

- Every example in E+ is covered by H
- No negative example in E- is covered by H

A rather trivial example that can facilitate the comprehension of the ILP way of learning follows. Assume that several facts are asserted regarding individuals and family relationships:

Persons	**Children**
male(markus).	hasChild(stefan,markus).
male(stefan).	hasChild(markus,anna).
male(heinz).	hasChild(markus,heinz).
male(bernd).	hasChild(bernd,gabi).
female(anna).	
female(gabi).	

Moreover, assume that we want to define a new concept "father" for which we provide the following training examples (+: positive example, -: negative example): +stefan, +markus, +bernd, -heinz, -anna, -gabi

The ILP system would provide us with a list of possible definitions. One of them would be: father(X) :- male(X), hasChild(X,Y)
another one:
father(X) :- male(X), hasChild(X,Y), male(Y), hasChild(Y,Z)
and so on. All of these solutions are assigned a degree of accuracy, based on how many examples are supported by each one of them.

The language used by an ILP system is an important factor for its performance [36]. By selecting a less expressive language, the search space becomes smaller and, thus, learning becomes more efficient. This, however, may prevent the system from finding a solution which cannot be represented by that specific language. In our case, we prefer using Datalog [37] which is a language compatible with the OWL ontologies and Semantic Web technologies in general.

To summarize, ILP seems a suitable tool for learning user profiles when they are expressed through ontologies. Moreover, ILP can support several techniques for noise handling and completion/replacement of imperfect data. This is extremely important in LBS applications since almost all input data and training examples are generated by sensors.

5.2 Learning User Profiles for LBS

To better illustrate the ILP-based creation and update of user profiles for LBS, we describe a scenario that is currently being implemented.

The system is evaluated in a building with numerous deployed sensors. These sensors measure the noise level at several locations, and sense the presence of pedestrians (e.g., infrared beacons). Furthermore, positioning devices are carried by each user (e.g., PDA with dead-reckoning system) [28]. Scattered around the building there are maps of the building. Server-side infrastructure is also deployed, where all the middleware components are running (including the ILP system). Our aim will be to learn when someone is lost in the building. Of course, there is no simple rule for deciding this situation of a user.

The learning process involves the following steps:

Training Step

When a user is lost, she can press a button on the device and get information about her current position (Where-Am-I service). This is perceived as a positive example by the ILP system. Specifically, the following set of assertions constitutes a positive example:

   lost_in_building(uid), location(uid, loc)

where *loc* is the current user position, *uid* the user id and *time* the current timestamp. This set is then extended from the knowledge based with all facts related, either to *uid* or *loc* instances. For example, if *loc* is the location of a map, then the facts *map(generalmap)*, *POILocatedIn(generalmap, loc)* is also included in the set of the training example. We assume that the background knowledge (consisting of several domain models as described in Section 6) specifies that an instance of map class is also an instance of the Point Of Interest (POI) class and the latter has a *POILocatedIn* property.

Similarly, *hasAge(uid,elderly)* is added to the set if the user stated that he is over 65 years old during her registration. As it becomes apparent, this training step is continuous (i.e., online learning).

Learning Step

Once the learning algorithm receives a number of new training sets, it re-executes and produces a list of rules (with variable accuracy) that describe when a user is lost. For example, the following rules could result from our sample scenario:

lost_in_building(u) ← location(u, l), map(m), POILocatedIn(m, l)

lost_in_building(u) ← location(u, l), POI(m), POILocatedIn(m, l)

The second rule is more general than the first one, which is also somewhat coarse-grained. If we want to make these rules more specific we can add some kind of temporal reasoning and take also into account the N last positions of the user or the time that is standing in front of the map, before she invokes the "Where-Am-I" service.

After the learning step of the algorithm, the new rules can be used so that we can automatically decide when a user is lost and act accordingly (e.g., "push" some guiding instructions to her).

Implementation Details

The initial implementation of this learning step is based on the DL-Learner [37] software, which is an ILP system relying on Description Logics (DL) [38] for knowledge representation. Its basic advantages are that it can be easily extended and used to learn classes in OWL ontologies and that can easily perform supervised learning tasks. Ontological reasoning functionality for classifying user classes and other domain classes is provided by Pellet [22][1].

6   MNISIKLIS System for Personalized Universal LBS

6.1   System Overview

UNO was used along with other domain models in MNISIKLIS system that provides real-time, indoor Location Based Services (LBS) to a wide range of users [28]. The main novelties of this system are that it relies on location data fusion from several positioning sensors (i.e., passive UHF RFID, Wi-Fi and Dead Reckoning), and it implements the Design for All paradigm. Specifically, it provides a multimodal user interface for LBS that can tailor the man-machine interaction to the individual user's profile (i.e., abilities). The implemented services heavily rely on semantic models and knowledge reasoning techniques. Hence, the overall service logic is highly human-centered.

---

[1] Currently, the ILP system is not integrated with the MNISIKLIS platform described in the following section.

The MNISIKLIS platform includes three main subsystems (as shown in Fig. 4):

Positioning Subsystem. It comprises the overall equipment and the algorithms used to estimate the user's position. Specifically, it consists of the sensors and the positioning techniques, the location fusion component and the interfaces between them.

Middleware. The middleware consists of the services and the navigation algorithms developed as well as the application models. It is also responsible for gluing together the other subsystems.

User Interaction Subsystem. The user interaction subsystem involves the user device (hardware and software), the input/output interfaces and the content selection and representation algorithms.

Apart from these core platform ingredients, a peripheral infrastructure for LBS content provisioning and management has been developed. Such infrastructure includes a GIS system and a Semantic Content Management System (SCMS).

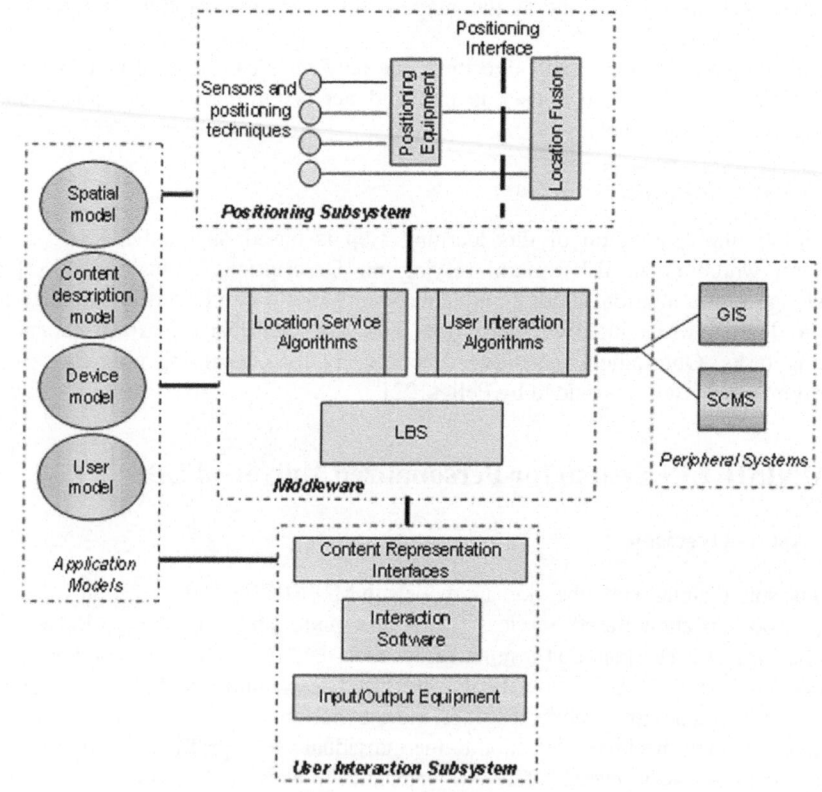

Fig. 4. MNISIKLIS Architecture

6.2 Services

The MNISIKLIS platform supports the following services:

- *Static Navigation.* The user asks the system to determine a "suitable" route to a certain destination. The service takes into consideration the application models (e.g., user profile) in order to compute the "best" path and guide the user with the most suitable landmarks.
- *Dynamic Navigation.* An extension of static navigation that periodically traces the user position. In case it detects a significant deviation of the user from the predetermined path, it helps her to find her way by providing more detailed information.
- *Where-Am-I.* The user asks for her current position inside a building. The system responds by providing details about the last known user position. The information about a specific location is organized and presented in different levels of detail.
- *Exploration.* While the user is moving inside the building, the system provides ("pushes") information about the nearest locations that she may be interested in. Such Points Of Interest (POIs) may have been explicitly stated by the user or not (e.g., significant exhibits in a museum).
- *Nearest POIs.* The system computes the POIs that are closer to the user. The main difference from the exploration service is the push-based nature of the latter. Hence, the system may always return points that are not located close to the user.

6.3 Application Domain Models

Four ontologies are the basis for MNISIKLIS: i) the spatial ontology (Indoor Navigation Ontology – INO), ii) the User Navigation Ontology (UNO), iii) the Device Ontology (DO), and iv) the Content Ontology (CO). The instances of the aforementioned ontologies are connected through semantic relationships in order to provide the aforementioned LBS. A short description for these follows:

Indoor Navigation Ontology (INO): The spatial ontology is an extended version of the INO [29], based on the OWL-DL language. Specifically, it describes concepts and relationships that correspond to every basic spatial element typically found in indoor environments.

Device Ontology (DO): Our approach adopts a device ontology in order to represent basic features and the functionality supported by various user devices (e.g., mobile phones, PDAs, headphones). The knowledge captured by the ontology refers to hardware capabilities (e.g., display size, resolution) as well as device supported modalities (e.g., input/output modes).

Content Ontology (CO): Content Ontology describes general categories of content with their properties and relations. CO includes two main categories of concepts: high-level concepts related to the general characteristics of the described content and low level concepts that describe each specific content type (e.g., Text, Image and Video). More details on these models can be found in [28].

By representing everything with ontologies, we can write rules and integrate them within the various algorithms implementing the MNISIKLIS services.

6.4 Related Systems

Several interesting efforts towards human-centered and personalized LBS systems can be found in the related literature. However, as we point out, most of them do not rely on formal modeling of users, space, etc.

iNAV [42] is a navigation framework aiming to providing guidance in indoor environments. Nevertheless, iNAV mainly targets at typical users, since it does not provide any advanced user interaction features. CoINS [43] is a context-aware indoor navigation system that involves a complex mechanism for spatial modeling and room detection. With regard to the route selection process, the system exploits an optimized version of the Dijkstra algorithm. However, CoINS does not currently support any multimodal interfaces to support diverse user classes.

IRREAL [44] is another indoor navigation system, based on infrared beacons, that adapts the presentation of route directions to the specific device capabilities. The application does not fully support interaction with disabled users. A pedestrian navigation system that investigates complex aspects like multi-criteria path selection and integrated positioning for both indoor and outdoor environments is described in [45]. Although the system supports audio guidance, it is not targeting to disabled users. In [46], the authors exploit Semantic Web technologies in order to develop a context ontology for supporting indoor navigation services. However, this approach does not examine in detail the efficiency of positioning techniques and the presentation of path instructions to the user.

Hua Wu et al [30], introduce an Indoor Navigation Model for the blind and visually impaired individuals. For Path planning uses the A* and Dijkstra's shortest path algorithms, to operate on an "Intelligent Map", that is based on a new data structure termed "cactus tree" which is predicated on the relationships between the different objects that represent an indoor environment. The paths produced are termed "virtual hand rails", which can be used to dynamically plan a path for a user within a region. The path following algorithm is based on dead reckoning, but incorporates human factors as well as information about the flooring and furnishing structures along the intended planned path. The overall system is based on the Euclidean characteristics of the space and does not exploit semantic technologies.

Riehle et al [31], are presenting a small portable personal navigation device that provides current position, useful contextual wayfinding information about the indoor environment and directions to a destination that improve access and independence for people with low vision. They also present some interesting results on how navigation devices can improve navigation performance of visually impaired individuals.

Dandan and Lee [32], propose a lattice-based semantic location model (LSLM) for the indoor environment. LSLM is based on the exit-location model and the theory of "formal concept analysis." The model can provide an explicit representation of the basic relationships between two entities such as containment and overlap. The nearest neighbor relationship on the concept lattice is used to define the optimal distance between two entities. Furthermore, the dual (location/exit) property of the model can cater for different navigation needs.

Chang et al [33], [34], are introducing a wayfinding system with an aim to increase workplace and life independence for cognitive-impaired patients such as people with traumatic brain injury, cerebral palsy, mental retardation, schizophrenia, and Alzheimer's disease. It is based on passive RFID tags and Bluetooth sensors. Passive RFID tags, which can be imagined as a new traffic sign system, are posted to selected positions on routes. The navigational photos are served on demand to the user who uses the built-in RFID reader to sense the RFID tag when it is in her proximity. A tracking function is integrated to timestamp the visited positions and issue alerts in case of anomalies. The system, while it utilizes a lot of the technologies used in MNISIKLIS, it does not provide enough tools for personalizing the wayfinding procedure according to user preferences.

7 Discussion on Personalization through Ontology-Based User Models

In order to build advanced personalized systems, many rather complex features have to be modeled and, thus, expressive formalisms are required that are able to capture such knowledge. Nowadays, mature ontology languages (e.g., OWL), as expressive subsets of first-order logic, have set up a suitable knowledge framework for defining complex concepts and relationships between them. However, more expressive languages and ontology design patterns are required in order to capture complex types of information. For example, fuzzy extensions of ontology languages may be useful in order to deal with knowledge uncertainty issues.

Furthermore, more and more applications call for adaptive behavior in order to achieve optimum performance. An increasing demand of effective management of knowledge concerning user data and profiles has been identified over the years. Hence, the embedment of intelligence into the personalization process seems to become a challenging task. Contrary to other approaches, ontologies do not constitute static models and views of the application domain. Due to the reasoning capabilities they provide, ontologies allow for the inference of new knowledge. Specifically, the addition of knowledge may refer to new concepts, relationships, individuals or axioms that describe the domain of discourse. This modification of the user model may lead to the entailment of new conclusions that may, in turn, dynamically lead the adaptive system behavior. Moreover, knowledge representation methodologies (and, thus, ontologies and rules, as well) enable the application of learning techniques (as already shown in Section 5). Hence, systems that take advantage of such technologies may be updated dynamically according to history information or training data.

However, some problems arise with regard to the management of knowledge. Firstly, current reasoning modules do not provide efficient reasoning support for large knowledge bases. Specifically, the management of ontologies that contain a large number of instances (e.g., more than a few hundreds) is still a challenging task. On the other hand, most of the reasoning modules can handle ontological models with a huge number of classes and properties. Finally, the integration of rules with ontologies should be further investigated in order for the Semantic Web to conclude in a standard formalism that will combine the required expressiveness and decidability.

8 Open Issues and Conclusions

In this paper we have presented some background knowledge on navigation theory from various disciplines (e.g., psychology, physiology), which directly affects any navigation-oriented user model. Furthermore, we have taken into consideration these theoretical implications in order to construct a user ontology. For that purpose, we used tools from the Knowledge Representation domain, and specifically the Semantic Web. We have also shown how such ontology is actively involved in the navigation procedure of the MNISIKLIS system through inference rules. Finally, we briefly described a way to (semi-)automatically refine and learn user classification rules with the aid of Inductive Logic Programming tools.

This latter work on profile learning, which is still in progress, addresses one of the most interesting and important issues: the (semi-)automatic user model creation. Another challenging issue, and "common" with respect to user profiles, is privacy protection (since UNO describes also personal information such as health/physical/mental status). Finally, as become obvious from the related literature referenced in the paper, most navigation systems (and thus user modeling, too) focus on specific aspects of user profiles (e.g., visually impairments, moving disabilities). Some other aspects of a user profile, such as cognitive characteristics have not been investigated so deeply and are usually not take into consideration in implemented LBS.

Acknowledgement

The MNISIKLIS system was has been partially funded by the Greek General Secretariat for Research and Technology (GSRT) under grant PABET 2005 – Project Code: 282. The project implementation consortium was comprised by Unisystems, National and Kapodistrian University of Athens and Technical Educational Institute of Athens.

References

[1] Gluck, M.: Making Sense of Human Wayfinding: A Review of Cognitive and Linguistic Knowledge for Personal Navigation with a New Research Direction. Syracuse University Technical Report 3 (1990)
[2] Downs, R.J., Stea, D.: Cognitive Maps and Spatial Behavior. Image and Environment, pp. 8–26. Aldine Publishing Company, Chicago (1973)
[3] Allen, G.: Spatial Abilities, Cognitive Maps, and Wayfinding - Bases for individual Differences in Spatial Cognition and Behavior. In: Golledge, R. (ed.) Wayfinding Behavior - Cognitive Mapping and Other Spatial Processes, pp. 46–80. Johns Hopkins University Press, Baltimore (1999)
[4] Timpf, S., Volta, G., Pollock, D., Egenhofer, M.: A Conceptual Model of Wayfinding Using Multiple Levels of Abstraction. In: Frank, A.U., Formentini, U., Campari, I. (eds.) GIS 1992. LNCS, vol. 639, pp. 348–367. Springer, Heidelberg (1992)

[5] Siegel, A.W., White, S.H.: The Development of Spatial Representation of Large-Scale Environments. In: Reese, H.W. (ed.) Advances in Child Development and Behavior. Academic Press, New York (1975)

[6] Lynch, K.: The Image of the City. MIT Press, Cambridge (1960)

[7] Weisman, J.: Evaluating architectural legibility: Wayfinding in the build environment. Environment and Behavior 13, 189–204 (1981)

[8] Schmitz, S.: Gender Differences in Acquisition of Environmental Knowledge Related to Wayfinding Behavior, Spatial Anxiety and Self-Estimated Environmental Competencies. Sex Roles 41(1/2) (1999)

[9] Kirasic, K.: Age differences in adults' spatial abilities, learning environmental layout and wayfinding behavior. Spatial Cognition and Computation 2, 117–134 (2000)

[10] Lawton, C.A., Kallai, J.: Gender Differences in Wayfinding Strategies and Anxiety About Wayfinding: A Cross-Cultural Comparison. Sex Roles 47(9/10) (2002)

[11] Raubal, M., Winter, S.: Enriching Wayfinding Instructions with Local Landmarks. In: Egenhofer, M.J., Mark, D.M. (eds.) GIScience 2002. LNCS, vol. 2478, pp. 243–259. Springer, Heidelberg (2002)

[12] Antoniou, G., van Harmelen, F.: A Semantic Web Primer. The MIT Press, Massachusetts (2004)

[13] Tsetsos, V., Anagnostopoulos, C., Kikiras, P., Hasiotis, T., Hadjiefthymiades, S.: A Human-centered Semantic Navigation System for Indoor Environments. In: IEEE International Conference on Pervasive Services (ICPS 2005), Santorini, Greece (2005)

[14] OntoNav Web site,
     http://p-comp.di.uoa.gr/projects/ontonav/index.html

[15] Horrocks, I., Patel-Schneider, P., Harold, B., Tabet, S., Grosof, B., Dean, M.: SWRL: A Semantic Web Rule Language Combining OWL and RuleML. World Wide Web Consortium Member Submission (2004),
     http://www.w3.org/Submission/SWRL/

[16] Heckmann, D., Schwartz, T., Brandherm, B., Schmitz, M., von Wilamowitz-Moellendorff, M.: Gumo – the general user model ontology. In: Ardissono, L., Brna, P., Mitrović, A. (eds.) UM 2005. LNCS (LNAI), vol. 3538, pp. 428–432. Springer, Heidelberg (2005)

[17] Heckmann, D., Krüger, A.: A User Modeling Markup Language (UserML) for Ubiquitous Computing. In: Brusilovsky, P., Corbett, A.T., de Rosis, F. (eds.) UM 2003. LNCS (LNAI), vol. 2702. Springer, Heidelberg (2003)

[18] W3C Semantic Web Best Practices and Deployment Working Group,
     http://www.w3.org/2001/sw/BestPractices/

[19] WHO, International Classification of Functioning, Disability and Health,
     http://www.who.int/classifications/icf/en/

[20] Resource Description Framework (RDF)/W3C Semantic Web Activity,
     http://www.w3.org/RDF/

[21] Dean, M., Schreiber, G., Bechhofer, S., van Harmelen, F., Hendler, J., Horrocks, I., McGuinness, D.L., Patel-Schneider, P.F., Stein, L.A.: OWL Web Ontology Language Reference. W3C Recommendation February 10 (2004),
     http://www.w3.org/TR/owl-ref/

[22] Sirin, E., Parsia, B., Grau, B.C., Kalyanpur, A., Katz, Y.: Pellet: A practical OWL-DL reasoner. Journal of Web Semantics 5(2) (2007)

[23] RacerPro,
     http://www.racer-systems.com/products/racerpro/index.phtml
     (retrieved April 10, 2008)

[24] Jess, The Rule Engine For the Java Platform,
     http://www.jessrules.com/jess/index.shtml (retrieved April 22, 2008)
[25] Jang, M., Sohn, J.C.: Bossam: An Extended Rule Engine for OWL Inferencing. In:
     Antoniou, G., Boley, H. (eds.) RuleML 2004. LNCS, vol. 3323, pp. 128–138. Springer,
     Heidelberg (2004)
[26] Papataxiarhis, V., Tsetsos, V., Karali, I., Stamatopoulos, P., Hadjiefthymiades, S.:
     Developing rule-based applications for the Web: Methodologies and Tools. In: Giurca,
     A., Gasevic, D., Taveter, K. (eds.) Handbook of Research on Emerging Rule-Based
     Languages and Technologies: Open Solutions and Approaches, Information Science
     Reference (2009)
[27] Tsetsos, V., Papataxiarhis, V., Hadjiefthymiades, S.: Personalization based on Semantic
     Web Technologies. In: Cardoso, J., Lytras, M. (eds.) Semantic Web Engineering in the
     Knowledge Society, Information Science Reference (2008)
[28] Papataxiarhis, V., Riga, V., Nomikos, V., Sekkas, O., Kolomvatsos, K., Tsetsos, V.,
     Papageorgas, P., Vourakis, S., Hadjiefthymiades, S., Kouroupetroglou, G.: MNISIKLIS:
     Indoor Location Based Services for All. In: 5th International Symposium on LBS &
     TeleCartography (LBS 2008), Salzburg, Austria (2008)
[29] Tsetsos, V., Anagnostopoulos, C., Kikiras, P., Hadjieftymiades, S.: Semantically
     Enriched Navigation for Indoor Environments. International Journal of Web and Grid
     Services (IJWGS) 4(2) (2006)
[30] Wu, H., Marshall, A., Yu, W.: Path Planning and Following Algorithms in an Indoor
     Navigation Model for Visually Impaired. In: Second International Conference on
     Internet Monitoring and Protection (2007)
[31] Riehle, T.H., Lichter, P., Giudice, N.A.: An indoor navigation system to support the
     visually impaired. In: 30th Annual International Conference of the IEEE Engineering in
     Medicine and Biology Society (2008)
[32] Li, D., Lee, D.L.: A Lattice-Based Semantic Location Model for Indoor Navigation. In:
     9th International Conference on Mobile Data Management (2008)
[33] Chang, Y.J., Chen, C.N., Chou, L.D., Wang, T.Y.: A novel indoor wayfinding system
     based on passive RFID for individuals with cognitive impairments. In: Second
     International Conference on Pervasive Computing Technologies for Healthcare (2008)
[34] Chang, Y.J., Chu, Y.Y., Chen, C.N., Wang, T.Y.: Mobile computing for indoor
     wayfinding based on bluetooth sensors for individuals with cognitive impairments. In:
     3rd International Symposium on Wireless Pervasive Computing (2008)
[35] Rehrl, K., Leitinger, S., Gartner, G.: The SemWay Project – Towards Semantic
     Navigation Systems. In: Proceedings of the 4th International Symposium on LBS &
     TeleCartography, Hong Kong (2007)
[36] Lavrak, N., Dzeroski, S.: Inductive logic programming, techniques and application. Elis
     Howrwood, New York (1994)
[37] Lehmann, J.: Hybrid Learning of Ontology Classes. In: Perner, P. (ed.) MLDM 2007.
     LNCS (LNAI), vol. 4571, pp. 883–898. Springer, Heidelberg (2007)
[38] Baader, F., Calvanese, D., McGiuness, D., Nardi, D., Patel-Schneider, P.: The
     Description Logic Handbook: Theory, Implementation, and Applications. Cambridge
     University Press, Cambridge (2003)
[39] Malerba, D., Lisi, F.A.: An ILP method for spatial association rule mining. In: Knobbe,
     A., van der Wallen, D. (eds.) Notes of the ECMIPKDD 2001 workshop on multi-
     relational data mining (2001)

[40] Huang, J., Pearce, A.R.: Collaborative Inductive Logic Programming for Path Planning. In: Proceedings of the Twentieth International Joint Conference on Artificial Intelligence (2007)

[41] Maclaren, H.: A Divide and Conquer Approach to Using Inductive Logic Programming for Learning User Models. The University of York, UK (2005)

[42] Kargl, F., Gessler, S., Flerlage, F.: The iNAV Indoor Navigation System. In: Ichikawa, H., Cho, W.-D., Satoh, I., Youn, H.Y. (eds.) UCS 2007. LNCS, vol. 4836, pp. 110–117. Springer, Heidelberg (2007)

[43] Lyardet, F., Grimmer, J., Muhlhauser, M.: CoINS: Context Sensitive Indoor Navigation System. In: Proceedings of the Eighth IEEE International Symposium on Multimedia, pp. 209–218. IEEE Computer Society, Washington (2006)

[44] Baus, J., Krüger, A., Wahlster, W.: A Resource - Adaptive Mobile Navigation System. In: International Conference on Intelligent User Interfaces IUI 2002, San Francisco, USA (2002)

[45] Gartner, G., Frank, A., Retscher, G.: Pedestrian Navigation System for Mixed Indoor/Outdoor Environments - The NAVIO Project. In: Schrenk, M. (ed.) Proceedings of the CORP 2004 and Geomultimedia04 Symposium, Vienna, Austria, pp. 165–171 (2004)

[46] Bikakis, A., Patkos, T., Antoniou, G., Papadopouli, M., Plexousakis, D.: A Semantic-based Framework for Context-aware Pedestrian Guiding Services. In: 2nd International Workshop on Semantic Web Technology For Ubiquitous and Mobile Applications (SWUMA), Riva del Garda, Trentino, Italy (2006)

[47] Stephanidis, C., Savidis, A.: Universal access in the information society: methods, tools, and interaction technologies. Universal Access in the Information Society 1(1), 40–55 (2001)

Semantic Integration of Adaptive Educational Systems

Sergey Sosnovsky[1], Peter Brusilovsky[1], Michael Yudelson[1],
Antonija Mitrovic[2], Moffat Mathews[2], and Amruth Kumar[3]

[1] University of Pittsburgh, School of Information Sciences,
135 North Bellefield Ave. Pittsburgh, PA 15260, USA
[2] University of Canterbury,
Department of Computer Science and Software Engineering
Private Bag 4800, Christchurch 8140, New Zealand
[3] Ramapo College of New Jersey
505 Ramapo Valley Road, Mahwah, NJ 07430-1680, USA
sosnovsky@gmail.com, peterb@pitt.edu, myudelson@gmail.com,
Tanja.Mitrovic@canterbury.ac.nz, moffat@cosc.canterbury.ac.nz,
amruth@ramapo.edu

Abstract. With the growth of adaptive educational systems available to students, integration of these systems is evolving from an interesting research problem into an important practical task. One of the challenges that needs to be addressed is the development of mechanisms for student model integration. The architectural principles and representation technologies employed by adaptive educational systems define the applicability of a particular integration approach. This chapter reviews the existing mechanisms and details one of them: the evidence integration.

Keywords: Adaptive Educational System, Semantic Integration, User Model Interoperability, Ontology.

1 Introduction

Over the last 10 years, a number of adaptive systems have migrated from research labs to real life. Web recommender systems [1], mobile tourist guides [2] and adaptive educational systems (AES) [3] are now employed by thousands of real users. In some application areas, the "density" of practical adaptive systems is reaching the point where several adaptive systems are available. Yet, in most cases, these systems do not compete, but rather complement each other, while offering unique functionality or content. This puts the problem of using several adaptive systems in parallel on the agenda of the user modeling community. This problem has been explored over the last few years by several research teams and from several perspectives: architectures for integrating adaptive systems [4], cross-system personalization [5], [6], user model ontologies [7], [8], and user modeling servers [9], [10], [11].

The main challenge of using several adaptive systems in parallel (or a distributed adaptive system) is making the whole more than the sum of its parts. In this context, it means that each of the systems should have a chance to improve the quality of user

T. Kuflik et al. (Eds.): Advances in Ubiquitous User Modelling, LNCS 5830, pp. 134–158, 2009.

modeling and adaptation based on integrated evidence about the user collected by all participating systems. At this point, the most popular approach to solving problem is *translation* [12] (or *mediation* [13]) from one user model to another. This approach is very attractive if two adaptive systems are used in a sequence, one after another. However, when two adaptive systems have to be used in parallel (i.e., the user models on both sides are being constantly updated within the same session), a translation of the whole user model from one representation to another becomes a relatively costly approach. To account for the combined information about the user, the integrated systems will need to translate the each other's user models before any adaptive decisions can be made.

Good examples of such a scenario are distributed adaptive E-Learning frameworks such as Medea [14] or KnowledgeTree [4], where students can work with educational activities provided by several independent adaptive systems. Each of the involved systems receives evidences about student knowledge and attempts to build the student knowledge model. To make this model reliable, each of the involved systems should take into account evidences produced by the student during his/her work with the systems. Our previous experience with distributed E-Learning systems shows that a student can switch from one system to another many times even within a single session [15]. To avoid multiple translations from one user model to another within the same session, we explored an alternative approach to user modeling in distributed adaptive systems called *evidence integration*. With this approach, adaptive systems do not exchange entire user models, but instead exchange elementary evidences produced as results of the student's actions. In this case, the problem of student model integration is actually a problem of evidence integration. While evidence integration is a relatively simple task in some domains (i.e., user's ratings for a specific movie can be easily taken into account by multiple recommender systems), it is not the case in e-learning. In e-learning, each educational activity (i.e., problem, quiz, or example) is typically described in terms of a system's internal *domain model*. Using this knowledge and the outcomes of student's actions (e.g. correct or incorrect solutions to problems), the user modeling component updates student knowledge model. In a rare case, where the component systems share the same domain model, integrating evidences from two or more adaptive systems is a relatively simple problem [14], [16]. However, in reality, two adaptive systems developed for the same domain (such as Java programming or SQL) can rely on very different domain representations. In that case, evidence integration becomes a difficult task, which requires some kind of translation from one *domain model* to another.

This paper details two practical examples of distributed student modeling using evidence integration. Each example involves two e-learning systems with considerably different domain models for the same subject (Java and SQL languages). One of these examples (Section 3) demonstrates fairly simple and straightforward evidence integration, while another (Section 4) presents a more sophisticated case based on the alignment between two large domain models relying on very different representation formalisms. Taken together, these cases stress the problems of distributed user modeling in the field of e-learning and demonstrate how the evidence integration approach can support conceptual and architectural integration in the context of a real college-level course. To make our example more useful, we preface it with a discussion of existing integration approaches in the area of e-learning (Section 2) and present the implementation details of our approach (Section 5). We conclude with a summary of our results and a discussion of future work.

2 Existing Integration Approaches

This analysis focuses on a particular aspect of adaptive system integration. Due to the wide spectrum of existing adaptive technologies, there are many ways to integrate user modeling information collected and inferred by adaptive systems. In the field of recommender systems, this task can be transformed into aggregation of user ratings collected by several systems [17], or mediation between content-based and collaborative user models [18]. In the field of pervasive adaptation exploiting rich, multifaceted user profiles, integration of adaptive systems will require matching complex user modeling ontologies [19]. AESs focus on the modeling of student knowledge, which includes representation of the domain structure in terms of its elementary units and estimation of knowledge levels for these units. Hence, we will limit our discussion to the integration of AESs modeling student knowledge. Such integration will require target systems to achieve a certain level of mutual understanding of the domain semantics. Once the systems agree on the domain model, they can exchange student models for the equivalent or related parts of the domain and incorporate them into adaptive inference.

The general task of domain model alignment potentially involves resolution of multiple model discrepancies on two principle levels. The language–level mismatches, such as different syntax, expressiveness, or varying semantics of used primitives, need to be resolved first. However, the more critical are the model-level mismatches that occur due to the difference in structure and/or semantics of the domain models. Resolution of these kinds of discrepancies involves dealing with such problems as:

- Naming conflicts (the same concept is defined in two models by different terms or the same term defines different concepts);
- Different graph structure (the models choose to connect relevant sets of concepts in different ways);
- Different scope (two models cover parts of the domain that only partially inter-sect or the scope of one model includes that of another model);
- Different granularity (the size of concepts differ across the models; a single con-cept of one model represents a piece of domain knowledge covered by several concepts in another model);
- Different focus (the models examine different modeling paradigms or adhere to different modeling conventions).

This list does not include the mismatches specific to those formal models employing advanced modeling primitives, such as typed relations and axioms (e.g. the same entity can be modeled as a concept and as an attribute).

The next sections outline several approaches to semantic integration of adaptive educational systems described in the literature.

2.1 Single-Ontology Integration

One of the first steps toward interoperable adaptive systems would be implementation of domain models as ontologies. Ontologies express the shared view on domain semantics and come with a full package of technologies developed within the framework of the Semantic Web initiative. When user models of two systems rely on a common domain ontology, they can be exchanged and consistently interpreted when necessary. The OntoAIMS project provides a good example of such integration [20]. Two components of OntoAims: OWL-OLM [21] and AIMS [22] – were developed as separate systems, but with a mutual concern about interoperability. Both AIMS and OWL-OLM represent their domain models as OWL-ontologies and model user knowledge as ontology overlays. As a result, merging these two systems into an integrated adaptive environment providing a rich learning experience was a straightforward task. The long-term user model in OntoAIMS is shared by both its components. During a session with either AIMS or OWL-OLM, a short-term user model is populated and then used to update the long-term model.

Several research teams have generalized this approach to the level of integrated architectures based on central user modeling servers (e.g. Personis [23], ActiveMath [24], CUMULATE [25]). These servers perform centralized domain and user modeling, and supply this information to the individual adaptive systems. As a result, the adaptive systems themselves do not need to support domain and user modeling. They update the central user model and request the modeling information from the server.

2.2 Central-Ontology Integration

The single-ontology integration can work only if the participating systems fully agree on a single ontology for modeling the domain of discourse. Unfortunately, the practice of AES is still far from the use of common ontologies. Although the designers of AES more and more frequently choose to represent the domain models as ontologies, they tend to employ different ontologies for the same domain.

In some cases, this problem can be remedied without much effort. If domain models of adaptive systems have a common reference ontology, it can facilitate the exchange of modeling information through the "hub" concepts shared by the domain models of both systems. This becomes important in the situation when several small adaptive systems model student knowledge in tightly related domains (or parts of a single domain). A central ontology can act as a meta-translator for the shared concepts and "bootstrap" the user modeling through such concepts. Mitrovic and Devedzic describe such a scenario in [26] and introduce M-OBLIGE – an architecture for centralized exchange of user-modeling information among multiple intelligent tutoring systems acting in related parts of SQL and Relational Algebra.

This scenario still requires a certain level of ontological commitment from the participating systems – their models should rely on the same reference ontology, which is hard to ensure when the systems are designed by different research teams. In general, adaptive systems use completely different ontologies to model student knowledge. These models can still be integrated; however, it requires more effort on both the architectural and conceptual sides. One of the first steps in this direction has been made in Medea [27]. Medea combines the functionality of an adaptive learning portal that help students navigate through available learning resources and one of a user modeling server that keeps track of student's actions and computes her/his knowledge of course topics. Medea does not host the learning content itself; instead, it provides access to the participating adaptive services. On the modeling side, Medea allows adaptive services to report their local user modeling information into the central user model. The important feature of Medea is the possibility to manually map the domain model of participating services into the central Medea ontology. As a result, the user model updates (received from adaptive services) can be translated into the concepts of Medea's ontology and fused into the central user modeling storage.

2.3 Integration Based on Automatic Ontology Mapping

Both Medea and M-OBLIGE provide practical solutions for semantic integration of multiple AESs into distributed platforms for coherent student modeling and adaptation. However, they both have limitations. The applicability of M-OBLIGE is reduced to those situations where the domain models of participating systems share the references to the central ontology. The approach implemented in Medea relies on manual ontology mapping, which is a time-consuming task that requires a high level of expertise both in knowledge engineering and the domain of discourse.

Using ontologies for domain modeling enables a more general solution for semantic integration of adaptive systems based on automatic ontology mapping [28]. Ontology mapping techniques help to automatically identify matching elements (concepts, relations, axioms) in different ontologies. They rely on a set of technologies from natural language processing, graph theory and information retrieval to discover similar lexical patterns, conceptual sub graphs and statistical regularities in texts accompanying the ontologies.

Once the mapping between the domain ontologies is established it can be used as a translation component for user model mediation. We are not aware of any fully-implemented components based on this approach; however the first step in this direction has been made. Authors of [29] investigate the applicability of automatic ontology mapping for translation between two overlay models of student knowledge based on two different domain ontologies. The practical evaluation shows that automatic ontology mapping results in user model translation, which is statistically close to the best possible translation done by human experts.

2.4 Evidence Integration

Several ontology-based techniques for semantic integration have been discussed; however, many successful adaptive e-learning systems do not employ ontologies for knowledge representation. They implement adaptation and user modeling technologies relying on formalisms that are different from the conceptual networks, which are the core components of ontologies.

Integration of such models is still possible, although is becomes subject to the two major limitations. First, numerous automatic ontology mapping techniques are not applicable for such models, nor can one expect these models to refer to some common upper ontology. Hence, the alignment of underlying domain models of such systems can only be done manually. Even though, the participating models can be of any kind (as long as they support the general principle of composite domain modeling) we argue that ontologies could still be useful as a common denominator and facilitate future integration.

Second, the differences in modeling principles and inference mechanisms make the coherent merging of user modeling information harder to achieve. Even when the mapping between two domain representations has been established, the consequent translation of user models can result in noisy and inadequate modeling. This becomes critical when the integration of user modeling information is organized as a rare holistic model exchange (e.g. at the end of the learning session). To remedy this problem, the user model exchange should be triggered as soon as the modeling event is observed. In this case, the influence of internal model inference (e.g., a student has learned this) on the objective event (e.g., a student has answered a problem correctly) is reduced and is maximally close to the evidence exchange happening in central user modeling servers. We call such a mechanism evidence integration.

The next sections of this chapter describe two examples of evidence integration of real adaptive E-Learning systems. The first case implements simple, server-side evidence integration, where the integrated models are fairly close and the user model exchange is not intensive. The second case is an example of more complex evidence integration, where a lot of the work is done on the system side and the user model reports to the server are much bigger.

3   Simple Evidence Integration

This section describes an example of simple evidence integration. Two e-learning systems helping students to practice Java, Problets and QuizJET, rely on different domain models. While QuizJET uses Java ontology, Problets model student knowledge in terms of pedagogically-oriented domain elements called learning objectives. There is not much difference between these two domain models, other than a shift in modeling focus, granularity, and scope. Each learning event observed and registered by Problets results in a small knowledge level update of corresponding learning objectives. The integration has been implemented within the framework of ADAPT[2] architecture on the CUMULATE user modeling server. The next three subsections detail the implementation of Problets and QuizJET as well as describe the integration procedure.

3.1 Ramapo College's Problets

Problets (www.problets.org) are problem-solving tutors on introductory programming concepts in C/C++/C#/Java. They present programming problems, grade the student's answer, and provide corrective feedback. Problets sequence problems adaptively [30], and generate feedback messages that include a step-by-step explanation of the correct solution [31]. Students can use Problets for knowledge assessment and self-assessment, as well as for improving their problem-solving skills. Fig. 1 presents the student interface of a Problet on *if/if-else* Statements in Java. The bottom-left panel contains a simple Java program. The students need to evaluate the program and answer a question presented in the top-left panel. The system presents student's answers in the right-bottom panel, and indicates the correct and incorrect answers by marking them in green, and red correspondingly. The detailed help on how to use the system, submit the answers and read the system's feedback messages can be always opened in the right-top panel of the Problet interface.

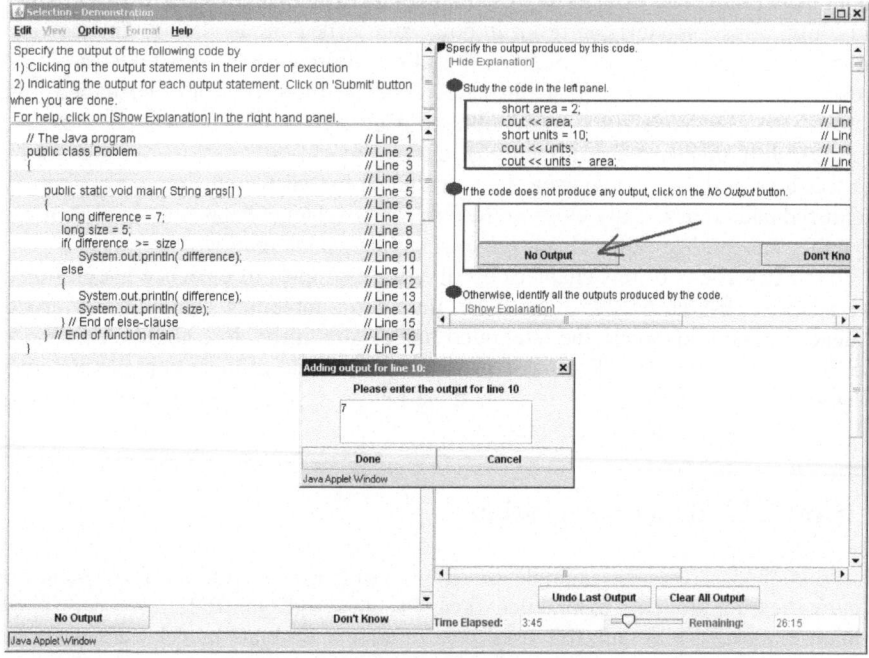

Fig. 1. A Problet on *if/if-else* statements in Java

Problets rely on the concept map of the domain, enhanced with pedagogical concepts called learning objectives, as the overlay student model [32]. Each learning objective is associated with the proficiency level calculated based on the student's answers. The student model provides the basis for adaptive decisions made by the tutor, through associating a proficiency model with each learning objective. The system propagates the proficiency values to the top levels of the concept hierarchy. At any point in the tutoring session, a student can observe the current state of her/his user model. Fig. 2 demonstrates an example of the user model snapshot for the *if/if-else* Statements in Java.

3.2 University of Pittsburgh's QuizJET

QuizJET (Java Evaluation Toolkit) is an online quiz system for Java programming language. It provides authoring and delivery of quiz questions and automatic evaluation of students' answers. A typical question in QuizJET is implemented as a simple Java program. The students need to evaluate the program code and answer a

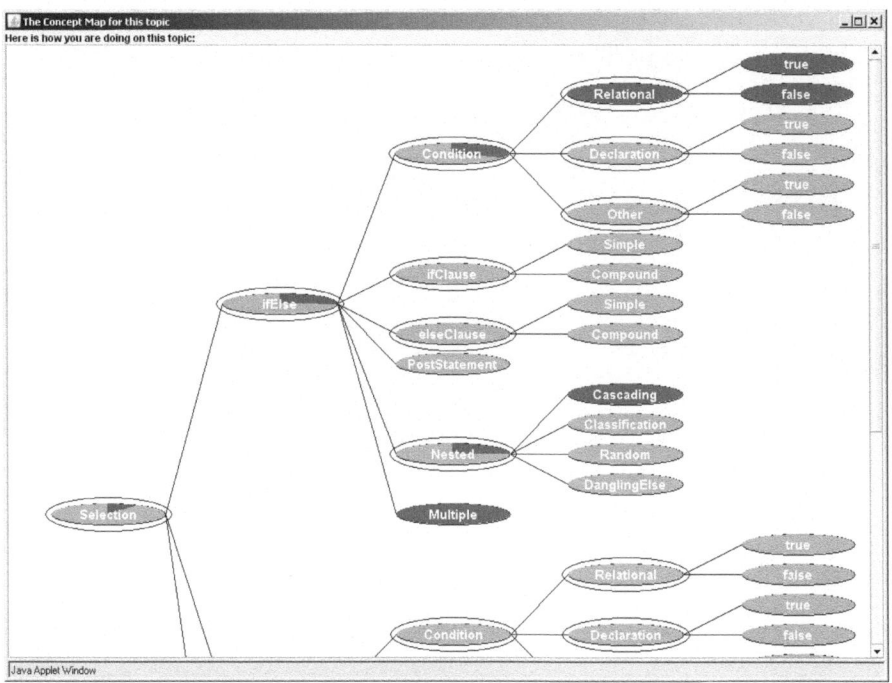

Fig. 2. A part of the domain hierarchy on *if/if-else* statements in Java. Learning objectives are associated with each concept in the hierarchy.

follow-up question, which can take one of two forms: "What will be the final value of the marked variable?" or "What will be printed by the program to the console window?" Upon evaluation of the student's answer, QuizJET provides brief feedback specifying the correctness of the answer and the right answer in case a student has made a mistake.

Fig. 3 demonstrates the student interface of QuizJET. The Java programs constituting QuizJET questions can consist of one or several classes. To switch between classes, QuizJET implements tab-based navigation. The driver class containing the main function (the entry point to the program) is always placed in the first tab, which also presents the question itself, processes the student's input and presents the system's feedback.

The important feature of QuizJET is parameterized questions. One or more numbers in the code of a driver class are dynamically replaced with a random value every time the question is delivered to a student. As a result, the students can practice QuizJET questions multiple times, and every time the question will be different and have a different correct answer.

Every QuizJET question is indexed by a number of concepts from the Java ontology. A concept in a question can play one of two roles: it acts either as a prerequisite for a question (if it is introduced earlier in the course), or as a question outcome (if the concept is first introduced by this question). Fig. 4 presents an extract from the Java ontology.

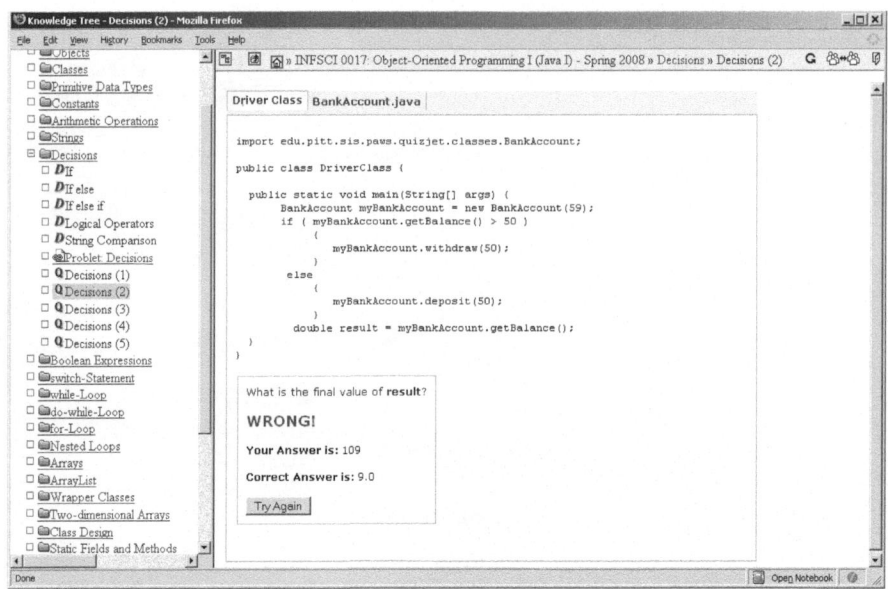

Fig. 3. An example of QuizJET question on Decisions in Java accessed through the Knowledge Tree Learning Portal

3.3 Integration Details

Both Problets and QuizJet questions rely on conceptual content models that provide detailed representation of underlying domain knowledge. In order to maintain consistent interpretation of the evidence reported by these two types of learning content, perform unifying user modeling and implement adaptive mechanisms taking into account a student's work with both systems we need to integrate the underlying domain models on the level of concepts constituting them.

Unlike QuizJET questions that are indexed with the concepts from the same ontology, each Problet relies on a separate model of learning objectives. These models cover six large topics of Java programming language: (1) Arithmetic Expressions, (2) Relational Expressions, (3) Logical Expressions, (4) *if/if-else* Statements, (5) *while* Loops, and (6) *for* Loops.

The combined scope of these topic models is several times more narrow than the one of the Java ontology. At the same time, the granularity of Problets' models is much higher. The total number of concepts in the Java ontology is approximatelly 500; the cumulative number of nodes in the Problets' models is more than 250. The most important problem we had to deal with is the difference in the modeling approaches (or different focus of modeling) used in Java ontology and Problets' domain models. Every learning objective models the application of a concept in a particular learning situation (e.g. different objectives model the simple *if* clause in the *if-else*-statement and the simple *if* clause in the *if*-statement). In other words, a learning objective can be described as a concept put in a context. In order to properly map the

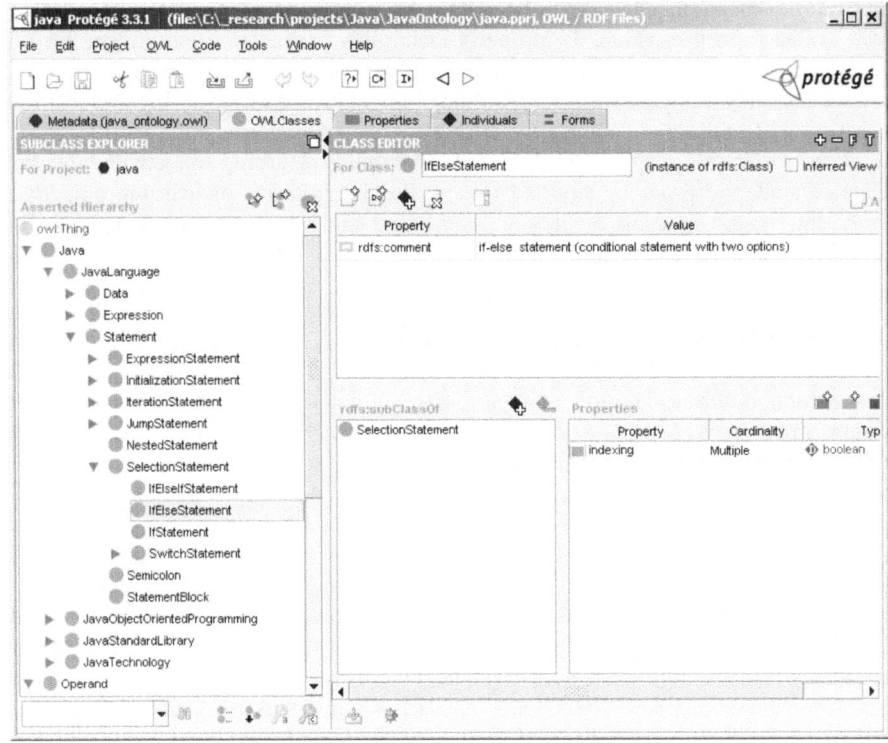

Fig. 4. An extract from the Java ontology

context of a learning objective we often had to connect one learning objective to several concepts from the Java ontology. To prevent aggressive evidence propagation to the concepts modeling context of learning objectives, we also provided weights (from 0 to 1) that define how much knowledge of a particular concept defines the proficiency of the learning objective. An example of mapping a learning objective to concepts is given ion Fig. 5. This terminal-level learning objective from the Selection

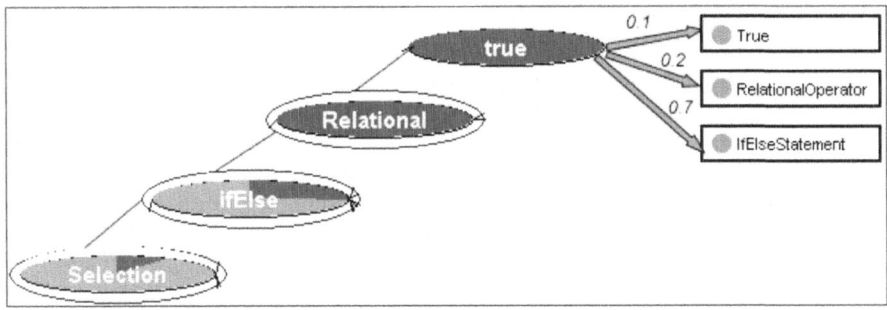

Fig. 5. An example of mapping between learning objectives and ontology concepts

topic defines the application of *if-else* statement, when the condition part of the statement evaluates to *true* value. To properly match this particular situation, we need to use three concepts from the Java Ontology. The assigned weights indicate that the main concept is still *IfElseStatement*, although the evidence of mastering this learning objective will contribute slightly to the knowledge of concepts *RelationalOperator* and *True*. Once this mapping is done for all Problets' learning objectives, any evidence of students' progress reported by any Problet in terms of learning objectives can be interpreted in terms of the ontology-based student model maintained by CU-MULATE and used by QuizJET.

4 Complex Evidence-Based Integration

This section describes a more complex case of evidence-based integration. Two systems implement adaptive support of learning SQL. One of the integrated systems, SQL-Guide, models user knowledge as an overlay of a domain ontology, while the other, SQL-Tutor, employs constraint-based student modeling. While both modeling approaches try to represent elementary knowledge in the domain (with concepts and constraints), the difference between these two models is significant, which results in many-to-many mappings of high modality. Another integration problem occurs due to the fact that learning events in SQL-Tutor trigger knowledge level updates for many constraints. As a result, multiplicative mapping propagations over a number of constraints lead to large user model updates even from a single learning event. The next subsections describe the details of participating systems and overview the implemented integration mechanisms.

4.1 SQL-Tutor and Constrained-Based User Modeling

SQL-Tutor is a constraint-based intelligent tutoring system [33] designed to help students learn SQL. It is part of a family of tools created and maintained by the Intelligent Computer Tutoring Group (ICTG[1]) [34]. SQL-Tutor has been evaluated in twelve studies since 1998 and has been shown to be effective in supporting students' learning.

SQL-Tutor contains approximately 300 problems relating to a number of databases; the databases provide a context for each problem. The pedagogical module presents students with problems appropriate to their knowledge state. It does so by combining its knowledge of the student, the domain (including meta-information about each problem, such as the complexity level), and the implemented teaching strategies. Students have the freedom to ignore the system's suggestions and choose other problems.

The SQL-Tutor interface is shown in Fig. 6 and contains the problem definition area, the solution workspace, the feedback message pane, controls, and the problem context area. The problem definition area presents the details of the problem (usually in text form). The student enters their solution in the solution workspace. The controls enable the student at any time to submit their solution, request more help, view their student model, execute their query on a real database, and view their session history.

---

[1] http://www.cosc.canterbury.ac.nz/tanja.mitrovic/ictg.html

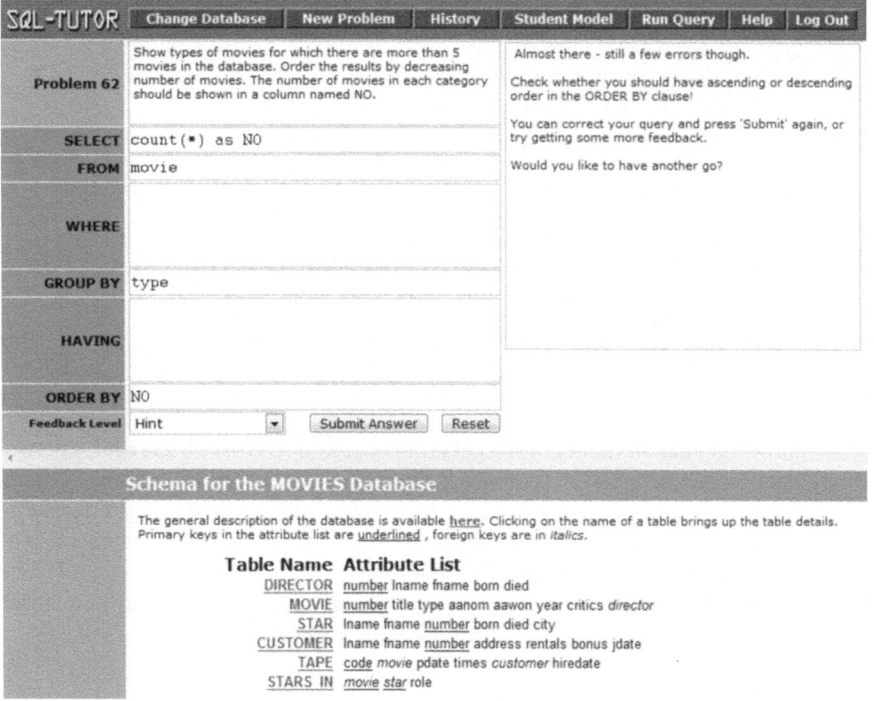

Fig. 6. The SQL-Tutor interface

The problem context provides information about the problem; the student can view the database schema, information about each relation (including detailed information about all the attributes), and the data in each table. The interface is designed to reduce the working memory load on the student by providing the appropriate information for each problem, while helping the student visualize the current goal structure. This enables students to balance their cognitive load by focusing on learning higher-level query definition problems rather than on checking low-level syntax.

After evaluating a submitted solution and identifying mistakes, SQL-Tutor provides students with adaptive feedback. Students can also request further help from one of the six feedback levels; this includes the option of viewing the ideal solution.

The domain module contains domain knowledge represented as *constraints*. Constraints are domain principles that must be satisfied in any correct solution. Each constraint contains two conditions: the relevance condition and the satisfaction condition. A constraint is relevant if the features within the student's solution match the same features described in the relevance condition. The satisfaction condition describes what must be true in order for the solution to be correct. If the student solution violates the satisfaction condition of any relevant constraint, the solution is incorrect. Feedback messages attached to each constraint allow the system to present detailed and specific feedback on violated constraints. The constraint set in SQL-Tutor contains about 700 constraints, which check for syntactic and semantic correctness of the solution. Fig. 7 illustrates two constraints.

```
(16 "You have to specify the grouping in the GROUP BY clause before you can
specify how to restrict grouping in the HAVING clause!"
(not (null (having ss)))
(not (null (slot-value ss 'group-by)))
"GROUP BY")

(635 "Check the condition involving the nested SELECT!"
(and (not (null (where ss))) (not (null (where is)))
   (match '(?*d1 ?a1 "NOT" "IN" "(" "SELECT" ?d5 "FROM" ?t ?*d2)
          (where is) bindings)
   (not (member "IN" (where ss) :test 'equalp))
   (member "EXISTS" (where ss) :test 'equalp)
   (match '(?*d3 ??n "EXISTS" "(" "SELECT" ?a2 "FROM" ?t ?*d4)
          (where ss) bindings))
(equalp ?n "NOT")
"WHERE")
```

Fig. 7. Two example constraints

The short-term student model in SQL-Tutor consists of the list of relevant, satisfied and violated constraints. The long-term student model consists of the general information about the student. In addition, this model contains the history of usage of each constraint found relevant in submissions made by a particular student. The history is a record of how the constraint was used on each occasion it was relevant. The long-term model also contains an estimate of the student's knowledge of each constraint. This model is used for adaptive problem selection.

4.2 SQL-Guide and SQL Ontology

SQL-Guide is an adaptive hypermedia system helping students to practice SQL skills. A typical SQL-Guide problem description contains a set of predefined databases and a desired output, for which a student is asked to write a matching query (see Fig. 8). The system evaluates the student's answer and provides simple feedback. All problems in SQL-Guide are dynamically generated using a set of parameterized templates. An average template is capable of generating several dozens of unique SQL problems with the predefined level of difficulty and the same set of related concepts.

To assist students in choosing the appropriate problem to practice, SQL-Guide employs an adaptive hypermedia technique called adaptive annotation. Every problem in SQL-Guide is annotated with an adaptive icon reflecting the progress of the student with the learning material underlying this problem. The CUMULATE user modeling server keeps track of all answers the student has given to SQL-Guide's problems and computes the long-term model of student knowledge for the related concepts. SQL-Guide requests the state of the model from CUMULATE and dynamically annotates links to topics and problems with the appropriate icons. The student's progress is double-coded: as the knowledge level grows, the icon fades and the bar level rises. By means of this abstraction, SQL-Guide delivers to a student two kinds of information: where the progress has been made (higher bar level) and where the attention should be focused (brighter target color). The checkmarks over the problem icons designate problems that have been solved correctly at least once. To help a student understand the meaning of annotations, QuizGuide dynamically generates mouse-over hints for all icons. A more detailed description of the system can be found in [35], [36].

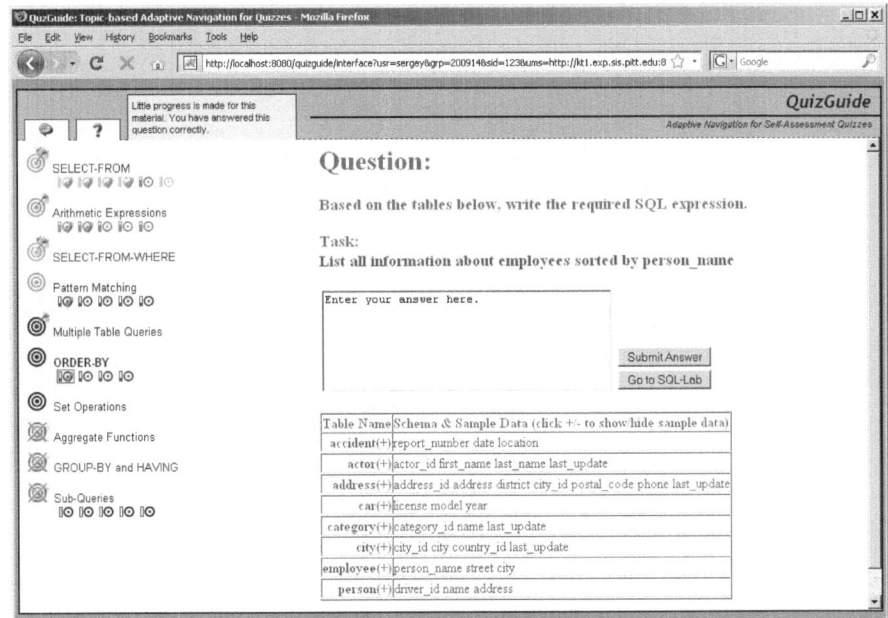

Fig. 8. The interface of SQL-Guide

Every problem template (and, naturally, every problem) in SQL-Guide is indexed with several concepts from the SQL Ontology, which was developed as a collaborative effort between the PAWS Lab of the University of Pittsburgh, and the ICT Group of the University of Canterbury [37]. The main purpose of this ontology is to support the development of adaptive educational content for SQL and facilitate the integration of educational systems in this domain, while ensuring the objective modeling of SQL semantics. The ontology can be accessed at http://www.sis.pitt.edu/~paws/ont/SQL.owl. It is a light-weight OWL-Lite ontology, with more than 200 classes connected via three relations: standard rfs:subClassOf (hyponymy relation) and a transitive relation pair sql:isUsedIn – sql:uses, which models the connection between two concepts, where one concept utilizes another. Fig. 9 gives some examples of the SQL ontology relations.

The level of granularity of the terminal concept in the SQL ontology was chosen to support the adequate modeling of students' knowledge with the necessary details. At the same time, our goal was not the comprehensive representation of the current SQL standard, therefore certain parts of the domain remain out of the scope of this ontology (Fig. 10).

```
<sql:WhereClause>        <rdfs:subClassOf>    <sql:Clause>
<sql:SelectStatement>    <rdfs:subClassOf>    <sql:Statement>
<sql:WhereClause>        <sql:isUsedIn>       <sql:SelectStatement>
<sql:SelectStatement>    <sql:uses>           <sql:WhereClause>
```

Fig. 9. Example of relations from SQL Ontology

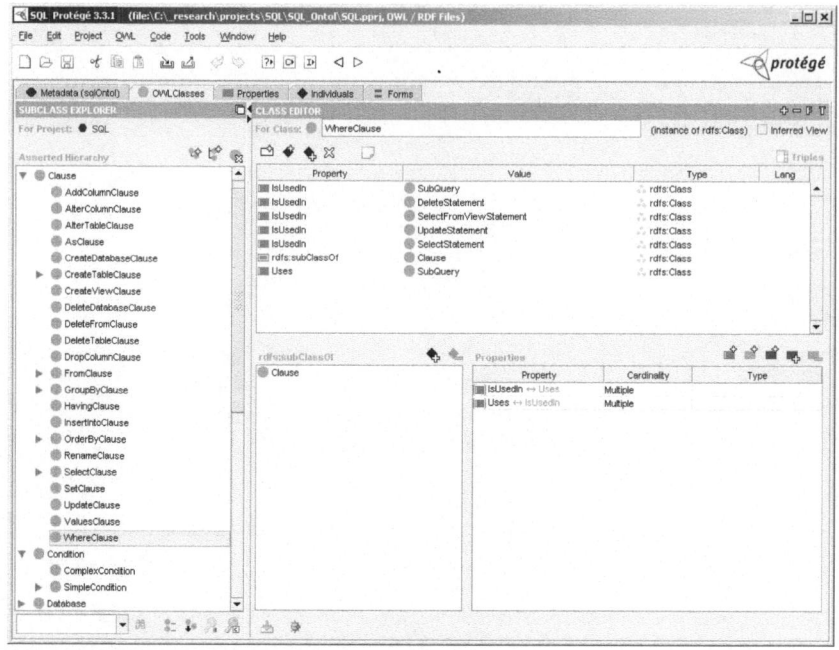

Fig. 10. SQL Ontology

4.3 Integration Details

SQL-Tutor is an independent (stand-alone), web-based, intelligent tutoring system. To use SQL-Tutor within the context of a complex evidence-based integration structure, we created a new system, SQL-Tutor Resource Component (STRC) containing four main modules. We describe the architecture of the new system first, followed by the details of its components and integration.

The SQL-Tutor Resource Component (STRC). The four modules of STRC are shown in Fig. 11 and include SQL-Tutor, the mapping module, the authentication module, and the external communications module. The STRC makes it possible for SQL-Tutor to be used as a teaching resource within the framework of a larger teaching system.

Within the STRC, the core engine and modules of SQL-Tutor are treated as a "black box". A simple internal API allows for basic control requests (for example, requesting a particular problem from SQL-Tutor) while the SQL-Tutor solution evaluator reports student progress.

The Mapping Module. The fundamental differences in the domain models of SQL-Tutor and SQL-Guide make reliable automatic alignment of these models rather impractical. A well-established set of ontology mapping techniques cannot be applied to this task due to the unique nature of SQL-Tutor's constraints. A constraint is not directly related to a single concept or a sub-tree of the ontology; instead, it models the

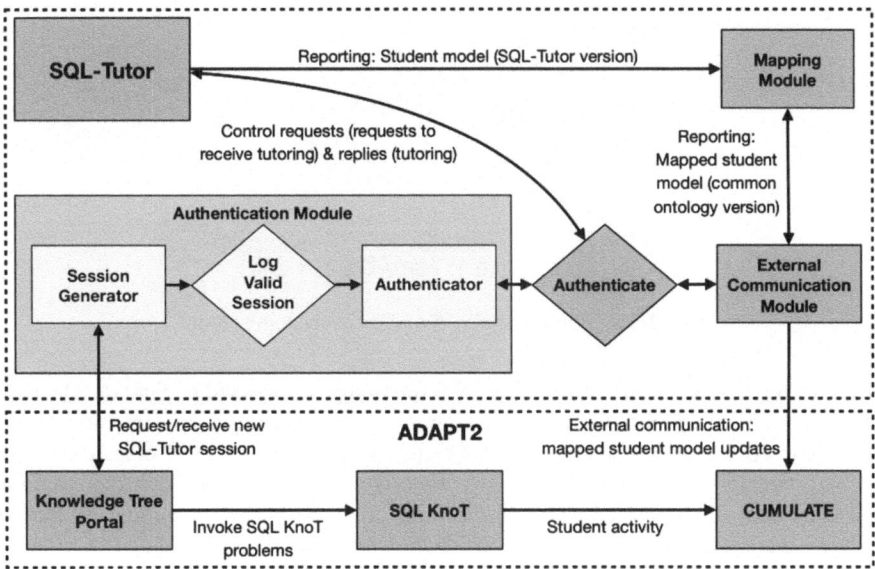

Fig. 11. High-level view of the SQL-Tutor Resource Component (STRC)

syntactic or semantic relations between various concepts. The development of the algorithm even for partial resolution of the modeling discrepancies between ontologies and constraint-based models is not a trivial task.

SQL-Tutor models students' knowledge in terms of constraints. When a student submits his/her solution, SQL-Tutor evaluates it and reports on the correctness of the submission as a set of satisfied and violated constraints (i.e. the short-term student model). Feedback on the student's solution is displayed directly in the student's browser while the report is sent to the mapping module (see Fig. 11).

The purpose of the mapping module is to take the short-term student model and convert it to a report based on a common ontology used by a particular external server. The mapping module therefore consists of the mappings between constraints and the common ontology, a student knowledge score calculator, and functions to convert the SQL-Tutor report to the mapped report.

The Mapping. Each constraint links to one or more concepts from the common SQL ontology. The degree to which each concept is associated to the constraint is called the weight, such that a concept with a higher weight has higher relevance in that constraint. Weights are small (1), medium (2), or large (3). Domain experts manually created the ontology while an expert in both SQL and Constraint-based Modeling (CBM) manually created the mapping. For more detail on the process used to derive the mapping, please refer to [37], [38].

Fig. 12 shows a part of the mapping, which is implemented as a list of lists. Each list contains a constraint ID followed by one or more concept/weight lists. For example, constraint 705 maps to two concepts, the *CommaCharacter* (with weight 1) and the *OrderByClause* (with weight 2).

Mapping

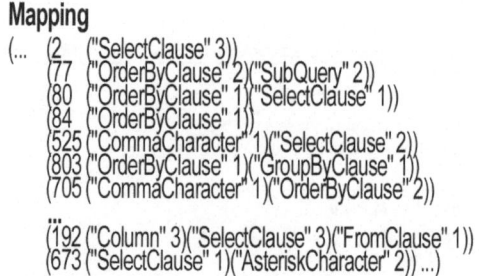

Fig. 12. Part of the mapping found in the mapping module

Calculating the Student's Evidence of Knowledge (Knowledge Score). On each attempt, the mapping module receives a report of the short-term student model consisting of two sets of constraints: satisfied and violated. Two sets of concepts (satisfied and violated) are created by parsing the sets of constraints through the mapping described above. As with constraints, the same concept can appear multiple times in both sets depending on the context in which they were satisfied or violated.

A student knowledge score is then calculated for each concept using equation 1 below. The score for each concept ranges from -1 to 1. A score of -1 means that the student violated all the instances of all constraints relating to that particular concept and vice versa for a score of 1.

$$Student's\ knowledge\ score\ for\ each\ concept$$
$$= \frac{sum\ of\ satisfied\ concept\ weights - sum\ of\ violated\ concept\ weights}{sum\ of\ relevant\ concept\ weights} \quad (1)$$

The mapped student model (the report of mapped concepts with associated calculated knowledge scores) is then sent to the external communications module, which is converted into the right format before sending it to CUMULATE user modeling server. Fig. 13 shows a part of SQL-Tutor student model report, containing the two lists of satisfied and violated constraint ID numbers. To keep the example uncluttered, only a small portion of each list is shown.

Satisfied constraints (partial list)
(... 2 77 80 84 525 705 803 ...)
Violated constraints (partial list)
(... 192 673 ...)

Fig. 13. Part of the student model showing the satisfied and violated constraints

Using the mapping (Fig. 12) and equation 1, a knowledge score is calculated for each concept. In our example, the *OrderByClause* has a knowledge score of 6/6, i.e. 1, as all constraints relating to it were satisfied. On the other hand, the *SelectClause* has a knowledge score of (6-4)/10 i.e. 0.2. The list of concepts and related knowledge scores form the mapped short-term student model. This information is then sent to CUMULATE, which integrates it with the global student model, as described in Section 5.3.

The Authentication Module. The authentication module contains the session generator and the authenticator and provides basic authentication at the server level to the STRC. Server-level authentication operates on the belief that user authentication occurs at the external server. This means that anyone using STRC via an authenticated external server is already authorized and does not require further validation. This is different from the stand-alone SQL-Tutor version, which provides authentication at the user-level.

Before communications with the STRC, an external server (e.g CUMULATE) identifies itself and requests a new session code from the session generator. Using this code and a secret key, the external server begins communications with the external communications module, which, after successful authentication, processes its request.

The purpose of this module is:

– to correctly identify and recognize the external server. This allows the STRC to adapt to the needs of each external server. This includes the particular communication protocols agreed upon between STRC and the external server, inclusion of specific information about each student (relevant to the external server), and potentially even the type of mapping (e.g. mapping to a different common ontology).
– to correctly identify and recognize each student. A username is unique within the domain of each external server. Recognizing each individual student is an essential part of providing customized content.
– to provide basic security. Unauthorized tampering with an educational system could significantly reduce its tutoring performance.

The External Communications Module. The external communications module is responsible for all communications (apart from the session code request) between the STRC and external servers. Communications adhere to the agreed-upon protocols defined within this module. This module also converts generated reports (such as the mapped student model reports) to the appropriate format for each external server. This allows STRC to be connected to multiple external servers.

5 ADAPT^2 and Knowledge Integration in CUMULATE

In this section, we describe the ADAPT^2 architecture that hosts all of the applications discussed above and provides the means for their integration. Special attention is given to CUMULATE – a centralized user modeling server. We explain how user knowledge is computed and integrated.

5.1 ADAPT^2 – Architecture for Semantic Integration of Adaptive Educational Systems

ADAPT^2 (read adapt-square; stands for Advanced Distributed Architecture for Personalized Teaching & Training [39]) is an extension of the earlier KnowledgeTree architecture [4]. ADAPT^2 provides a general framework for organizing multiple adaptive and non-adaptive educational tools into a distributed learning environment. The four main types of components in this framework are:

- Learning Portal, which organizes the learning material and provides students and teachers with the fanctionality necessary for participating in learning process;
- User Modeling Server, which stores students' activity and infers information about their characteristics;
- Activity Server, which implements one or more kinds of learning activities in either an adaptive or non-adaptive manner;
- Value-added Service, which adds some additional capabilities to the raw content provided by Activities Servers, e.g. it can provide adaptive navigation support or add annotation mash-up, etc.

All applications described in this paper act as components of ADAPT^2. Several of them have been developed for ADAPT^2 specifically (SQL-Guide, QuizJET) and are able to submit learning evidences to CUMULATE and request user model reports from it. Others have been enhanced to make them compatible with ADAPT^2 (Problets, SQL Tutor) by implementing ADAPT^2 authentication and event-reporting components. From the student perspective, all applications are accessible through the single entry point – the Knowledge Tree portal. Knowledge Tree employs a folder-document paradigm and is a link level aggregator for a variety of educational resources. Knowledge Tree provides authentication, authorization, and access to the resources. The conceptual integration of the components is provided by the CUMULATE server as described in the next section.

5.2   Student Modeling with CUMULATE

CUMULATE [9] is a second-generation user modeling server developed for ADAPT^2. CUMULATE accepts reports of user activity from ADAPT^2 systems and infers overlay user knowledge model for a related domain. CUMULATE maintains awareness about users and educational content by storing and/or caching several types of information: user identities and credentials, user memberships in groups (classes), identities of the resources, with which ADAPT^2 users interact, domain ontologies with concept hierarchies, and resource-concept metadata indices.

CUMULATE accepts and processes two kinds of activity reports. For the learning activities with a fixed set of domain concepts, CUMULATE can accept *brief event reports*, which mention only user, group, and resource IDs. For processing brief reports, the ontological metadata for the application's resources needs to be known in advance. CUMULATE caches the resource metadata and uses it to determine the activated domain concepts as soon as the evidence of user activity with a particular resource arrives. For the dynamic learning resources with mutable sets of concepts (can be different for different attempts), CUMULATE requires *extended reports*, which include a full set of activated domain concepts. In addition, CUMULATE keeps per-resource progress measures, tracking user advancement in working with a particular problem or exercise.

Following each positive activity report, which provides evidence of student knowledge, CUMULATE updates the state of all confirmed concepts related to the activity. For the brief reports, CUMULATE performs a cache lookup to determine activated concepts and then updates knowledge of the determined concepts. For the extended reports, the respective knowledge is updated directly.

To update user knowledge based on evidences received through activity reports, CUMULATE applies a specific inference mechanism that builds upon the paradigm of power-law learning. The idea of this approach is that with every successful attempts to apply a certain concept, the increment of actual user knowledge is diminishing, asymptotically approaching 100%. The specific version of this approach implemented in CUMULATE was designed to meet the following guidelines:

- Knowledge of a concept is updated with every successful solution to the problem involving this concept. There is no knowledge decay or punishment applied for incorrect answers.
- Knowledge level updates for an activated concept are directly related to the weight between the concept and the solved problem. This update is inversely related to the sum of weights of all activated concepts.
- Knowledge level updates for an activated concept are inversely related to the number of successful attempts for a particular problem. It was designed to encourage users to access different problems instead of trying to increase their knowledge by solving just one.

The current state of user knowledge represented by CUMULATE can be requested by any ADAPT^2 component. These requests can be general; for example, a snapshot of a full domain model can be acquired. Or they can be specific, requesting only a limited subset of the user model. The format of the reports can be plain text, XML, or Java Objects.

5.3 Knowledge Integration in CUMULATE

Evidence information can be processed by CUMULATE in three different ways. The student action reports received from QuizJET or SQL-Guide problems (which are ADAPT^2 native applications) go through a straightforward knowledge modeling cycle. They are combined with the ontology-based metadata to identify the activated concepts and then the knowledge levels for these concepts are recalculated based on the modeling formula taking into account the status of the report (success/failure), the concept weights (from metadata entries) and the historical information (previous knowledge for a concept, number of successful attempts for a problem). The propagation path of user modeling information for this case is shown in Fig. 14.

In the case of Problets, the learning objectives are mapped to ADAPT^2's Java ontology, i.e., each Problet's objectives are related to some ontology concept. Instead of reporting problem solving events, Problets report the evidence in terms of learning objectives. Each time a learning objective is evaluated, Problets report it to CUMULATE using brief reports and indicating the unique ID of a learning objective. To process this evidence, CUMULATE registers every learning objective as a "virtual problem". Hence, the mapping is captured in relations between the virtual exercises and the mapped ontology concepts. The strength of the relation between a learning objective and an ontology concept is denoted by a weight. When a new report of a user's work with Problets arrives, CUMULATE identifies activated concepts and performs a knowledge update in the same way as for ADAPT^2 native applications.

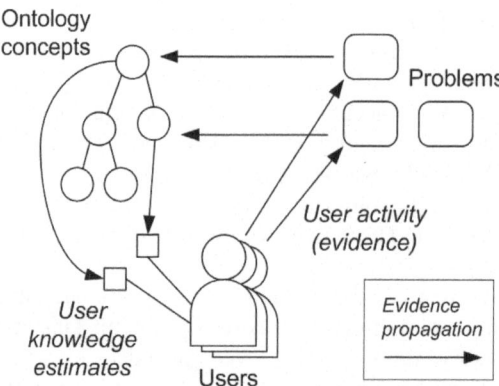

Fig. 14. Propagating reports of user activity (evidence) in CUMULATE

SQL-Tutor also has its own domain model. However, unlike Problets, each problem solving attempt in SQL-Tutor results in dozens of new evidences about learned or violated constraints. Hence, the simple conversion on the CUMULATE side, as implemented for Problets, is not feasible. Instead, a dedicated conversion component is developed on the SQL-Tutor side (refer to Section 4.3 for details). SQL-Tutor uses the extended report protocol to augment the simple evidence information (whether or not the problem has been solved correctly) with a list of activated SQL concepts from the ADAPT[2] SQL ontology. Along with concepts it also reports values between -1 and 1. These values signify the change in knowledge levels computed based on the constraints activated inside SQL-Tutor and the strength of relations between these constraints and ontology concepts. The negative values and corresponding concepts designate student's mistakes and are ignored by CUMULATE, since it does not allow negative evidence propagation. The knowledge levels for the filtered list of concepts are updated using the same modeling formula.

6 Discussion

In this paper, we discussed several ways of integrating adaptive learning systems, focusing on evidence integration, a lightweight solution for integration of user modeling information collected by different educational systems. The resulting infrastructure allows two applications developed by different research teams and relying on considerably different domain models to be used by students in the same course. The applications separately collect the evidence about student knowledge and communicate it to the user modeling server, which allows to maintain more holistic user models.

Our approach is based on manual mapping of domain models and timely evidence reports for user modeling. It was implemented within ADAPT[2] architecture, which supports distributed adaptive e-learning systems. While ADAPT[2] was originally developed for distributed student modeling based on the same domain model, the flexibility of our user modeling server CUMULATE allowed us to deal with a more general scenario involving essentially different domain and student models. The exploration of this approach in two different case studies, featuring Problets and SQL-Tutor allowed us to distill and generalize this approach and argue that it has a broader applicability for the cases where two applications with different domain models have to work with and model the student simultaneously.

Currently, evidence integration is uni-directional: e.g., information about the student's problem solving results within SQL-Tutor is mapped to the target domain model first (converted from constraints to the ontological concepts) and propagated to CUMULATE, which integrates it with other evidence within the global student model. In future work, we plan to develop a "reverse" mechanism for integrating evidence from other components of ADAPT² with the local student models maintained by SQL-Tutor.

While the necessity for manual domain model mapping could be considered a shortcoming of cross-model integration approach, we believe that it is necessary in the case of conceptually different model. At the same time, if both domain models are implemented as Semantic Web ontologies, a good quality mapping can be obtained using automatic mapping techniques. In our recent study, this approach was applied for translation between the student knowledge models of related parts of C and Java programming languages. The C and Java ontologies were developed by different research teams and differed significantly in concept naming conventions and granularity. Student knowledge about a small subset of Java and C concepts were evaluated using several quizzes. The resulting models were compared based on the manual mapping provided by a human expert and the mapping produced automatically by an ontology mapping algorithm. The results of that experiment show that the automatic mapping can generate a user model translation, which is not statistically different from the translation done by a human expert [29].

One of the questions, which require further investigation, is the quality of user models obtained in the process of this multi-system modeling. We argue that our solution based on domain model mapping, while introducing some noise, can result in better student modeling than if we simply ignore a stream of evidence coming from a system with a different user model. At the moment, we are running a multi-semester user study to evaluate the quality of multi-system user modeling using predictive validity and other approaches to user model evaluation.

We are also planning to explore the evidence-based integration approach with other adaptive systems, such as University of Malaga's SIETTE [40] and Trinity College's APeLS [41].

References

1. Schafer, J.B., Frankowski, D., Herlocker, J., Sen, S.: Collaborative filtering recommender systems. In: Brusilovsky, P., Kobsa, A., Nejdl, W. (eds.) Adaptive Web 2007. LNCS, vol. 4321, pp. 291–324. Springer, Heidelberg (2007)
2. Krüger, A., Baus, J., Heckmann, D., Kruppa, M., Wasinger, R.: Adaptive mobile guides. In: Brusilovsky, P., Kobsa, A., Nejdl, W. (eds.) Adaptive Web 2007. LNCS, vol. 4321, pp. 521–549. Springer, Heidelberg (2007)
3. Brusilovsky, P., Peylo, C.: Adaptive and intelligent Web-based educational systems. International Journal of Artificial Intelligence in Education 13(2-4), 159–172 (2003)

4. Brusilovsky, P.: KnowledgeTree: A distributed architecture for adaptive e-learning. In: Proceedings of 13th International World Wide Web Conference, WWW 2004 (Alternate track papers and posters), New York, NY, May 17-22, pp. 104–113 (2004)
5. Niederée, C., Stewart, A., Mehta, B., Hemmje, M.: A Multi-Dimensional, Unified User Model for Cross-System Personalization. In: Proceedings of Workshop on Environments for Personalized Information Access at AVI 2004, Gallipoli, Italy, pp. 34–54 (2004), http://www.di.uniba.it/avi2004/e4pia/EPIA2004_proceedings.pdf
6. Carmagnola, F., Dimitrova, V.: An Evidence-Based Approach to Handle Semantic Heterogeneity in Interoperable Distributed User Models. In: Nejdl, W., Kay, J., Pu, P., Herder, E. (eds.) AH 2008. LNCS, vol. 5149, pp. 73–82. Springer, Heidelberg (2008)
7. Heckmann, D., Schwartz, T., Brandherm, B., Schmitz, M., von Wilamowitz-Moellendorff, M.: Gumo - The General User Model Ontology. In: Ardissono, L., Brna, P., Mitrović, A. (eds.) UM 2005. LNCS (LNAI), vol. 3538, pp. 428–432. Springer, Heidelberg (2005)
8. Dolog, P., Nejdl, W.: Semantic Web Technologies for the Adaptive Web. In: Brusilovsky, P., Kobsa, A., Nejdl, W. (eds.) Adaptive Web 2007. LNCS, vol. 4321, pp. 697–719. Springer, Heidelberg (2007)
9. Yudelson, M., Brusilovsky, P., Zadorozhny, V.: A User Modeling Server for Contemporary Adaptive Hypermedia: An Evaluation of Push Approach to Evidence Propagation. In: Conati, C., McCoy, K., Paliouras, G. (eds.) UM 2007. LNCS (LNAI), vol. 4511, pp. 27–36. Springer, Heidelberg (2007)
10. Kobsa, A., Fink, J.: An LDAP-based User Modeling Server and its Evaluation. User Modeling and User-Adapted Interaction 16(2), 129–169 (2006)
11. Kay, J., Kummerfeld, B., Lauder, P.: Personis: A server for user modeling. In: De Bra, P., Brusilovsky, P., Conejo, R. (eds.) AH 2002. LNCS, vol. 2347, pp. 203–212. Springer, Heidelberg (2002)
12. Sosnovsky, S., Dolog, P., Henze, N., Brusilovsky, P., Nejdl, W.: Translation of overlay models of student knowledge for relative domains based on domain ontology mapping. In: Luckin, R., Koedinger, K.R., Greer, J. (eds.) Proceedings of 13th International Conference on Artificial Intelligent in Education, AI-ED 2007, Marina Del Rey, CA, July 9-13, pp. 289–296 (2007)
13. Berkovsky, S., Kuflik, T., Ricci, F.: Cross-technique mediation of user models. In: Wade, V.P., Ashman, H., Smyth, B. (eds.) AH 2006. LNCS, vol. 4018, pp. 21–30. Springer, Heidelberg (2006)
14. Trella, M., Carmona, C., Conejo, R.: MEDEA: an Open Service-Based Learning Platform for Developing Intelligent Educational Systems for the Web. In: Proceedings of Workshop on Adaptive Systems for Web-based Education at 12th International Conference on Artificial Intelligence in Education, AIED 2005, Amsterdam, July 18, pp. 27–34 (2005)
15. Brusilovsky, P., Sosnovsky, S., Lee, D.H., Yudelson, M.V., Zadorozhny, V., Zhou, X.: An open integrated exploratorium for database courses. In: Proceedings of 13th Annual Conference on Innovation and Technology in Computer Science Education, ITiCSE 2008, Madrid, Spain, June 30-July 2, pp. 22–26 (2008)
16. Denaux, R., Dimitrova, V., Aroyo, L.: Integrating Open User Modeling and Learning Content Management for the Semantic Web. In: Ardissono, L., Brna, P., Mitrović, A. (eds.) UM 2005. LNCS (LNAI), vol. 3538, pp. 9–18. Springer, Heidelberg (2005)
17. Berkovsky, S.: Decentralized Mediation of User Models for a Better Personalization. In: Wade, V.P., Ashman, H., Smyth, B. (eds.) AH 2006. LNCS, vol. 4018, pp. 404–408. Springer, Heidelberg (2006)

18. Berkovsky, S., Kuflik, T., Ricci, F.: Cross-Technique Mediation of User Models. In: Wade, V.P., Ashman, H., Smyth, B. (eds.) AH 2006. LNCS, vol. 4018, pp. 21–30. Springer, Heidelberg (2006)

19. Heckmann, D., Schwartz, T., Brandherm, B., Schmitz, M., von Wilamowitz-Moellendorff, M.: Gumo – The General User Model Ontology. In: Ardissono, L., Brna, P., Mitrović, A. (eds.) UM 2005. LNCS (LNAI), vol. 3538, pp. 428–432. Springer, Heidelberg (2005)

20. Denaux, R., Dimitrova, V., Aroyo, L.: Integrating Open User Modeling and Learning Content Management for the Semantic Web. In: Ardissono, L., Brna, P., Mitrović, A. (eds.) UM 2005. LNCS (LNAI), vol. 3538, pp. 9–18. Springer, Heidelberg (2005)

21. Denaux, R., Aroyo, L., Dimitrova, V.: OWL-OLM: Interactive Ontology-based Elicitation of User Models. In: Proceedings of Workshop on Personalisation for the Semantic Web (PerSWeb 2005) at UM 2005, Edinburgh, UK, July 23-29 (2005),
http://www.win.tue.nl/persweb/full-proceedings.pdf

22. Aroyo, L., Dicheva, D.: AIMS: Learning and Teaching Support for WWW-based Education. International Journal for Continuing Engineering Education and Life-long Learning (IJCEELL) 11(1/2), 152–164

23. Kay, J., Kummerfeld, R.J., Lauder, P.: Personis: A Server for User Models. In: De Bra, P., Brusilovsky, P., Conejo, R. (eds.) AH 2002. LNCS, vol. 2347, pp. 203–212. Springer, Heidelberg (2002)

24. Melis, E., Goguadze, G., Homik, M., Libbrecht, P., Ullrich, C., Winterstein, S.: Semantic-Aware Components and Services of ActiveMath. British Journal of Educational Technology 37(3), 405–423 (2006)

25. Brusilovsky, P., Sosnovsky, S., Shcherbinina, O.: User Modeling in a Distributed E-Learning Architecture. In: Ardissono, L., Brna, P., Mitrović, A. (eds.) UM 2005. LNCS (LNAI), vol. 3538, pp. 387–391. Springer, Heidelberg (2005)

26. Mitrovic, A., Devedzic, V.: A Model of Multitutor Ontology-based Learning Environments. Continuing Engineering Education and Life-Long Learning 14(3), 229–245 (2004)

27. Trella, M., Carmona, C., Conejo, R.: MEDEA: an Open Service-Based Learning Platform for Developing Intelligent Educational Systems for the Web. In: Proceedings of Workshop on Adaptive Systems for Web-Based Education: Tools and Reusability at AIED 2005, Amsterdam, The Netherlands, pp. 27–34 (2005)

28. Kalfoglou, Y., Schorelmmer, M.: Ontology Mapping: the State of the Art. The Knowledge Engineering Review 18(1), 1–31 (2003)

29. Sosnovsky, S., Dolog, P., Henze, N., Brusilovsky, P., Nejdl, W.: Translation of Overlay Models of Student Knowledge for Relative Domains Based on Domain Ontology Mapping. In: Luckin, R., Koedinger, K.R., Greer, J. (eds.) Proceedings of 13th International Conference on Artificial Intelligence in Education (AIED 2007), Marina Del Ray, CA, USA, July 9-13, pp. 289–296 (2007)

30. Kumar, A.N.: A Scalable Solution for Adaptive Problem Sequencing and its Evaluation. In: Wade, V.P., Ashman, H., Smyth, B. (eds.) AH 2006. LNCS, vol. 4018, pp. 161–171. Springer, Heidelberg (2006)

31. Kumar, A.: Explanation of step-by-step execution as feedback for problems on program analysis, and its generation in model-based problem-solving tutors. Technology, Instruction, Cognition and Learning 3 (2006) (in press)

32. Kumar, A.N.: Using Enhanced Concept Map for Student Modeling in a Model-Based Programming Tutor. In: Proceedings of International FLAIRS conference on Artificial Intelligence, Melbourne Beach, FL, May 11-13 (2006)

33. Mitrovic, A., Ohlsson, S.: Evaluation of a Constraint-based Tutor for a Database Language. Int. J. on Artificial Intelligence in Education 10(3-4), 238–256 (1999)

34. Mitrovic, A., Martin, B., Suraweera, P.: Intelligent tutors for all: Constraint-based modeling methodology, systems and authoring. IEEE Intelligent Systems, special issue on Intelligent Educational Systems 22(4), 38–45 (2007)
35. Brusilovsky, P., Sosnovsky, S., Lee, D.H., Yudelson, M., Zadorozhny, V., Zhou, X.: An Open Integrated Exploratorium for Database Courses. In: Proceedings of 13th Annual Conference on Innovation and Technology in Computer Science Education (ITiCSE 2008), Madrid, Spain, June 30 - July 2, pp. 22–26 (2008)
36. Sosnovsky, S., Brusilovsky, P., Lee, D.H., Zadorozhny, V., Zhou, X.: Re-assessing the Value of Adaptive Navigation Support in E-Learning Context. In: Nejdl, W., Kay, J., Pu, P., Herder, E. (eds.) AH 2008. LNCS, vol. 5149, pp. 193–203. Springer, Heidelberg (2008)
37. Sosnovsky, S., Mitrovic, A., Lee, D.H., Brusilovsky, P., Yudelson, M.: Ontology-based integration of adaptive educational systems. In: Proceedings of 16th International Conference on Computers in Education (ICCE 2008), Taipei, Taiwan, October 27-31, pp. 11–18 (2008)
38. Sosnovsky, S., Mitrovic, A., Lee, D.H., Brusilovsky, P., Yudelson, M., Brusilovsky, V., et al.: Towards Integration of Adaptive Educational Systems: Mapping Domain Models to Ontologies. In: Dicheva, D., Harrer, A., Mizoguchi, R. (eds.) Proceedings of 6th International Workshop on Ontologies and Semantic Web for E-Learning (SWEL 2008) at ITS 2008, Montreal, Canada, June 23 (2008), http://compsci.wssu.edu/iis/swel/SWEL08/Papers/Sosnovsky.pdf
39. Brusilovsky, P., Sosnovsky, S., Yudelson, M.: Ontology-based framework for user model interoperability in distributed learning environments. In: Richards, G. (ed.) Proceedings of World Conference on E-Learning, E-Learn 2005, Vancouver, Canada, October 24-28, pp. 2851–2855 (2005)
40. Conejo, R., Guzman, E., Millán, E.: SIETTE: A Web-based tool for adaptive teaching. International Journal of Artificial Intelligence in Education 14(1), 29–61 (2004)
41. Conlan, O., Wade, V., Bruen, C., Gargan, M.: Multi-model, metadata-driven approach to adaptive hypermedia services for personalized eLearning. In: De Bra, P., Brusilovsky, P., Conejo, R. (eds.) AH 2002. LNCS, vol. 2347, pp. 100–111. Springer, Heidelberg (2002)

Author Index